Rancière and Literature

Critical Connections

A series of edited collections forging new connections between contemporary critical theorists and a wide range of research areas, such as critical and cultural theory, gender studies, film, literature, music, philosophy and politics.

Series Editors
Ian Buchanan, University of Wollongong
James Williams, Deakin University

Editorial Advisory Board

Nick Hewlett
Gregg Lambert
Todd May
John Mullarkey
Paul Patton
Marc Rölli
Alison Ross
Kathrin Thiele
Frédéric Worms

Titles available in the series
Badiou and Philosophy, edited by Sean Bowden and Simon Duffy
Agamben and Colonialism, edited by Marcelo Svirsky and Simone Bignall
Laruelle and Non-Philosophy, edited by John Mullarkey and Anthony Paul Smith
Virilio and Visual Culture, edited by John Armitage and Ryan Bishop
Rancière and Film, edited by Paul Bowman
Stiegler and Technics, edited by Christina Howells and Gerald Moore
Badiou and the Political Condition, edited by Marios Constantinou
Nancy and the Political, edited by Sanja Dejanovic
Butler and Ethics, edited by Moya Lloyd
Latour and the Passage of Law, edited by Kyle McGee
Nancy and Visual Culture, edited by Carrie Giunta and Adrienne Janus
Rancière and Literature, edited by Grace Hellyer and Julian Murphet
Agamben and Radical Politics, edited by Daniel McLoughlin

Forthcoming titles
Balibar and the Citizen/Subject, edited by Warren Montag and Hanan Elsayed

Visit the Critical Connections website at www.euppublishing.com/series/crcs

Rancière and Literature

Edited by Grace Hellyer and Julian Murphet

EDINBURGH
University Press

Edinburgh University Press is one of the leading university presses in the UK. We publish academic books and journals in our selected subject areas across the humanities and social sciences, combining cutting-edge scholarship with high editorial and production values to produce academic works of lasting importance. For more information visit our website:
www.edinburghuniversitypress.com

© editorial matter and organisation Grace Hellyer and Julian Murphet, 2016
© the chapters their several authors, 2016

Edinburgh University Press Ltd
The Tun – Holyrood Road
12(2f) Jackson's Entry
Edinburgh EH8 8PJ

Typeset in 11/13 Adobe Sabon by
Servis Filmsetting Ltd, Stockport, Cheshire

A CIP record for this book is available from the British Library

ISBN 978 1 4744 0257 6 (hardback)
ISBN 978 1 4744 0259 0 (webready PDF)
ISBN 978 1 4744 0260 6 (epub)

The right of Grace Hellyer and Julian Murphet to be identified as the editors of this work has been asserted in accordance with the Copyright, Designs and Patents Act 1988, and the Copyright and Related Rights Regulations 2003 (SI No. 2498).

Contents

Acknowledgements vii
Notes on Contributors viii

Introduction: Rancière and Literature 1
Julian Murphet and Grace Hellyer

SECTION I Coordinates

1. Fictions of Time 25
   Jacques Rancière

2. Jacques Rancière in the Forest of Signs: Indiscipline, Figurality and Translation 42
   Eric Méchoulan

3. Rancière and Tragedy 58
   Oliver Feltham

4. Rancière Lost: On John Milton and Aesthetics 76
   Justin Clemens

5. 'A New Mode of the Existence of Truth': Rancière and the Beginnings of Modernity 1780–1830 99
   Andrew Gibson

SECTION II Realisms

6. The Novelist and Her Poor: Nineteenth-Century Character Dynamics 125
   Elaine Freedgood

7. 'Broiled in Hell-fire': Melville, Rancière and the
   Heresy of Literature   143
   Grace Hellyer

8. Why Maggie Tulliver Had To Be Killed   164
   Emily Steinlight

9. The Meaning in the Detail: Literature and the
   Detritus of the Nineteenth Century in Jacques
   Rancière and Walter Benjamin   183
   Alison Ross

SECTION III Contemporaneities

10. Ineluctable Modality of the Sensible: Poverty and
    Form in *Ulysses*   207
    Julian Murphet

11. The Politics of Realism in Rancière and Houellebecq   226
    Arne De Boever

12. Literature, Politics and Action   249
    Bert Olivier

Index   269

Acknowledgements

Elaine Freedgood, 'The Novelist and Her Poor', first appeared in *Novel*, vol. 47, no. 2, pp. 210–23. © 2014, *Novel*, Inc. All rights reserved. Republished by permission of the copyright holder, and the present publisher, Duke University Press, www.dukeupress.edu.

Notes on Contributors

Arne De Boever teaches American studies in the School of Critical Studies at the California Institute of the Arts, where he also directs the MA Aesthetics and Politics programme. He is the author of *States of Exception in the Contemporary Novel* (2012) and *Narrative Care: Biopolitics and the Novel* (2013) and editor of *Gilbert Simondon: Being and Technology* (2012) and *The Psychopathologies of Cognitive Capitalism: Vol. 1* (2013). He edits *Parrhesia: A Journal of Critical Philosophy* and the critical theory/philosophy section of the *Los Angeles Review of Books*. He is also a member of the *boundary 2* collective and an Advisory Editor for *Oxford Literary Review*.

Justin Clemens's books include *Psychoanalysis is an Antiphilosophy* (Edinburgh University Press, 2013) and, with A. J. Bartlett and Jon Roffe, *Lacan Deleuze Badiou* (Edinburgh University Press, 2014). He currently holds an Australian Research Council Future Fellowship on contemporary Australian poetry. He is Associate Professor at the University of Melbourne.

Oliver Feltham is professor of philosophy at the American University of Paris. He has published on the philosophy of change in contemporary French philosophy, critical theory and early modern philosophy. His current project is to develop a history of models of political action, playing historical episodes of political innovation, such as in the English, American and French Revolutions, against philosophers' attempts to theorise those moments in their systematic accounts of politics and social justice. The first instalment of this project was published in March 2013 by Bloomsbury under the title *Anatomy of Failure: Philosophy and Political Action*. It focuses on the Leveller-agitators in the English

Revolution and the philosophies of John Locke and Thomas Hobbes. The sequel to this book will focus on the American and French Revolutions, and on the philosophies of action present in Adam Smith, David Hume, Jean-Jacques Rousseau and Edmund Burke. Feltham is also interested in contemporary poetics and aesthetics, in particular with regard to theatre.

Elaine Freedgood, professor of English at NYU, is the author of *Victorian Writing about Risk: Imagining a Safe England in a Dangerous World* (Cambridge, 2000) and *The Ideas in Things: Fugitive Meaning in the Victorian Novel* (Chicago, 2006) and the editor of *Factory Writing in Victorian Britain* (Oxford, 2003). Her current work is on metalepsis in the realist novel.

Andrew Gibson is former Research Professor of Modern Literature and Theory at Royal Holloway, University of London, and a former Carole and Gordon Professor of Irish Literature at Northwestern University, Chicago. He is a member of the Conseil scientifique and has been a member of the Comité de sélection of the Collège international de philosophie in Paris. His many books include *Joyce's Revenge: History, Politics, Aesthetics in 'Ulysses'* (Oxford, 2002), *Beckett and Badiou: The Pathos of Intermittency* (Oxford, 2010), *Intermittency: The Concept of Historical Reason in Contemporary French Philosophy* (Edinburgh, 2011) and *The Strong Spirit: History, Politics and Aesthetics in Joyce's Writings 1898–1915* (Oxford, 2013). He is currently writing *Modernity and the Political Fix* for Bloomsbury.

Grace Hellyer completed her PhD thesis at the University of New South Wales on the philosophy of Jacques Rancière and the nineteenth-century American Romance. She has published in the field of American literature and her research interests include the novel, literature and philosophy, and aesthetics.

Eric Méchoulan teaches at the Université de Montréal and was Directeur de programme at the Collège international de philosophie. He has written books and papers about literature, philosophy and history: *Lire avec soin: critique, justice et médias* (Presses de l'ENS, forthcoming); *D'où nous viennent nos idées? Métaphysique et intermédialité* (VLB Éditeur, 2010); *Pour une histoire esthétique de la littérature* (Presses universitaires de France,

2004). He co-organised for the US journal *SubStance* a special issue on Jacques Rancière in 2004.

Julian Murphet is Scientia Professor of English and Film Studies and Director of the Centre for Modernism Studies in Australia at the University of New South Wales. He is the author of *Multimedia Modernism* (Cambridge, 2009) and *Literature and Race in Los Angeles* (Cambridge, 2001) and the co-editor of *Modernism and Masculinity* (Cambridge, 2014) and *Faulkner in the Media Ecology* (LSU, 2015). He edits the journal *Affirmations: of the modern*.

Bert Olivier works as Senior Research Fellow in Philosophy at the University of the Free State, South Africa, and is also an adjunct professor in the School of Education at the University of KwaZulu-Natal. His work is interdisciplinary and he has published academic articles and books across a wide variety of disciplines such as philosophy, architecture, literature, psychoanalysis, cinema and social theory, although his home discipline is philosophy. Bert was awarded the Stals Prize for Philosophy by the South African Akademie vir Wetenskap en Kuns in 2004, and a Distinguished Professorship by the Nelson Mandela Metropolitan University, South Africa, in 2012.

Jacques Rancière, born in Algiers (1940), is Emeritus Professor of Aesthetics and Politics at the University of Paris VIII, where he taught from 1969 to 2000 in the Department of Philosophy. He has also taught at the Collège international de philosophie, the European Graduate School and in various American universities. His work crosses over the fields of social history, politics, aesthetics, film studies and literature. He is notably the author of *The Flesh of Words: The Politics of Writing* (Stanford University Press, 2004), *Mute Speech: Literature, Critical Theory, and Politics* (Columbia University Press, 2011), *The Politics of Literature* (Polity Press, 2011) and *Aisthesis: Scenes from the Aesthetic Regime of Art* (Verso, 2013). His last book is *Le Fil perdu. Essais sur la fiction moderne* (La Fabrique, 2014).

Alison Ross is an Australian Research Council Future Fellow in Philosophy at Monash University. She is the author of *The Aesthetic Paths of Philosophy: Presentation in Kant, Heidegger,*

Lacoue-Labarthe and Nancy (Stanford, 2007) and *Walter Benjamin's Concept of the Image* (Routledge, 2014).

Emily Steinlight is the Stephen M. Gorn Family Assistant Professor of English at Penn. She is currently completing a book manuscript titled *The Biopolitical Imagination*, which focuses on the nineteenth-century novel's engagement with the politics of population.

Introduction: Rancière and Literature
Julian Murphet and Grace Hellyer

It would be difficult to construe the course of modern French philosophy apart from its remarkably intimate relationship with literature, both as a prime material for thinking and as the very medium in which many of its best propositions are framed. Of all the great modern national traditions in philosophy, none is so circumvolved with its culture's literary heritage, or indeed with that 'world republic of letters' whose headquarters and Greenwich meridian will always have been Paris.[1] In no other country, for instance, can a figure like Sartre – novelist, playwright, philosopher, essayist – even be imagined, at least since the *sui generis* intellectuals of the Renaissance and Enlightenment: Bacon, Rousseau and Goethe himself. The difficulty simply in classifying thinkers like Bataille, Blanchot, Lacan, Cixous and Derrida rests largely upon the degree to which their prose is defined by an acute self-consciousness and 'literariness' that deconstructs in advance any too-rigid distinction between philosophy and poetry, theory and *écriture*. The unique importance of a journal like *Tel Quel* (1960–82), both to the leading philosophical *and* to the avant-garde literary figures of its moment, is emblematic. In France, or at least in its capital, *to think* is above all *to write*, in a way quite distinct from the empirical traditions of the anglophone world, or the speculative idealism of German thought.

Each luminous name in the pantheon of 'French Theory' summons up its own minor canon of literary auteurs, who in one way or another allowed the thinker in question to articulate otherwise intractable problems. Derrida's critical relationships with Artaud, Joyce, Celan, Mallarmé and Kafka shadow his more celebrated engagements with Rousseau, Lévi-Strauss, Husserl and Heidegger; Kristeva, a novelist in her own right, began her career in Theory with penetrating researches into the avant-garde poetics of Lautréamont and Mallarmé; Foucault's well-known love of Dostoevsky, Borges and de Sade, alongside his major study of Roussel, clarify the literary foundations of his thinking; Deleuze predicated much of his extraordinarily heterodox project on the works of Lewis Carroll, Kafka, Woolf, Melville and Proust; and while Lyotard was more of a student of the visual arts, there is no denying the prodigious debts owed by Badiou (also a playwright), Nancy, Irigaray, Kofman and Lacan to their own constellations of presiding literary geniuses.

The Althusser school is something of an exception to this overarching pattern. Althusser himself was an almost uniquely 'non-literary' French writer; his own style was crude and pedantic and he drew on no deep literary sources of inspiration. In the division of labour that characterised his ambitious programme for reading *Capital*, the literary responsibilities fell largely to Pierre Macherey, though Balibar certainly brought more literary sensibility to his prose than his boorish master. Of all the contributors to that momentous project, however, none has ultimately fulfilled the promise of a 'literary philosophising' better than Jacques Rancière, whose life's work might be said to have amounted to a wholesale de-distinction between the privileged philosophical terrain and the open territory of the 'mute and wandering letter'. Taking an image from Nietzsche's *Gay Science*, where the great 'free spirit' complains that 'conscious thinking *takes place [only] in words, that is, in communication symbols*', and so belongs 'to the community- and herd-aspects of [man's] nature' – i.e., that 'everything which enters consciousness thereby *becomes* shallow, thin, relatively stupid, general, a sign, a herd-mark'[2] – we could say that Rancière's entire project has been to gloss that very image, but to *transvaluate* its imperious complaint into a demotic celebration. It is precisely the levelling, democratic genesis of all 'communication symbols' in the 'net connecting one person with another' (212) that makes thought available to anybody whatever, and demolishes the barriers that philosophy would erect between its 'truths' and the masses of people excluded from them. Philosophy is writing, and writing belongs, as language, to the *demos*.

Rancière's account of literature

Few modern thinkers have been so marked by the instance of Plato as Rancière, whose work consistently challenges the tenacious 'distribution of the sensible' enshrined in the various Socratic dialogues, especially the division of roles and functions in the *Republic*, and the denigration of writing in the *Phaedrus*. That denigration, indeed, amounts to something like a theoretical prolepsis for making sense of Rancière's 'aesthetic regime' in the modern era, as we shall see, but its animus is rooted in Plato's entirely different conception of the value of the arts in society, interpreted by Rancière as a wholly distinct 'regime', namely the *ethical regime*. The ethical regime of images (plastic and literary) is one in which the arts (ways of doing and making) are adjudged according to the faithfulness with which they illustrate truths, or wickedly dissemble untruths, and so affect the living substance of the collective *ethos*: the character of a people. What distinguishes acts of literary mimesis in the ethical regime is 'their end or purpose, [...] the way in which the poem's images provide the spectators, both children and adult citizens, with a certain education and fit in with the distribution of the city's occupations'.[3] Insofar as a poem reinforces and reinscribes the prevailing partition of social space – accords its own immanent 'distribution of the sensible' with that extrinsic separation – it is deemed good; to the extent that it fosters impermissible thoughts about the gods, about fate, or about morals, it is unworthy of admission to the city at all.

The next regime of images that Rancière nominates is the *representative regime* of the arts. Here, the principle of mimesis is elevated from a means to an end, the ultimate end of all artistic and literary production itself: imitation. Only, it is no longer the external world, let alone transcendent philosophical truths, that the new principle of mimesis is charged with representing; rather, imitation here refers circularly to *poesis* or the various arts themselves. Now the governing tautology is not set by the rules of the social space in which literary praxis takes place, but by the established norms of literary production themselves, 'the normative principle of inclusion' which allows that certain ways of writing are 'good' and others are 'bad'.[4] Of course this corresponds ultimately to a distribution of social roles, but rather than addressing the *ethos* as a single substance, the various genres and modes here respond differentially to the stratification of social classes, professions and identities that constitute 'society'. What we call 'classicism' is precisely the exhaustive canon of permissible moves according to which certain acts are acceptable and others not, so that a sonnet can be rigidly defined, a tragedy accurately accredited, and an ode praised or blamed to the extent that it performs the conventional qualities of 'odeness'. Moreover, the 'representative regime' allows for minute regulations within, without and between the various arts that silently map the reification of social space: 'partitions between the representable and the unrepresentable; the distinction between genres according to what it represented [comedy for lower-class characters, tragedy for nobles, etc.]; principles for adapting forms of expression to genres and thus to the subject matter represented; the distribution of resemblances according to principles of verisimilitude, appropriateness, or correspondence; criteria for distinguishing between and comparing the arts; etc.'[5]

Yet in both regimes, one associated with Plato and the other with Aristotle, a problem silently insists, and that problem is the very medium of literature itself, about which Socrates had anxiously complained that words, once written down, 'remain most solemnly silent', and cannot respond to the living touch of interlocution. Moreover, 'once it has been written down, every discourse roams about everywhere, reaching indiscriminately those with understanding no less than those who have no business with it, and it doesn't know to whom it should speak and to whom it should not.'[6] It is this promiscuous indifference of the written sign that troubles both the ethical and the representative regimes from within their most sacred precinct: the poem as the hymn to the gods, or as the template for all mimesis. For such mute indifference both corrodes the living substance of a communitarian bond cast in virtuous images, and proliferates the classical tautologies of mimesis in a *mise en abîme* that unstitches their constitutive authority, disseminating them willy-nilly into the *demos*. And it is this mute, wandering letter that finally comes into its own in what Rancière dubs the 'aesthetic regime of the arts' (of which, more below).

Though it is typical to construe these three regimes as arranged in a historical sequence – ancient, Renaissance, modern – and although certainly the aesthetic regime is first properly announced only in the passion of Romanticism and then progressively developed over the nineteenth century, there is in truth no strict adhesion of any regime to a historical period or epoch. In fact, all three are veritably 'eternal' possibilities that come into dominance in certain social and historical conditions: for example, slavery, feudalism and bourgeois 'democracy'. There is thus some consonance between Rancière's tripartite model of regimes and Badiou's three schemata linking art and philosophy: the didactic schema, the classical schema and the romantic schema, which loosely correlate to the ethical, the representative and the aesthetic regimes, respectively, though with some important differences.[7] This might explain, for instance, the recrudescence of an ethical regime of images in the Soviet Union, or the constant tendency to retreat to this or that classicism as a redoubt from the ravages of capitalist nihilism. Nevertheless, if there is a metanarrative in Rancière's account of aesthetics, it is that there came a tipping point in the career of the 'mute and wandering letter', after which both ethical and representative aesthetics lost most of their root systems in the topsoil of modernity.

And that tipping point has a very particular name: Literature. The Romantic inauguration of an aesthetic regime of the arts, under the impetus of Hegel and the French Revolution, cleared a space for the emergence of literature as such, which is to say practices of writing and of reading that seized the significance of the literary act as paradoxically its *indifference* to the rules of art and the ethos of a people (its asymptotic approach to the 'prose of the world'), and its *aspiration* to an absolute rapport with Spirit itself – with 'the "religion" of artifice: the institution of artifacts and rituals that transfer to the community [. . .] the pulverized gold of setting suns and agonizing natures, purified by the religion that [. . .] celebrates the real presence of absence'.[8] In Rancière, this aporia assumes the twin-star name of Flaubert-Mallarmé. On the one hand, Flaubert, with his notorious ambition to write 'a book about nothing', adapts the literary apparatus so radically that henceforth not this, not that literary 'subject' is appropriate to any given genre, but *any-subject-whatever* can become the bearer of a literary signal – provided the intensively worked quality of the language shifts our attention from narrative 'content' to style. Writing becomes autonomous from purpose and decorum, inasmuch as it is indifferent to everything but the inhuman music of which it is capable. On the other, Mallarmé writes a rather different 'book about nothing', espousing a negative theology in which 'the nothing [is] put forward as everything that emblematizes the all',[9] embowered in a sacred overestimation of language as what now substitutes for the God who died. 'The "realistic" excess of things and the "aesthetic" superstition about words form a system. And the proper name for this system is literature.'[10] From the generative grammar institutionalised by these two proper names, all 'literature' is woven, which thus gives the lie to any substantive distinction between those immutable literary-historical classifications: Romantic, Realist, Modernist and Postmodernist.

For Rancière, these are nothing but pseudo-distinctions. In a series of interventions (sometimes rehearsing identical themes and arguments) on literary subjects from Balzac to Mandelstam, Wordsworth to James Agee, he has described a stubbornly transverse and counterintuitive line of approach to the subject of literary specificity, slashing through 'period' discriminations and disciplinary proprieties with the impolitic brusqueness of an impassioned amateur. The vital question is not 'what distinguishes modernism from realism?' (for Rancière an academic question of the worst kind), but *what makes literature literature*? And the answer to that has everything to do with the radical novelty of the *'partage du sensible* [distribution of the sensible]' that this new kind of writing makes possible in the 'aesthetic regime of the arts'. What makes literature literature under this regime is not its ethical purpose, nor its exemplary mimetic function, but its new-found capacity to alter the very Kantian categories through which we are permitted to perceive the world itself, its ability to dissociate names and bodies, to uncouple hidebound correspondences between *les mots et les choses* and effect entirely novel modes of association. It finds itself charged with the power to disturb 'the system of *a priori* forms determining what presents itself to sense perception'.[11] Literature is thus instrumental in reshaping the way the world is 'seen' by a reading public increasingly *au fait* with an undisciplined deluge of reading matters. It is the mode of writing best adapted to 'the democracy of the mute letter, meaning the letter that anybody can retrieve and use in his or her way', since it is 'the art of writing that specifically addresses those who *should not* read'.[12] It is therefore, but in a way scarcely theorised before, *political* through and through, inasmuch as the 'political' (the accepted distribution of subjects, classes, groups, etc., in a given social space) is itself always 'aesthetic', revolving 'around what is seen and what can be said about it'.[13] Literature, however, is not 'political' in the conventional sense; it does not 'represent' the interests or subject-positions that populate the political terrain proper. It represents nothing but a new and open relation to things as such. It uncouples the sign from the referent so that the human sensorium, its doors of perception cleansed by what the formalists called *Ostranenie*, is given the wherewithal to break its 'mind-forg'd manacles' and so espy the worm within the rose, feel out the misery hidden in the fruitful land, or hear the lowly crickets in the grass. That inaugural Romantic promise is only confirmed and extended by all the subsequent 'literarity' of the nineteenth and twentieth centuries, however such extensions may have been classified by literary history.

Literature as such is to be approached, on this understanding, not so much for its stories, characters, plots or situations as for the evidence it gives of a wholesale reorientation of the very means of perception and of the new distributions of matter it makes sensible. Empirical reality itself ceases to be self-evident thanks to the ministrations of literary 'perception': its common-sensical forms give way under the discrete pressure of linguistic autonomism, dissolving into lower and lower orders of being, more and more inchoate patterns of materiality, driven by

> the visionary power that imperceptibly lifts [an action] up, sentence after sentence, in order to make us perceive, under the banal prose of social communication and ordinary narrative plotting, the poetic prose of the great order or great disorder, the music of unbound affections and perceptions, mixed together in the great indifferent flux of the Infinite.[14]

From Deleuze, the philosopher to whom Rancière's aesthetic and literary vocabulary is most indebted, he takes the notion that art liberates percepts, affects and sensations from their habitual constellations in fixed genres and forms, and sets them loose upon devious paths, drawn into new configurations and hybrid formations.[15] And from Deleuze, as well, he borrows the distinction between 'molar' distributions of the sensible associated with the ethical and representative regimes (recognisable bodies, figures, names, objects, all in their proper places), and the new aesthetic domain of 'molecularity', where these molar forms are subject to disaggregation, dissociation, progressive dissolution into what Flaubert called 'the dance of atoms'.[16] At this level, literature strips knowable forms of their constitutive qualities, and weaves new tissues of association between perceptions, affects, names and ideas no longer embedded in immemorial plots.

Rancière reading literature

As a literary critic, then, Rancière shares a familiar trait with other philosophers for whom literature is a crucial 'proof' of certain fundamental theorems – Derrida, Blanchot, Badiou and many others. Namely, his acts of reading consist largely in a repetitive iteration of the assertion that *this text is doing what all literature does* (for instance: it deconstructs binary oppositions; it stakes a wager on the night; it tarries in the wake of an Event; etc.). In Rancière's case, the singular tale being told by any number of literary acts under the aesthetic regime of the arts is that now *everything talks, equally* – there is nothing that cannot now be heard to speak, to flash its own hieroglyphs and flourish the sibilant sound of its own dissolution into the flux of atoms. In the pure equality of 'literarity' as such, everything and nothing speak indifferently and interminably in the resonant hollows of all matter.

His 'interpretive' method is always immanent and makes excellent use of the stylistic contagion that obtains between a source text and its commentary. That impulse is taken from his ignorant master, Jacotot: it consists in a refusal to 'explain'. As he puts it, 'every explanation is a fiction of inequality [. . .]. Explanation turns all *wishing to say* into a scholar's secret,' and what Rancière is most at pains to establish is the discursive 'community of equals' whose presupposition is absolutely incompatible with any authoritative 'social institution', such as the one that confers upon the scholar-critic the right to assume the acquiescence of his auditor or reader to a privileged interpretation.[17] So the task is patiently and even 'ignorantly' to let the text speak in its own voice the full radicalism of its aesthetic dissensus. Rancière finds himself constantly in the position of *ventriloquising* his specimen text, not with an eye to unpacking its secrets but simply in order to allow it to skirt the rim of the void in a discourse immanently afflicted by the 'great prostitution of things'.[18] There is typically some scene-setting by way of an authorial biographical sketch or an account of the text's initial reception; but, the discussion under way, the prose moves inexorably toward an intimate encounter with the substance of the text itself, drawing from its style a lesson of how language dissolves the hierarchical logics that long kept base from noble, serious from comedic, inside from outside, in the propriety of erstwhile regimes. Each reading, which is also a kind of extended sympathetic paraphrase, shows how the sudden availability of 'everything' to the most ambitious literary attention results in a movement towards pure nothingness: books about nothing, with no purpose beyond the perfection of their own music, their own dramatic presentation of a void that subtends all sensible appearance.

It is therefore a rather different approach from the one we might expect from a famous leftist philosopher. Rancière has little interest in literature's 'representationality', its capacity to flatter and shore up the various identities and subjectivities that animate the boisterous public sphere. In that sense, he takes very seriously the many claims for 'autonomy' that have characterised literary acts in the aesthetic regime. For Rancière, we may say, this autonomy is tendentiously absolute. Whereas a Badiou might insist upon the militant fidelity a true literary act must demonstrate 'subjectively' to the Event of which it is an affirmation (and so the larger *truth procedure* it swears fealty to against the otiose pressures of opinion and common sense in the general *service des biens*); or a Jameson might delineate the socially symbolic and therefore political gesture any work of literature must perform in its reorganisation of prefabricated ideological materials into a novel formal complex; Rancière is interested only in the extent to which a literary text refashions the *partage du sensible* – the way it disorders existing ways of seeing and saying. There is no 'affirmative' moment here, no political or philosophical 'meaning' as such, only a negative process of dissociation, dissolution and entropy, as the literary signal approaches ever closer to the babble and murmur of the prose of the world. Every 'reading' of a text, then, is designed to proffer not a moment of epiphany or recognition, but a sense of semantic crumbling and loss, in which aesthetic heat death all-new intensities and vibrations can be detected. 'The written sign turns into any old bit of garbage or into sheer difference in intensity – to the point where nothing more can be read except the indifferent vibration of atoms in their random variations.'[19]

His major literary investigations enact such readings in long, often chronological sequences. *Short Voyages to the Land of the People* (1990/2003) looks at texts by Wordsworth, Büchner, the proletarian Claude Genout, Michelet, Rilke; the monograph on *Mallarmé* (1996/2011) considers that poet in great depth; *The Flesh of Words* (1998/2004) analyses major works by Wordsworth, Mandelstam, Rimbaud, the Bible, Balzac, Proust, Cervantes and Melville; *Mute Speech* (1998–2011), his literary masterpiece, offers an extraordinary history lesson in the emergence of literarity, and covers Victor Hugo, Schlegel, Hegel, Novalis, Taine, Balzac, Zola, Flaubert, Mallarmé, Proust and Valéry, amongst others; the essays collected in *The Politics of Literature* (2006/2011) extend the invitation not only to the regulars (Flaubert, Mallarmé) but also to Brecht, Tolstoy and Borges; while the superb *Aisthesis* (2011/2013), which blends literary with art-historical, performance and cinematic criticism, introduces Stendhal, Emerson, Whitman and Agee. His canon is idiosyncratic and almost parochial in its nationalism (though from Deleuze he has borrowed an interest in the American writers); Wordsworth and Keats are the only English writers he has any interest in, his engagement with German literature seems limited to Rilke and Brecht (though he has a good deal to say about the German philosophers of the Hegel era), and one looks in vain for any mention of Asian or Third World writers or those of the Global South – not for Rancière the paradigm of 'world literature' or comparative literary studies! Rather, his myopic attention to a narrow cast of essentially French, nineteenth-century authors is supposed to serve heuristically for any investigation launched into the literature of the aesthetic regime (which, we understand, is international and connected somehow to the penetration of capitalism and formal 'democracy'); the lesson seems to be that, wherever you look, the same derangement of categories, the same dissociation between words and things, the same dissolution of molar forms into vibrating molecules, will be taking place.

Molecular politics?

As the delineation of a politics of literature is at the heart of Rancière's work, this begs the question of what relationship this pure molecularity could possibly have to politics. Rancière often positions his conception of the efficacy proper to art and literature against a so-called 'critical art' that stakes its claim to producing effects in the world on a fundamentally consensual conception of reality – on the conviction of a sameness between cause and effect; an art that 'is presumed to be effective politically because it displays the marks of domination', or assumes that it 'compels us to revolt when it shows us revolting things'.[20] He is speaking here of a *mimetic* paradigm that posits a causal logic assuming that what the reader or viewer experiences is 'a set of signs formed according to the artist's intention'. He calls this the *'pedagogical model* of the efficacy of art'.[21]

For Rancière, the efficacy of art under the aesthetic regime is always related to the gap between the author, the work and the experience of the work. He often presents literature as the primary form of artistic production in the aesthetic regime, and this is linked to writing's peculiar capacity to bear witness to this gap. In *The Ignorant Schoolmaster*, it is the existence of the book as a 'third thing' simultaneously mediating and blocking the encounter between intelligences that creates a space where demonstrations of equality can take place. Here writing as such, separated from determinate modes of address, makes it possible to suspend the hierarchical relation of teacher and student and facilitate the student's coming into possession of his or her own intellectual capacity. Literature is, in Rancière's thought, the most significant artistic medium of the aesthetic regime because of its privileged relationship to this suspension. It is for this reason that he underlines the 'muteness' of writing, as opposed to living speech, as its most important characteristic.

For Rancière, as we have pointed out, the aesthetic regime in literature amounts to the overturning of the hierarchies of *belles lettres* by the apotheosis of this muteness. There is a reordering of the sense of the power of language wherein its 'sonorous and imagistic power' becomes more important than 'the syntax that subordinates those words to the expression of thought and the logical order of an action'.[22] In *Mute Speech*, the primacy of fiction over language is framed as one of the four principles that define the representative regime with one of the aesthetic regime's chief moves being the reversal of this opposition: the subordination of fiction to language. The problem with the representative regime is that '[t]he system of poetic fiction is placed in the dependence of an ideal of efficacious speech, which in turn refers back to an art which is more than an art, that is, a manner of living, a manner of dealing with human and divine affairs: rhetoric';[23] that the intellectual part of art commands the material part, and 'can equally well espouse the hierarchical order of the monarchy or the egalitarian order of republican orators'.[24] The novel, the type of literature that best characterises the aesthetic regime, offers a solution to this problem because its particular type of fiction is indeterminate, lacking any fixed principle of decorum. At the same time, it is not prose fiction but poetry that is presented as a manifestation of the pure power of literary language. The specificity of literature is shown to lie in the continuity of its medium with the 'materials' that are used to express a thought in other modes of artistic production – in the poetic use of language it becomes inert, like paint or stone. In *Mute Speech*, this is the power specific to the poetic use of language and opposed to the power of language that comes into play with the use of language to construct a plot or a fiction. This poetry expresses '[w]hat is proper to art', namely 'the realization of a pure intentionality through any subject whatsoever'.[25] Here Rancière raises Hegel's critique of Romantic art as ushering in the dissolution of art and of literature by allowing poetry to become 'nothing more than the continual dissolution of representation, the act of self-exhibition, the exhibition of an empty intention at the expense of every object'.[26] This Hegelian denunciation pertinently raises what is perhaps the most troubling aspect of Rancière's characterisation of literature – his resolute valorisation of the principle of indifference.

This principle of indifference calls the assumptions of critical and 'mimetic' art into question, contrasting an ideal of 'ethical immediacy' with a conception of 'aesthetic distance' that draws heavily on Romantic philosophy.[27] Aesthetic distance is constituted by 'the suspension of a determinable relation between the artist's intention, a performance in some place reserved for art, and the spectator's gaze and state of the community'.[28] The art of the aesthetic regime and its effects are defined by the suspension of any determinate relation between *poesis* and *aesthesis* – between particular forms and particular effects or social functions. In the place of those determinate effects and functions, Rancière nominates 'dissensus' as the only mode of effectivity proper to the art of aesthetic regime, also claiming this particular efficacy as the only property that art shares with politics.

> Dissensus is a conflict between a sensory presentation and a way of making sense of it, or between several sensory regimes and/or 'bodies'. This is the way in which dissensus can be said to reside at the heart of politics, since at bottom the latter itself consists in an activity that redraws the frame within which common objects are determined. Politics breaks with the sensory self-evidence of the 'natural' order that destines specific individuals and groups to occupy positions of rule or of being ruled, assigning them to public or private lives, pinning them down to a certain time and space.[29]

Politics consists of deformations of the shared 'sensible' world wherein those destined for the mere reproduction of life, or those not previously counted within the partitioning of the community, affirm their stake in a common world. While both art and politics are defined by and define a certain form of dissensus – a particular ability to reconfigure common, sensible experience – they do so in distinct, if overlapping, ways. The aesthetics within politics consists of the reconfiguration of the common through determinate instances of political subjectification, the 'framing of a *we*, a subject, a collective demonstration whose emergence is the element that disrupts the distribution of social parts'.[30] Such a reframing could be represented in literature, but the effects of that representation would be ultimately uncertain and Rancière argues time and again that the dissensual capacity proper to literature cannot simply be identified with this representative capacity. In fact, he suggests that to depend on this fundamentally pedagogical mode of efficacy is to betray the particular democratic force that he ascribes to literature. The distinction between the action that is specific to politics and that which belongs to art and literature is central to Rancière's thought and it is only when the specificity of this distinction is maintained, he seems to suggest, that literature can properly attain its own power of acting in the world. He argues that the mode of dissensus proper to aesthetic and literary activity can *only* inhere in reconfigurations of the fabric of sensory experience and that in this mode of activity, unlike politics, there can be no direct cause-effect relationship. The literary work's multiplication of the sensible reality defined by a given consensus is polemical, to be sure, but it does not function in the direct pedagogical manner that the critical art tradition might suppose. The fact that there is no necessary link between the intention realised in a literary work and a capacity for political subjectification or the formation of an intention to actively intervene in a shared world is even what allows literature to carry the promise of a new community. Literature, in this account, cannot 'give a collective voice to the anonymous' or provide impulses and new modes of awareness that are directly *for* politics, but it can call the self-evidence of the shared sensible into question by inventing new variations of how the world could appear, new modes of intelligibility and 'commonsense', and 'new forms of individuality' by reframing the world of common experience as 'the world of a shared impersonal experience'.[31]

In this volume, and elsewhere, Rancière identifies this activity as 'the labour of fiction'.[32] In the chapter included in this volume, the paradox of this labour of fiction is identified with Erich Auerbach's claim that the staging of the random moment, disconnected from the causal sequences of plot, constitutes the greatest achievement of modern literary fiction. Here, the random moment is taken up as the time of modern literature, a time disconnected from the integration of moments in either intentional action or mechanical repetition, a time that collapses the distinction between activity and passivity and in which all moments are equal. The abdication of the literary fiction from those powers of sense-making that it shares with the 'fictions' that structure everyday life at the very moment of its apotheosis is represented as constitutive of the modern literature of the aesthetic regime. Against the Marxist science of history that Rancière here identifies with the fictional proprieties and implicit hierarchies of the representative regime, realist literary fiction is claimed as bearing witness to the loss of the link between knowledge and action. Rather than mourning for the loss of the efficacy of this kind of plot, however, Rancière claims that this literary temporality of causal disconnection is capable of revealing the 'truth' of a certain experience of time. He returns again to the classical schemata, opposing the 'poetic convocation of events' to the 'prosaic connection of activities' arguing that the time of modern literature collapses that distinction, thereby calling into being the time of the community to come. Here the pure power of temporal disconnection and dis-identification is said to concretely disclose the commonality of experience, 'the elementary things which our lives have in common'.[33]

That this power of revelation should come at the expense of the loss of the power of making sensible fictions, the loss as it were of a more clearly pedagogical efficacy, is indeed a starkly minimal rendering of the powers of literature and the most singular and problematic aspect of the literature of Rancière's aesthetic regime. It is founded on a total identification of aesthetics with equality – the aesthetic regime is constituted by the opening of the field of *aesthesis* to absolutely anyone – 'the world itself as something to be sensed, perceived, and thought, for modes of expression to be reinvented'.[34] However, the commonality of *aesthesis* also signals an irrevocable rupturing of sense by contingency. Jean-Philippe Deranty has characterised this as a co-implication of *logos* and *pathos*. When the materials of logos are revealed as mute things then, along with the opening up of new possibilities for the mobilisations of sense, new avenues of sense-making and ways of showing how there is logos and pathos, there emerges a 'blind spot' constituted by the fact that there is also 'pathos in logos' so that 'sense itself runs the risk of collapsing into "muteness", the absurd, the dead.'[35]

Rancière's foregrounding of materiality in sense-making is the basis of the link that he forges between political dissensus and the aesthetic dissensus that he claims as literature's defining affect. In his readings of particular works the implications of this procedure become apparent as a kind of knot. His careful delineation of the meta-politics of a certain kind of narrative rupture in *The Red and the Black* and their relation to a politics of plebeian feeling founded on the equality of shared sensation coalesces in a valorisation of the renunciation of the world of determinate actions and political struggles. This is a familiar gesture, part of a line of thought that runs through his writing on literature and emerges with particular emphasis in his work on Flaubert and in *Aisthesis* with his framing of Winckelmann's analysis of the Belvedere Torso as the constitutive articulation of the emergence of the aesthetic regime. In the introduction to that volume, he identifies this knot with particular clarity, naming the troubling separation between the curiously ineffective efficacy of the aesthetic and the paths of action that are forged in the political life of a community as central to his paradoxical account of the politics of literature. He tells us that the aesthetic paradigm of the community holds the promise of 'men free and equal in their sensible life' but that it also 'tends to cut this community off from all the paths that are normally used to reach a goal'.[36] The emancipatory energies of art, he tells us, do not suceed in 'reintegrating the strategic patterns of causes and effects'.[37] Instead of interpreting this statement as a pessimistic abdication of literature from politics, Rancière asks that we see it as a necessary prerequisite of the identification of literature's particular power. Only '[h]asty minds', he tells us, 'will see this as the sign of an irremediable breach between aesthetic utopia and real political and revolutionary action'.[38] Here, more clearly than ever before, he frames the function of literature's paradoxical relation to political action, 'the equivalence of strategic action and radical inaction', as bearing witness to a paradox that accompanies theories of political agency and emancipation:

> Emancipated workers could not repudiate the hierarchical model governing the distribution of activities without taking distance from the capacity to act that subjugated them to it. [. . .] The scientific Marxist revolution certainly wanted to put an end to the workers' reveries, along with utopian programmes. But by opposing them to the effects of real, social development, it kept subordinating the end and means of action to the movement of life, at the risk of discovering that this movement does not want anything and does not allow any strategies to lay claim to it.[39]

Here, Rancière implicitly invokes the possibility of a politics that is identical with 'the movement of life', one operating at the level of shared sensible experience. Aesthetic experience, in its very separation from determinate action, is claimed as bearing witness to that possibility. This vision, of course, bears a strong affinity with the romantic idealism of Schiller's model of aesthetic education where the cancellation of the opposition between reason and sensation in aesthetic experience is claimed as bearing the promise of a non-polemical, consensual reframing of a shared world. Here, that romantic ideal becomes incorporated into a framework for understanding the conditions under which political action can take place. The opposition between the logic of actions and the 'movement of life' in the political world is invoked in order to locate the significance of the aesthetic suspension of that opposition. Rancière's assertion of the literary work's separation from the logic of politics is staked on the claim that it is only in that space of aesthetic suspension and indifference that literature can bear witness to the possibility of emancipated action.

The book in your hands

Our first suite of essays, which opens with Rancière's own magisterial intervention on the matter of 'fiction', seeks to establish the broad parameters of his philosophical estimation of literary practice. Beginning from the deceptively obvious proposition that Rancière is, before anything else, an exemplary *reader*, Eric Méchoulan demonstrates with delightful perspicacity how the philosopher's aversion from disciplinary thought propels him towards a theoretical *indiscipline* that has much to teach contemporary literary studies. This studied amateurism offers a path away from masterful interpretations in 'depth', and toward a distributed horizontal immanence, but this begs the questions of figurality and translation. For Méchoulan, Rancière's hostility toward hermeneutics heralds a conception of the 'figure' as a 'movement of active interpretation', an unauthorised adventure in indeterminate meaning-making, rather than a sanctioned substitution. Translation, meanwhile, ceases to be a specialist intervention between national tongues, and comes to constitute the very essence of understanding itself, as the mind shifts cannily between a surface distribution of equivalences within a single language. Oliver Feltham takes up the absence of any prolonged examination of the genre of tragedy in Rancière's writing and links it to the prevalence of the theme of 'inegalitarian distortion in the sharing out of roles in the city' in his political thought. Here the miscount becomes like the fatal flaw of the tragedy and Feltham goes on to suggest that there also could be a fatal flaw in Rancière's political thinking, a melancholy errancy that refuses to name any determinate good and becomes trapped in the postures of demystification. Following a limpid and exact rehearsal of the essential lineaments of Rancière's political aesthetics, Justin Clemens brilliantly explores the case of John Milton, in particular his late pamphlet *Of True Religion*, as a test of the scope and limits of Rancière's 'three regimes' of aesthetic specificity. Establishing Rancière's implication in a fairly traditional account of aesthetic finitude, Clemens then shows how Milton's 'paradoxy' – his classical representationalism as a poet alongside his occasional partisanship as a pamphleteer – establishes a participatory politics of contrarieties, and an epistemology of indistinction, that is irreducible to any one of the three regimes of images. Concerned with an eternity that has nothing to do with theology, Milton bores a hole in Rancière's aesthetics with a rational messianism that will not be bounded by melancholy finitude. Finally in the opening section, tackling the curious position of the 'beginnings of modernity' (1780–1830) in Rancière's work, Andrew Gibson shows how he is both drawn to and repelled by the very concept of modernity, and can at best defend a very modest, ambivalent and intermittent account of it. Charting a comparative path through thinkers as various as Hobsbawm, Berman, Schmitt and Mannheim, Gibson allows us to see Rancière's distinctly less Promethean, less 'evental' conception of the 'age of revolutions' as relatively dispersed, anonymous, rhizomatic and lower-key. The fate of literature in this construal is to tend towards the 'insensible' or 'quasi-corporeal', never quite delivering on its promises, but straying literarily into a ghostly zone of suspension and orphaned speech. In which case, what we call literary modernity is nothing other than the registered experience of anachronism, untimeliness and weird temporal rifts that can never be adequately contained in a period concept like 'modernity', which truthfully only happens now and then, here and there, and cannot be used to define an entire century or more.

Our second section tackles the central problematic of nineteenth-century literary Realism in Rancière's thinking. Against Rancière's demand that philosophy not claim to speak or think for the poor, Elaine Freedgood takes up the work of the narrator in nineteenth-century fiction who seeks to give thoughts and words to her subjects. She explores the distance between the literary narration of the author, as well as the literary allusions that she wields, and the poor that she represents. This becomes an intentional strategy of removing the poor from the political sphere in which they would participate by representing them solely in terms of feeling. However, Freedgood inverts this procedure in a Rancièrian fashion by ingeniously comparing free indirect discourse with the capitalism that controls production and impoverishes its workers, arguing that the muteness of Gaskell's poor, her refusal to give them a voice in her text, paradoxically leaves open a space for their own self-representation. Grace Hellyer takes up Rancière's account of the distinction between the representative and aesthetic regimes to describe certain tensions animating the novel *Moby-Dick*, locating her account of these concepts in Rancière's earlier work on history. She reads the novel as shaped partly by the urge to confer democratic dignity on its characters that invokes the hierarchical generic proprieties of the representative regime and argues that these structures are deformed and complicated by the representation of the leviathan, an avatar of 'mute life' irreducible to those categories. Emily Steinlight explores George Eliot's literary murder of Maggie Tulliver under the presupposition of Rancière's foregrounding of the principle of indifference and indeterminacy in his account of the aesthetic regime; it is a provocative example given Eliot's mastery of a literary realism that, unlike Flaubert's, explicitly purports to take up the task of representation. The paradox inhering in the narrative foreshadowing and crafting of the 'chance' event of the flood is here linked to a Malthusian train of thought; to a logic of political economy that bears a 'sense of life's socio-economic status and its

Introduction 19

potential calculability' and makes the random loss of life part of a 'natural' regulatory system that governs life's tendency towards excess. Eliot, in this account, at once takes up this line of thought and invalidates it by fracturing 'any organic unity in the succession of events'. Alison Ross examines Walter Benjamin's and Rancière's conceptions of the ability of literature to convey truth and meaning via their respective representations of 'detritus'. She marks the impact of Rancière's conception of aesthetic regime on 'the semantic integrity of the category of literature' and, in particular, the role played by the 'anything whatever' in the creation of meaning. Here her alignment of Rancière's notion of aesthetic indifference with Benjamin's notion of intentionless truth provides a valuable perspective on Rancière's theories of history and the tenuous political outcomes of his theorising of the aesthetic shift in the nineteenth century.

The third section presses Rancière on the questions of modernism, modernity and the contemporary. Wondering whether Rancière's hostility toward the concept of modernism might occlude a certain conceptual problem in his own schema, Julian Murphet compares the relative achievements of Gustave Flaubert and James Joyce, and proposes that the shift from 'absolute style' to 'form' betokened by these two authors clarifies a determinate break inside the aesthetic regime itself. Murphet suggests that Joyce's inability to persevere within an autonomous notion of style is a reflex of the altered circumstances of textual production in the early twentieth century, and argues that his shifting of the locus of the problem of aesthetics towards the business of form marks a supersession of the 'distribution of the sensible' as the primary work of literary production. With Joyce, the problem is not what can be seen and said, purely, but what to do with all the ways of seeing and saying that are no longer tolerable, and how such rapid obsolescence affects the thinking of politics, and its most perdurable problem, the poor. Arne De Boever's article goes some way in the urgent task of bringing Rancière's categories and concerns into a productive dialogue with those of traditional literary criticism, as well as offering a solid grounding of his literary thought in his early preoccupation with workers' histories. His examination of the realist tradition in the light of Michel Foucault's concept of biopolitics aims to uncover the implications of Rancière's sidelining of representational accounts of the realist novel, his refusal to consider the novel's claim to generate representations of the world. This is linked to a problem that De Boever identifies with Rancière's inter-related approaches to politics and the politics of literature, namely that while his theory of literature privileges the inhuman, his politics remain limited by a resolute humanism. Bert Olivier takes up an instance of dissensus as represented within the diegetic space of Yaakunah's novel *The Woman Who Sparked the Greatest Sex Scandal of All Time* as potentially facilitating 'the possible subversion of the status quo in extant social reality'. The concept of the distribution of the sensible is taken up firstly as a theme in the fiction and secondly in terms of the text's possible capacity to generate dissensual effects under that suspension of intention that is the hallmark of Rancière's account of the aesthetic regime. Olivier bases his claim for the novel's 'extra-textual' capacity to create dissensual effects on its ability to trigger the recognition of an analogy with shared contemporary experience, suggesting that it aims to prepare the reader for social revolution.

Notes

1. See Pascale Casanova, *The World Republic of Letters*, trans. M. B. DeBevoise (Cambridge, MA: Harvard University Press, 2007).
2. Friedrich Nietzsche, *The Gay Science*, ed. Bernard Williams, trans. Josephine Nauckhoff and Adrian Del Caro (Cambridge: Cambridge University Press, 2001), 213.
3. Jacques Rancière, *The Politics of Aesthetics*, trans. Gabriel Rockhill (London and New York: Bloomsbury, 2006), 21.
4. Ibid.
5. Ibid., 22.
6. Plato, *Phaedrus*, 275 d–e, in John M. Cooper and D. S. Hutchinson (eds), *Plato: Complete Works* (Indianapolis: Hackett Publishing, 1997), 552.
7. Alain Badiou, *Handbook of Inaesthetics*, trans. Alberto Toscano (Stanford: Stanford University Press, 2004), 2–5.
8. Rancière, *Mallarmé: The Politics of the Siren* (London and New York: Bloomsbury, 2011), 30–1.
9. Rancière, 'The Intruder: Mallarmé's Politics', in *The Politics of Literature*, trans. Julie Rose (Cambridge: Polity, 2011), 93.
10. Rancière, 'Borges and the French Disease', in *The Politics of Literature*, 132.
11. Rancière, *The Politics of Aesthetics*, 13.

12. Rancière, *Dissensus: On Politics and Aesthetics*, trans. Steven Corcoran (London and New York: Bloomsbury, 2010), 158.
13. Rancière, *The Politics of Aesthetics*, 13.
14. Rancière, *Mute Speech: Literature, Critical Theory, and Politics*, trans. James Swenson (New York: Columbia University Press, 2011), e-book edition, loc. 2481.
15. See Gilles Deleuze and Félix Guattari, *What Is Philosophy?*, trans. Hugh Tomlinson and Graham Burchell (New York: Columbia University Press, 1994), 163–200.
16. Deleuze and Guattari, *A Thousand Plateaus: Capitalism and Schizophrenia*, trans. Brian Massumi (Minneapolis: University of Minnesota Press, 1987), 47–62.
17. Rancière, 'The Community of Equals', in *On the Shores of Politics*, trans. Liz Heron (New York and London: Verso, 1995), 63–4.
18. Rancière, 'Borges and the French Disease', in *The Politics of Literature*, 140.
19. Rancière, 'The Truth Through the Window', in *The Politics of Literature*, 157.
20. Rancière, *Dissensus*, 134, 135.
21. Ibid., 135, 136.
22. Rancière, *Mute Speech*, loc. 949.
23. Ibid., loc. 1058.
24. Ibid., loc. 1085.
25. Ibid., loc. 1537.
26. Ibid., loc. 1775.
27. Rancière, *Dissensus*, 137.
28. Ibid.
29. Ibid., 139.
30. Ibid., 141–2.
31. Ibid., 142, 149.
32. Ibid., 141.
33. See page XX, below.
34. Jean-Philippe Deranty, 'The Symbolic and the Material: A Review of Jacques Rancière's *Aisthesis: Scenes from the Aesthetic Regime of Art*', *Parrhesia*, 18 (2013), 140.
35. Ibid., 141.
36. Rancière, *Aisthesis: Scenes from the Aesthetic Regime of Art*, trans. Zakir Paul (London and New York: Verso, 2013), xv.
37. Ibid.
38. Ibid.
39. Ibid., xvi.

I Coordinates

I

Fictions of Time
Jacques Rancière

First, some preliminary remarks about the notion of fiction. Fiction does not mean the invention of imaginary beings in contrast with solid reality. Fiction is a structure of rationality that is required wherever a sense of reality must be produced. It is firstly a form of presentation of things that cuts out a frame and places elements within it so as to compose a situation and make it perceptible. It can be a look cast through a window by a character in a novel or in a film. It can be the report made by an editorialist in a newsreel, telling us, for instance, that the French are anxious about the future or that Europe is prey to doubt. The point is not whether the description is true or not. We are not behind the window and we will never meet a character called 'the French'. The point is about the sense of reality produced by the cutting out of the scene, the identification of its elements and the modality of the description. Politicians, journalists or social scientists must use fictions, just like novelists, whenever they have to say: this is the situation, these are the elements that compose it. They also need it to tell whence the situation comes, what its elements make possible and what future will follow from it. This is the second aspect of the rationality of fiction: it is a form of linkage between events that makes them coexist or follow one another, establishes causal connections between them, makes sense of that connection and gives to that connection the modality of the real, the possible or the necessary. The connection may simply be the fact that a woman in a novel commits suicide because she has got into debt and cannot reimburse her creditors. It may be the connection made by a politician who affirms that the Greek people are indebted because they have lived beyond their means, or the causal link made by a sociologist who tells us that the anti-authoritarian revolts of the 1960s paved the way for the triumph of neo-liberalism and individualism, and so on. Fiction is present wherever one must say: this is what is given, this is the reason why it is so, and this is the consequence that can be drawn from it.

Now, what distinguishes literary fiction is the fact that the reality of the situations and the linkage of the events cannot be supposed to be already known, that they are the object of an explicit construction. This is why avowed fiction, far from being the fantasy that must be explained by the rational arguments of theory, politics or science, is more rational than the discourses that pretend to account for it. Literary fiction – or avowed fiction in general – is not so much the object that social science has to analyse as it is the laboratory where fictional forms are experimented as such and which, for that reason, helps us understand the functioning of the forms of unavowed fiction at work in politics, social science or other theoretical discourses. It does so because it is obliged to construct what is at the heart of any fictional rationality but easily can be presupposed in the forms of unavowed fiction: time, which means the form of coexistence of facts that defines a situation and the mode of connection between events that defines a story. What I will try to show in this chapter is how some transformations in the realm of artistic fiction, by subverting the normal forms of coexistence and linkage of events, also question the distribution of the forms of temporality within which the sense of a common history is constructed.

I begin with an episode in a specific form of fiction: a theoretical fiction constructed in order to account for the transformations of literary fiction. In the last chapter of *Mimesis* Erich Auerbach must produce a fictional operation for which his extensive knowledge is of no help: he must designate the point of arrival – which also means the highest achievement – in the long history of Western literary fiction. He must do so by way of the same method that he has used in the whole book: selecting a short passage from a fictional work that presents a specific 'sense of reality'. He selects thus a passage from Virginia Woolf's novel *To the Lighthouse*. This seems to be an odd choice since the passage narrates a quite minimalist event: the housewife Mrs Ramsay is knitting a pair of stockings destined for the son of the lighthouse keeper and she tries to measure them on the legs of her son. Moreover the narration of this tiny incident is broken by two digressions, one of which tells the feelings of Mrs Ramsay, while the other evokes the way in which she is perceived by people who are not present in the episode. One insignificant event plus two digressions: this is a fictional construction that would be given a very poor grade by any professor. This passage, however, marks for Auerbach the highest achievement in the progress of Western literature, an achievement that he sums up in a sentence which exactly overturns the criteria of the professors: 'What takes place here in Virginia Woolf's novel is precisely what was attempted everywhere in works of this kind (although not everywhere with the same insight and mastery) – that is, to put the emphasis on the random occurrence, to exploit it not in the service of a planned continuity of action but in itself.'[1]

This is an extraordinary statement: Auerbach tells us that the greatest achievement in the history of Western literary fiction is the dismantlement of the continuity of narrative action. It is the isolation of the random occurrence – perhaps we had better translate in Deleuzian fashion, the any-moment-whatever. Far from being satisfied with this paradoxical statement, he draws a momentous consequence from that achievement. He tells us that this term of the progression of literary fiction also is a landmark in a broader historical process since it bears the promise of a human community to come. 'It is still a long way to a common life of mankind on earth, but the goal begins to be visible. And it is most concretely visible now in the unprejudiced, precise, interior and exterior representation of the random moment in the lives of different people'.[2]

This narration of the historical destiny of Western fiction presents us with a whole nest of dialectical paradoxes. First paradox: the *fact* that Auerbach sees achieved in this passage is the rupture of the continuity of action. He could perfectly have made another choice, since, after all, the same novel presents many aspects of continuity: the narration starts with the project of going to the lighthouse and ends, many years after, when the father and his children arrive at the lighthouse. In the meantime, like in most novels, years have gone by, the children have grown up and some characters have died. Nevertheless it is the disconnection between the moments that is selected as the last event in the progress of literary fiction. Moreover, this term of the history fiction is itself conceived as a landmark in another historical process: the process leading to the future of a human community. Since the random moment is at the same time what is most singular and what is most common in everyday experience, its autonomisation points toward a human community to come. So, fiction reaches its highest historical achievement when it loses what seemed to constitute it, namely the causal connection between the events. The ultimate destiny of fiction in modern times thus might be the abolition of fiction.

The second paradox has to do with the random moment, the moment disconnected from 'any planned action' that gives its destination to the whole of the connections which constitute the historical process. This destination, however, is not reached through any specific connection of historical forces. The mediation between the two paradoxes is made by a third one: the most singular in the life of the individuals, what anybody lives in the solitude of the random moment is also the most common; it is what links it with the experience of everybody. I would like to show that this paradoxical connection between fiction and the abolition of fiction, the isolation of the random moment and the movement of the historical process, the most singular and the most common is not the personal invention of a particular theoretician. Instead it defines a certain idea of modernity, meaning a certain idea of the link between three forms of temporal process: firstly, the system of temporal connections that constitutes a literary or an artistic fiction; secondly, the system of connections which defines a common historical process; thirdly, the temporality of the lived time in everyday experience. My contention is that the apparent paradoxes of this modernism may help us understand the deeper contradictions which lie at the core of the dominant model of political and artistic modernity. It may do so because it questions the understanding of history on which the dominant interpretation of modernity rests. Ultimately it calls into question the dependency of the modern understanding of historical rationality upon an antique model of fictional rationality.

To make this point, I will compare Auerbach's argumentation with another interpretation of the relation between time, fiction and politics that had been formulated at the end of the 1930s in the polemical essays of Georg Lukács on the history of the modern Western novel. The point is that what is praised by Auerbach in the story of an evening in the Ramsay family is exactly what had been condemned by Lukács in the story of a day in the life of Leopold Bloom. It is fragmentation, which means for Lukács the subjective dissolution of the experience of social and historical reality into the random and passive impressions of insignificant individuals. But there is no point for Lukács in opposing objectivism to subjectivism. On the contrary, the evil of the dissolution is already present in objectivism itself. It is present in its way of dealing with time. It is the treatment of time that makes the difference between good realist fiction and bad naturalistic fiction. It is an opposition between two ways of linking events in a time sequence, an opposition that he sums up in his essay 'Narrate or Describe?'.[3] At the beginning of his essay Lukács opposes two horse races, one in Zola's *Nana* and the other in Tolstoy's *Anna Karenina*. Zola, he admits, colourfully describes every possible detail at a race, from the saddling of the horses to the finish of the race, including the fashion show of the Parisian public and the manoeuvring behind the scenes. This accumulation of detail, however, presents us with nothing more than the passive point of view of a spectator looking at a show. Zola describes the race for us as 'a thing'. On the contrary, Tolstoy narrates a race that is dramatised by the fall of one character, Vronsky, under the anxious eye of his lover, Anna, whose reactions are watched by her husband, Karenin. It is no more spectacle, then, but action, described from the point of view of the participants. The same opposition can be drawn between two events in a theatre. Zola describes in full detail the opening night in Nana's theatre: the auditorium, the performance on the stage, the intermissions, the foyer, the dressing rooms and so on. In contrast, when Balzac in *Lost Illusions* describes a premiere in a theatre, he focuses on the drama of the characters: the success of Coralie as an actress, the success of Lucien de Rubempré as a journalist, their passionate love, the conflicts generated by Lucien's success, and the rest. By so doing he shows us the rising power of the press and the subordination of both the theatre and the press to capitalism. It can be objected that Zola also shows us this subordination and he does it all the better as he describes them as objective facts and not simply from the point of view of fictional characters. It can also be said that Vronsky's fall is a mere incident while Zola shows us the state of a society through the spectacle of the horse race. But Lukács overturns the objections: Zola describes things, one beside the other, one after the other; he represents the prostitution of the theatre under capitalism as a result of a social state, as a dead thing. On the contrary Balzac, because he shows us 'complete' characters striving for their goals, shows us how the theatre *becomes* prostituted under capitalism. And even the fact that Vronsky's fall is a chance incident shows us that we are dealing with active characters, submitted to the chance events and not to dead realities. There is a strict opposition between two times: the time of description which puts things beside one another like in a genre picture or a still life; and the time of action in which active characters interact with the movement of the social process.

This connection between the activity of complete personalities and the dynamism of the historical process deserves attention. For Lukács it witnesses the continuity from the great humanist tradition to the Marxist understanding of the laws of History. More radically, I think, it shows us the link between the logic of the Marxist narrative and the logic of the representative regime of fiction. The core of the alliance between those two logics is a conception of time; it is a hierarchical division of temporalities. The Lukácsian opposition between narration and description exactly follows the basic principles laid down in Aristotle's *Poetics*. Fiction, Aristotle stated, is an arrangement of actions, through which active characters move from ignorance to knowledge and from good fortune to misfortune – or the reverse. This arrangement of actions takes place according to necessity or verisimilitude. Therefore poetic fiction, which tells how facts might happen in general, through a necessary or plausible connection of causes and effects, is superior to the chronicle that only tells how facts happen, in their particularity, one after another. This poetic connection of events through which the characters shift from fortune to misfortune makes the content of the drama in opposition to the *opsis*, the visible setting of the performance on the stage which is, he says, the task of the props-man and not of the poet. This Aristotelian distinction had been revived in the times of the Italian Renaissance and of the French seventeenth century and it had become the basis of a canonical division of genres contrasting, for instance, tragedy, devoted to noble actions and characters, with comedy, devoted to the prose of the everyday, and history painting with genre painting. When Lukács contrasts Zola's chronicles or genre pictures with Balzac or Tolstoy's dramas revealing the historical process, he exactly follows the Aristotelian division. But the opposition of two ways of linking events in a horizontal connection rested itself on a vertical separation of temporalities which was a separation between two forms of life and two categories of human beings. The temporality of the causal connection of events fitted the condition of those men who were called active men: men able either to conceive of great ends and to pursue them against the strokes of fortune or to act for the sole purpose of acting, as an end in itself; the temporality of the chronicle, the comedy or the genre painting fitted the condition of those men who were called passive because they were enclosed in the time of the everyday, the time of the mere production and reproduction of life when things happen one after another and when any form of activity is only a means for an immediate end. As is well known, this division between two forms of activity also was a division between two forms of inactivity: active men's leisure was an end in itself while ordinary men's rest was only an interval between two expenses of energy.

Lukács's analysis thus casts light on the dependency of the Marxist narrative of the historical development upon the Aristotelian conceptualisation of fiction. His polemic emphasises more than ever the opposition between the rational structure of the causal fiction and the empirical character of the chronicle – which means that he endorses the opposition between the active men dealing with the strokes of fortune in their pursuit of ambitious ends and the passive men, enclosed in a world of things where everything is mere 'detail'. Lukács's insistence on the role of the epic individual characters may seem to contradict the Marxist theoretical revolution that has located the matrix of the causal linkage of events in the time of History and the motor of the rational development of history in the obscure domain of the production of material life. I think that this emphasis itself may be a way of concealing the questions that Lukács's object – the realist novel – raises with respect to his method – Marxist historical materialism. As a matter of fact, if the latter has based the historical process on the obscure life of everyday production, it has reinstated the hierarchy of temporalities at another level by opposing the time of science, the time of those who know the causal connection of the historical forces to the time of ideology, the time of those who live in the mere succession, the time of the things that appear one beside the other, one after another on the wall of the cave. It is true that, in return, Marxism has subverted the antique relation between knowledge and fortune. In the antique logic of tragedy, the shift from ignorance to knowledge used to be, for the elevated characters of the plot, a shift from good fortune to misfortune. In the science of history, necessity works in the opposite way: as it develops itself, the misfortune of capitalist exploitation produces a knowledge of the laws of history and society which becomes a weapon in the struggle that will open the way to good fortune for everybody. But it is precisely at this point that the logic of the realist novel gets in the way. It does not restore the antique consequence from knowledge to misfortune. More radically it calls into question the very idea of a consequence from knowledge to action. In its plots science does not produce either good fortune or misfortune. It has no effect in the domain of action.

This is the lesson that the good realist novelists Balzac and Tolstoy teach as well as the bad naturalistic novelist Zola. The analysis of the multiple layers of the modern town that Balzac displays at the beginning of *The Girl with the Golden Eyes* does not contribute anything to the success of the thirteen omniscient and omnipotent conspirers invented by the novelist. On the contrary, they fail in all their endeavours and the highest success of Vautrin, the great strategist imagined by Balzac, is winning his position as chief of the police. As for Tolstoy, he shows in *War and Peace* that the strategic science of the generals weighs nothing on the battlefield. Success or failure is determined by an incalculable connection of small actions and chance events. Their lesson thus is not different from that provided by Zola's cycle of the Rougon Macquart: at the end of the scientific exploration through which the history of a family reveals both the laws of heredity and the functioning of a society, the scientific records are burnt by the scientist's mother to protect the social respectability of her family; they are replaced on the shelves of the library by the layette of a baby who is the incestuous son of the scientist and whose demonstrations of hunger symbolise the triumph of a life instinct devoid of any purpose.

Lukács's emphasis on the opposition between the active 'participants' and the mere passive 'observers' might be a way of concealing the gap that modern fiction has opened between knowledge and action. What makes the decision, Lukács tells us, is the decision of acting instead of looking. But at this point the paradox takes on another form. Lukács's analysis shows that capacity of planning action is progressively lessened by the very development of the capitalist process and of its grip upon all social activities. In the 1830s the rise of capitalism was revealed by the failed businessman Balzac through the intrigues led by the naïve and ambitious Lucien de Rubempré. In the 1870s capitalism has extended its sway over French society and allows Zola to show in detail the mechanism of its power in theatres as well as in the mining industry or at the stock exchange. But this means that capitalism has become a state of things that can be accurately described but that no epic characters are able to confront. Things still get worse in the time of James

Joyce when a later development of capitalism is expressed by the 'most evolved subjectivism' which 'transforms the entire inner life of characters into something static and reified'.[4] Of course Lukács refutes the idea that such a dissolution of the 'human personality' is the necessary consequence of the development of capitalism. He makes it a consequence of the 'passive capitulation' of the descriptive writers before the development of the inhumanity of capitalism. There are, he says, 'great individual artists like Thomas Mann who struggle against the current' and can still make true humanist and realist fiction.[5] Lukács does not seem inclined to notice that the decline of the Buddenbrook family, the fascination with illness and inertia in *The Magic Mountain* or the passive expectation of death by the professor Aschenbach don't demonstrate a very high degree of active participation in the development of the historical process.

But the problem lies deeper: by overemphasising the role of the 'active characters' and the interconnection between their actions and the global linkage of causes and effects, Lukács revives the old Aristotelian rationality of fiction behind the modern Marxist rationality. The Marxist faith in the link between the development of necessity, the production of knowledge and the rise of resistance is overturned by the old tragic connection between the acquisition of knowledge and the shift to misfortune. Lukács's analysis leads to a strange conclusion: the progress of capitalism – and of its knowledge – is the progress of its decline which also means the growing incapacity to resist it. Consequently the form of artistic fiction which is required by this progress is the form of fiction that goes 'against the current' of that development. Such is the conclusion that the Marxist theoretician Georg Lukács seems to draw, without spelling it out, in 1936 in Moscow. Such is the conclusion that another Marxist theoretician, the young anti-Stalinist critic Clement Greenberg, spells out three years later in New York when he writes his famous essay 'Avant-garde and Kitsch': the task of the modernist avant-garde is to resist the movement of History. From that premise Greenberg draws a quite different conclusion: the artistic avant-garde has to move away from any kind of political concern and social commitment and to commit itself to the sole experimentation of the possibilities of its own medium.

I think that it is this paradoxical conclusion of the dominant model of the historical process that is questioned by Auerbach's strange emphasis on the 'random moment' disconnected from the continuity of any planned action. What is at issue in this conflict of modernities must, however, be clarified. The random moment is not the minimal unit of time isolated from the long line and the complex interconnections of the global historical process. It is a qualitatively different sort of time-unit. It is the scene on which appears the issue that is concealed by the simple opposition between the short time and the long time: a conflict of temporalities that is a conflict between forms of life. Beneath the opposition between the necessity of poetic fiction and the randomness of the chronicle, there is the hierarchy opposing two forms of life: on the one hand, the form of life of the active men, using time for the accomplishment of their ends or the mere pleasure of experiencing action or leisure as ends in themselves; on the other hand, the form of life of the passive men also called mechanical men: human beings enclosed in the temporality of the everyday where they only deal with means and never with ends. What can be modern, from this point of view, is the abolition of the very hierarchy of temporalities that links the representative poetics with a whole hierarchical distribution of the sensible. But the abolition of the representative hierarchy in fiction does not simply consist in introducing common people and the prose of the everyday into the realm of high art. It entails something more radical which is the destruction of the representational form of the event and of the connection of events as an 'arrangement of actions' which was based on the division between active and passive human beings. The typically 'modern' time is thus the time 'disconnected' from the integration of its moments into either the temporality of intentional action or that of mechanical repetition; a time wherein activity and passivity have become indiscernible, an inactive time within which the opposition between leisure and rest has also been abolished. Such is the 'disconnected' time whose formula had first been spelled out in Rousseau's *Reveries of the Solitary Walker*. It is the time that Stendhal's hero Julien Sorel enjoys in his prison when he has stepped out of the play of social intrigues. But it is also the time that the joiner Gauny, on whose texts I comment in *Proletarian Nights*, enjoys in the house where he is laying the floor while his look diverges from the activity of his hands and takes possession by imagination of the perspective through the window, or when, once back home, he devotes to the leisure of writing the time that should be devoted to rest. It is this time of disruption that literature takes over and transforms so as to make it its own form of temporality, the form of temporality in which all moments are equal, which ruins the opposition between the causal linkage of poetic events and the mere succession of facts.

Such is the issue at stake in the polemical texts in which Virginia Woolf calls into question the very logic of the plot, the logic of the story of love, social success or else determining how a moment must be followed by another moment and linked with it within an ordered totality. Her target is the apparently banal and innocuous idea of 'succession'. It is at this point that the horizontal connection of events is linked with a whole hierarchical distribution of the sensible whose principle can be summed up in three words: 'Everybody follows somebody.' This principle, she says, is clearly borrowed from the protocol of the official ceremonies in which the Archbishop of York follows the Lord High Chancellor who himself follows the Archbishop of Canterbury. The disruption of the old hierarchical regime of fiction thus entails two main transformations: first, the events of fortune and misfortune, the pursuits of social or sentimental ends, are replaced by a halo of sensory micro-events that are not determined by any goal; second, the mode of relation of those events is no more succession, it is coexistence and interpenetration. To become 'modern', that is to get rid of its dependency on the rules of social hierarchy, fiction simply must be faithful to what can be observed in the everyday life of any ordinary man: 'The mind receives a myriad impressions – trivial, fantastic, evanescent, or engraved with the sharpness of steel. From all sides they come, an incessant shower of innumerable atoms.'[6] It is not simply a matter of opposing the everyday to the long run. The everyday is the fictional framework inside which the truth of the experience of time must appear: the truth of the coexistence of the atoms, the multiplicity of micro-events which occur 'at the same time' and penetrate each other without any hierarchy, thereby drawing unpredictable arabesques that the novelist must record and transcribe *as they happen* – and no more in the Aristotelian way, as they *might* happen. At this point the revolution of the old 'liberal' art of words meets the revolution promised by the new mechanical art of the moving images. A few months before Virginia Woolf's manifesto, the young filmmaker Jean Epstein had written a manifesto for the new art, *Bonjour cinéma!*, in which he pitted against the lie of the story the truth of cinema, the truth of the 'tragic crystal' of time whose waves 'advance in concentric circles, expanding from relay to relay'. As it turns out, what is at issue in this emplotment of time as coexistence is the abolition of the old opposition between the liberal arts and the mechanical arts, between the free active men and the passive or mechanical men.

It can be said that this 'anti-hierarchical' emplotment of time contrasts the historical connection of causes and effects with a formalist play reserved to elitist artists dealing with the impalpable emotions of elitist characters. But things are more complicated. When Lukács opposes the Marxist knowledge of the interconnection of actions to formalist description, or when Auerbach makes the fictional democracy of the 'any-moment-whatever' the harbinger of a human community that will experience this democracy in real life, they both forget that this democratic subversion of time can also be staged and has effectively been staged as the connection between the artistic subversion of fiction and the Marxist revolution of real life. They forget or they ignore that it is this conjunction that has taken place in the work of the so-called avant-garde artists of the revolutionary Soviet Union. At the same time as James Joyce described the myriad impressions affecting the ordinary man Leopold Bloom during an ordinary day in Dublin, and Virginia Woolf described the walks of Clarissa Dalloway and Peter Walsh on an ordinary day in London, those artists drew a both logical and unexpected conclusion from the revolution of literary fiction. If it is taken seriously, the abolition of the hierarchy in fiction already is the abolition of the very distinction between the poetic connection of events and the prosaic connection of activities in the everyday life. 'Modern fiction' in this sense becomes a contradiction in terms. The destiny of fiction is to abolish itself, to equate itself with the interconnection of 'ordinary activities' that makes the life of the collective present in the microcosm of any ordinary day.

Such was notably the consequence drawn by a filmmaker, Dziga Vertov, when he proudly wrote at the beginning of *Man with a Movie Camera* that his film was 'an experiment in the visual transmission of visual phenomena without the help of intertitles, without the help of a script, without the help of actors'. This proclamation must not be misunderstood. It is not simply a matter of substituting the record of actual things for the invention of a plot. It is a matter of presenting the interconnection of all the activities that occur in an ordinary day as the reality of a 'common life', the reality of communism. The work of the cameraman who runs

Fictions of Time 37

everywhere all day long to shoot activities of any kind, and of the editor who cuts, arranges and pastes the fragments of film, is destined to a unique operation: the operation of manifesting the living link of this community. Now this operation itself must be shown as homogeneous to all the everyday activities that it records and connects. This is why the gesture of the hand that turns the crank of the camera and the hand that cuts and pastes fragments of film must continuously be connected with other gestures of other hands: a policeman turning the signs to regulate the traffic in the street, a seamstress plying her needle, a female worker packing cigarettes in a factory, a cashier turning the crank of his cash register, the operators of a telephone exchange inserting and removing jack plugs, but also a manicurist doing the nails of a customer in a beauty parlour, or a shoe-shiner in the street. All those handiworks, as they are connected together, make the reality of communism as a common fabric of life. This is why it is pointless to ask whether the doing of nails in a beauty parlour or the activity of a shoe-shiner are appropriate episodes in the narration of a day in the new communist society. What matters is not the content of the activity, which may link it with different ages and forms of society, it is its *form*: an activity of the hand which can be linked with any similar activity. Now the main point is the temporal form of the linkage. Even though it is the story of a day symbolised in a one-hour film, the time of the film, the time of the linkage is not the time of succession. It is the time of the existence and interpenetration of similar activities occupying equal fragments of time and proceeding at the same rhythm. It is the egalitarian temporality of the any-moment-whatever.[7]

This is what links the leisurely time of Mrs Ramsay or Mrs Dalloway with the speedy activity of their 'sisters' working on the assembly line in the tobacco factory. Apparently there is no relationship between the clouds of impressions and reveries whirling around the knitting of a pair of stockings in a petty bourgeois vacation home or the shopping of an upper-class woman in the fashionable areas of London and the accelerated movement of the great symphony of communist work constructed by Dziga Vertov. The latter's project was said to be the radical achievement of a modern anti-representative movement which is readily epitomised in a simple operation: substituting presence or direct performance for representation. On this basis, the avant-gardist self-suppression of art in the construction of new forms of life appeared as the most radical form of this artistic revolution: the apotheosis of action, brushing aside the whole universe of fiction. But it is a complete misunderstanding. The point is not to substitute direct performance for representation. It is to substitute a pattern of temporality for another. And *Man with a Movie Camera* does not present the apotheosis of action. It presents the apotheosis of movement. Movement is not action brought back to its quintessence. It is action deprived of what gives it its substance, namely a connection of causes and effects determined by the pursuit of specific ends. This is precisely what is lacking in the avant-gardist symphony of movement and what makes it similar to the literary exploitation of the random moment disconnected from the continuity of action. Far from any 'planned continuity of action', this symphony supposes that each specific activity be disconnected from the specific end that it pursues and reduced to a pure sequence of movement equal to any other sequence of movement, regardless of its specific nature and finality.

The pure performance opposed to the old representative fiction is a specific form of performance, whose idea, between the end of the nineteenth century and the 1920s, had been embodied by one art: dance, meaning modern dance that had substituted for the old representative and hierarchical art of the ballet, the pure power of free movement. As it had notably been theorised by one of the pioneers of modern dance, Isadora Duncan, free movement is an endless movement which means two things: firstly it is a continuous movement, a movement that unrelentingly engenders another movement, dismissing the very opposition of movement and repose. Secondly it is a movement with no purpose except movement itself. In this movement all the hierarchical oppositions between activity and passivity, action and inaction, leisure and rest have disappeared. It is exactly in this way that Vertov constructs communism as the reign of the equality of movement, the reign of the any-moment-whatever. It is no coincidence that, on the famous posters designed by the Stenberg brothers for the film, the movement of the film is symbolised by a ballerina instead of a factory worker. As it turns out, at the end of the film, at the moment when the link of all the activities of the day must be synthetised and symbolised, this visual synthesis of the collective movement is provided by the dance of three ballerinas in superimposition. This superimposition is not simply a technical device among all those that create a sense of community on the surface on the screen.

More radically the dance of the three ballerinas is the presentation of the form of temporality that connects the movements of their 'sisters', the female workers on the assembly line between whom the camera draws its straight lines. The presentation of the vibrant activity of the communist society may appear to be at the furthest distance from the evening reverie of the housewife Mrs Ramsay or the morning walk of the upper-class woman Clarissa Dalloway. But it implements the same basic principle. The vibrant activity and the idle fictional reverie are weaved in the same fabric of time: the time of coexistence and interpenetration wherein activity and inactivity have become equivalent.

Such an equivalence defines a certain communism. Communism, after all, had first been thought by Marx as the form of community in which the generic human activity, which had been subordinated to the mere necessity of the reproduction of life, has become an end in itself. The Vertovian symphony of work exactly implements this aesthetic communism. But the communist party of the Soviet Union implemented another communism, a communism defined as an end to be reached through the strict obedience to the laws of the social process and the calculations of the scientific avant-garde. From its point of view the communism of the any-moment-whatever could only be a formalist play. The task of the artists was not to substitute the construction of the sensory fabric of the community for the creation of fictions. It was to represent the reality of the action of the builders of communism and to entertain them after their efforts. In short they had to produce not only fictions but fictions obeying the rules of the old representative logic. We can describe this conflict as the conflict between aesthetic communism and representative communism. Now this conflict of two communisms also produced the splitting of the modernist emplotment of time. This splitting was witnessed in the 1930s by the two apparently opposite attitudes that I evoked earlier. On the one hand, there is the denunciation of modernist 'fragmentation' and the return to the 'humanist' fiction and its active characters engaged in the interconnection of social relationships, proclaimed by Lukács in 1936. The problem with this return is that it relies on a self-contradictory analysis of the historical process: the dynamism of the capitalist process means the development of its decline which also means the acceleration of fragmentation and the decline of the active capacity. In the future, the conceptualisation of 'late capitalism' will prove both the most efficient matrix for the analysis of any fiction or any cultural production and the most repetitive demonstration of the eternity of this lateness. This is perhaps that future which was anticipated in 1939 by Clement Greenberg when he gave the name of 'modernism' to the radical dismissal of what had been the core of historical modernism: the destruction of the hierarchy of temporalities. Modernism as he conceptualised it was a reaction against the development of capitalism that destroyed the conditions of high art. But reacting against capitalism firstly meant reacting against its most catastrophic effect as regards art. This most catastrophic effect was a subversion of the normal distribution of temporalities: by sending the sons and daughters of peasants to the industrial towns, capitalism had made them discover, along with the separation of the time of work and the time of rest, another experience of time, the time of boredom against which they asked for a culture of their own which could be nothing but the culture of *kitsch*. In order to resist that evolution, artists had to move away from both social commitment and fictional logic in order to explore the sole demands and possibilities of their medium.

In this distribution of the play, the evening in the Ramsay family and Auerbach's comment make a discordant tone resound. On the one hand, the microcosms and the epiphanies of the modern novel appear as the reduction of a lost dream, the dream that had been implemented in the great project of art becoming life, becoming identical with the breath of a new community. But things can be thought differently. It can be said that those literary moments have kept what the speedy rhythm of the Vertovian camera absorbed: the interval of time giving to the two women on the assembly line the possibility to dissociate their reverie or their conversation from the task of their hands. By doing so they may have faithfully kept what has been brushed aside by both the call to humanist fiction and the proclamation of so-called modernist autonomy, the promise encapsulated in the egalitarian revolution of time. Or rather we can see the great egalitarian symphony of movement and the tiny narrative of the random moments as the symmetric fragments of a project which may have been the most consistent form of the modernist dream: the identification of the modern revolution of the social conditions with a revolution in time itself, a revolution abolishing the division and the hierarchy of temporalities which is at the very core of the social hierarchy. In that sense, both the symphony of movement and the narratives of the random moments still keep, for an indefinite future, the promise made at the end of the eighteenth century by a German poet: the promise of a revolution that would not simply concern the art of poetry or any specific art but the art of life itself.

Notes

1. Eric Auerbach, *Mimesis: The Representation of Reality in Western Literature*, trans. Willard R. Trask (Princeton: Princeton University Press, 1968), 552.
2. Ibid.
3. See Georg Lukács, *Writer and Critic, and Other Essays*, trans. Arthur Kahn (London: Merlin Press, 1970), 110–48.
4. Ibid., 144.
5. Lukács, 'Es geht um den Realismus', in *Essays über Realismus* (Berlin: Neuwied, 1971), 322.
6. Virginia Woolf, 'Modern Fiction', in *The Crowded Dance of Modern Life*, ed. Rachel Bowlby (London: Penguin, 1993), 8.
7. See Gilles Deleuze, *Cinema 1*, trans. Hugh Tomlinson and Barbara Habberjam (Minneapolis: University of Minnesota Press, 1997), 29–32, 100–22.

2

Jacques Rancière in the Forest of Signs: Indiscipline, Figurality and Translation[1]

Eric Méchoulan

'I must verify the reason for my thought, the humanity of my feelings, but I can do it only by making them venture forth into the forest of signs that by themselves don't want to say anything, don't correspond with that thought or that feeling.'[2] What kind of *adventure* is this? Why must we *verify* our very humanity? Moreover, why should such verification be carried out in the middle of the obviously obscure forest of signs? In order to answer these questions, we first need to think about how we conduct our reflections, the means we can use, and the relations we are able to create.

Indisciplining

Let us begin with a question of method: though he studied and taught philosophy and conducted historical research on nineteenth-century workers' archives, Jacques Rancière is first of all a reader. As we all are. But he is a much more patient and attentive reader than most, and one who resists falling into disciplinary habits. Maybe he learned from the nineteenth-century workers he studied for years that one does not always need to walk on well-paved roads. He wrote a remarkable historical study about them, without being a historian or 'applying' a historical method. When he wrote about the methods of 'true' historians, it was less to criticise them or to propose other ways of interpreting archives than to reveal how they constituted, without acknowledging it, a poetics of knowledge. It was not a way of undermining their force or of assigning them the status of fiction (as has sometimes been done by philosophers or literary critics). It was a way to make visible the distribution of territories at work in specific historical research. Indeed, fiction should not be understood as the invention

Jacques Rancière in the Forest of Signs   43

of pure imaginary worlds; it is what Jacques Rancière calls a 'structure of rationality' – that is, a way of presenting and associating things, situations or events in order to make them perceptible and intelligible.³

Making these territories visible was a matter of reading surfaces and escaping disciplinary thought, since disciplines are above all ways of delimiting who has the right to speak and who does not, who is supposed to know and who is not:

> A well-ordered society would like the bodies which compose it to have the perceptions, sensations and thoughts which correspond to them. Now this correspondence is perpetually disturbed. [. . .] Disciplinary thought must ceaselessly hinder this haemorrhage in order to establish stable relations between states of the body and the modes of perception and signification which correspond to them.⁴

Disciplines are social stabilisations of knowledge. To come back to Michel Foucault's fundamental lesson: scrutinising ways of knowing is deciphering relations of power.

We then need a form of political as well as theoretical *indiscipline* in order to espouse the movement of social life. Asked if his work was interdisciplinary or a-disciplinary, Rancière answered:

> Neither. It is 'indisciplinary'. It is not only a matter of going besides the disciplines but of breaking them. [. . .] The apportionment of disciplines refers to the more fundamental apportionment that separates those regarded as qualified to think from those regarded as unqualified; those who do the science and those who are regarded as its object.⁵

What must be examined then is the distribution of fields and their means of arranging things and events, even if this is only to recognise how empirical data is perceived as a thing here or as an event there.

We could also use another word to describe his regime of thinking, a word sometimes used with a pejorative meaning, but in which we still should hear the important feeling of love: amateurism. He claims the 'amateur' label for himself on the cinema, about which he has written extensively without any major theorisation. But with his usual twist, Rancière asks us to think again about what an amateur is, since 'amateurism is also a theoretical and political position, one that contests the authority of specialists by re-examining how the borders of their domains are traced at the intersection of experience and knowledge'.[6] Against the experts who are supposed to know how to reveal the true meanings of events, the territorial distribution of experience and knowledge must be examined above all.

Contrary to any hermeneutical principle that assumes something to be hidden (and thus usually sacred) under trivial surfaces, Rancière's 'method' is to discern how appearances are brought together, and form new objects, even under the heading of institutions and fields of expertise. This is consistent with his emphasis on equality: hermeneuts show off their mastery over texts and events, and that is exactly what should be avoided. He explicitly claims,

> I always try to think in terms of horizontal distributions, combinations between systems of possibilities, not in terms of surface and substratum. Where one searches for the hidden beneath the apparent, a position of mastery is established. I have tried to conceive of a topography that does not presuppose this position of mastery. It is possible, from any given point, to try to reconstruct the conceptual network that makes it possible to conceive of a statement, that causes a painting or a piece of music to make an impression, that causes reality to appear transformable or inalterable. This is in a way the main theme of my research.[7]

As is well known, hermeneutics gives an important place to figurality and interpretation. Such an anti-hermeneutic stance implies that figurality be reconfigured and interpretation reinterpreted.

Figuring

For hermeneutics, classical figural interpretation establishes a link between two events or persons in such a way that the first signifies not only itself but also the second, while the second involves or fulfils the first. More broadly, a figure shows or means something other than what it seems to show or mean. It necessitates an operation connecting the two elements, with the idea that what is now discovered is the true being or meaning. One could feel that figurality denies any stable identity (after all, it was conceived as a disease or an abuse by many philosophers; Hobbes, for example, cautions against the contagious power of metaphors, tropes and other rhetorical figures). But, on the contrary, with this operation of ultimate identification, one plays only the old game of appearance and truth. Despite the acknowledgement of the power of figuration, its goal is still to stabilise identity, to master once and for all the operation of signification.

Rancière's practice detaches itself from such a goal and gives interpretation the flavour of adventure. It is a common ground for researchers and artists:

> Like researchers, artists construct the stages where the manifestation and effect of their skills are exhibited, rendered uncertain in the terms of the new idiom that conveys a new intellectual adventure. The effect of the idiom cannot be anticipated. It requires spectators who play the role of active interpreters. An emancipated community is a community of narrators and translators.[8]

I will later come back to the notion of translation. For the moment, let us emphasise the fact that the horizon of figurality is not the identification of a deep secret but the movement of active interpretation, not the substitution of one appearance for another as legitimate truth but the uncertain adventure of reading in a forest of signs.

Kant distinguishes between artistic forms, determined by intentions, and aesthetic forms, free from any strict determination and that open up a play of the imagination. As he says, 'by an aesthetic idea, however, I mean that representation of the imagination that occasions much thinking though without it being possible for any determinate thought, i.e. concept, to be adequate to it, which, consequently, no language fully attains or can make intelligible.'[9] Even if no language can make them completely intelligible, there is still some room in each language for figuration to manoeuvre. What interests Rancière here is the opening of the indeterminate. That is where figurality plays its role. He seems to be remarkably close to Kant's insights when he claims that 'I have tried to think about this art of "aesthetic ideas" by expanding the concept of "figure", to make it signify not only the substitution of one term for another but the intertwining of several regimes of expression and the work of several arts and several media.'[10] In this expansion of figurality, we have the opportunity to reshuffle the ancient cards of form and matter, activity and passivity.

It is in this framework, between the active and the passive, that Jacques Rancière explores the notion of 'pensiveness': something in an image that resists thought. According to Rancière, Godard's *Histoires du cinéma* offers us a good example of pensiveness through the very labour of figuration.[11] Godard shows us, first, how a double logic of articulation of elements can be used – that of narrative sequence and infinite metaphorisation; second, how different arts and media can exchange their respective powers; and third, how one specific art can constitute the imaginary of another one. Each time, Godard expands the necessary notion of figure through arts and media.

Rancière resists the vogue of technological determinism, and especially the Benjaminian thesis that mechanical arts would induce a shift in artistic paradigms and a new relation to aesthetics. On the contrary, for mechanical productions to be recognised as arts, they first need a new aesthetic paradigm, offering new topics or another character: the anonymous. 'Commonplace' (*quelconque*) appearances are not promoted by new techniques of visual capture such as photography; it is rather that photography can only become recognised as an art when a new aesthetic regime enables the anonymous and the commonplace to be visible as artistic appearances.[12] Aesthetics offers another link to politics, one that forces us to re-evaluate what a medium or a media can be.[13]

Close to Kant's – and, moreover, Schiller's – understanding of the aesthetic (etymologically, the 'sensation'), we can see aesthetics as playing with the two meanings of the word 'sense': the sensory and signification, or perception and discernment.

> Schiller's aesthetic state, by suspending the opposition between an active understanding and passive sensibility, aims at breaking down – with an idea of art – an idea of society based on the opposition between those who think and decide and those who are doomed to material tasks. [...] this suspension of work's negative value became the assertion of its positive value as the very form of the shared effectivity of thought and community.[14]

The question of activity and passivity does not belong only to spectatorship: it is, on the one hand, a question of policing – determining who has the right and the power to be active, and who has, at best, the right to remain silent and passive – and, on the other hand, a question of politics – emancipating people from these relations of power and rethinking what activity and passivity can be. 'There is a subversive virtue in the fact of not acting, or rather of making action inactive and inaction active.'[15] The subversion comes from the fact that the refusal of determination is not the simple love of pure beauty, outside of the world, but the voiding of the hierarchical difference between ends and means. What was once the privilege of the elite (to decide the nature of the ends, and who would be used as means) is nowadays at the disposal of everyone.

Acts of emancipation equalise anyone with anyone else. It is not an equalisation of identities[16] but a production of subjects-in-the-making. Rancière focuses on acts of subjectivation, but 'acts' here must redefine the borders of activity and passivity. Along the same lines, we should speak here less of the 'subject' and more of the processes of subjectivation. 'The refusal to theorize the subject is integral to his critique of the politics of theory.'[17]

In theorising the processes of subjectivation, Rancière circumvents any theory of stable identity, just as figuration gives identity its fluidity, its constant renewal and its seduction (etymologically, *se-ducere* means 'to lead away, apart'). As Donna Haraway says, 'Figures do not have to be representational and mimetic, but they do have to be tropic; that is, they cannot be literal and self-identical. Figures must involve at least some kind of displacement that can trouble identifications and certainties.'[18] For Rancière, figures are, moreover, ways of operating: they are not a representation of something, be it imaginary or real, but a construction of situations and their possible meanings, relations of inclusion or exclusion, borders marked or erased between perception and action.[19] This is why figuration is a matter of politics. It concerns the *texture* of the real.

Roland Barthes tried to show how, in realist novels, the little detail, pointless as far as the narrative is concerned, is a way of reinforcing the feeling of a description of something real. Rancière claims that the mention of the barometer in Flaubert's *Un Cœur simple* is not an 'effect of real', but a way to show the texture of this real, the type of life lived by the characters.[20] Figurality is a way of organising these textures. It operates like daydreaming (*rêverie*): daydreaming is not a refuge in an interior world for the person who does not want to act because reality is disappointing, but another mode of thinking, of building structures of rationality. Daydreaming erases the very division between the thinking head, clearly deciding what will be the ends, and the exterior world, where the effects of the thought would be perceptible.[21] Just like pensiveness, it reconfigures our uses of figurality between activity and passivity. What is at stake here is the status of action. An act is not only the fact of doing something in social space; it is also a hierarchical structure of both the perceptible and this social sphere.[22] Passivity is then not only the fact that one is submitted to an action, it is also a way of reproducing this hierarchical division. That is why Jacques Rancière tries to open a space and a time of thought where these divisions are called into question.

'To stand by' is to do nothing, but also to be ready to act or support somebody. In putting forward the possibility of an inactive activity, Rancière recalls feminist issues of care.[23] In order to be recognised and to be able to voice your concerns, you need to be standing in social space. You need to have a standing, a status – equal to anyone else's. What matters is not being in the centre but recognising the frontiers, and being willing to step to the side. *Standing by* is to be on somebody's side and to look edgewise at things and gestures. Side issues are actually the real issues.

Instead of territories of thought and fields of knowledge that are supposed to enclose the meanings of events and institute social identities, Rancière invites us to step aside into the position of the spectator, but an emancipated spectator free from wrong figurations of his or her passivity.[24] In his book *On the Shores of Politics* (whose title is already an invitation to watch and talk from the sides), he claims that the *demos* is 'forever drawing away from itself', that is, working on its own edges, experiencing its unlikeness to itself. That constitutes the emancipatory issue of figurality.

Translating

As we saw earlier, 'an emancipated community is a community of narrators and translators.'[25] Actually, the movement implied by the operation of figuration is already a translation inside one's own language. We should not consider there to be a strong division between native tongues and second languages. Even native tongues are foreign languages. Writers know better than any 'native' speakers that they are not respected artists because they have mastered the language, but on the contrary because they are constantly perplexed, even baffled, by the language they are supposed to use. Pascal Quignard expresses it with a surprising eloquence:

> I will have spent my life searching for words that failed me. What is a man of letters? One for whom words fail, leap, flee, lose sense. They always tremble a little before the strange shape they nevertheless end up inhabiting. They neither speak nor hide: they give signs tirelessly.[26]

The very use of the future perfect testifies to the uneasy temporal structure of such a feeling. Words offer forms, but they shiver as though under a torn coat in the windy forest of signs. And nevertheless they inhabit these forms; they are at home in this very strangeness. The slight reference to Heraclitus ('The lord whose is the oracle at Delphi neither speaks nor hides his meaning, but gives a sign') is also a sign of this strange familiarity of signs.

Side issues and second language practices are not marginal issues, they are the main operations at stake because language use is never purely literal and words never stick to the categories or the social order they are supposed to reproduce. They are never hermetic forms, perfectly woven around themselves. Another French writer describes with acuteness the relationship of the writer to words:

> What controls the effectiveness of a writer's use of words is not the capacity to clasp meaning tightly, it is an almost tactile knowledge of the layout of their property lines, and even more, their litigations over common ownership. For the writer, almost everything in the word is a border, and almost nothing is contained.[27]

The frontiers of meaning do not delimit words, they divide the word, and at the same time they open it to other words and different uses, provoking unexpected regroupings. The question of translation is then a fundamental one, because it engages not only the relation between languages, but also the relation between the literal and the figural, between systems of classification and their defiguration. These systems of classification are nothing else than figures that present themselves as something outside the regime of figurality. Hence the deep relation between uses of language and political situations:

> Man is a political animal because he is a literary animal who lets himself be diverted from his 'natural' purpose by the power of words. [. . .] This has always been, as is well known, the phobia of those in power and the theoreticians of good government, worried that the circulation of writing

would produce 'disorder' in the established system of classification. [. . .] It is true that the circulation of these quasi-bodies causes modifications in the sensory perception of what is common to the community, in the relationship between what is common to language and the sensible distribution of spaces and occupations. They form, in this way, uncertain communities that contribute to the formation of enunciative collectives that call into question the distribution of roles, territories, and languages. In short, they contribute to the formation of political subjects that challenge the given distribution of the sensible. A political collective is not, in actual fact, an organism or a communal body. The channels for political subjectivization are not those of imaginary identification but those of 'literary' disincorporation.[28]

Far from collective identities and systems of classification, the 'essence' of man as a political animal (according to the famous Aristotelian formula) is actually being engaged in storytelling and translations. The true arena of the political is the terrain of translation. Who is in charge of translations and who decides what sentences are deemed untranslatable delimits systems of power. The people in power fear all these words circulating in the social space, because one can never know exactly where they will end up, and how they will be interpreted and recycled.

Defiguration is then a cause for concern, since words can always move on/out/away 'without a legitimate father to accompany them toward their authorized addressee'.[29] This allusion to Plato's *Phaedrus* emphasises the fact that the condemnation of the medium of writing is far less ontological or epistemological than political.[30] Media matter because they always put communication in jeopardy when they are not strictly controlled. But even in the most controlled communication, words cannot stay exactly where they should be because the addressees are never completely determined or anticipated.

This constitutes one more reason for stepping outside any hermeneutical prejudice. The category of understanding, so often invoked by hermeneuts, does not open up hidden meanings, or something more reasonable standing under what has been said:

Understanding is never more than translating, that is, giving the equivalent of a text, but in no way its reason. There is nothing behind the written page, no false bottom that necessitates the work of an other intelligence, that of the explicator; no language of the master, no language of the language whose words and sentences are able to speak the reason of the words and sentences of a text.³¹

Translation is of paramount importance because it operates as the most usual way of understanding sentences, events, situations. In remaining at the surface, redistributing equivalences, we experience then the very texture of social life.

Far from the search for hidden truths in the depth of language, the movement important for Rancière is this surface distribution of equivalences, which should be verified: 'Men are political animals because they are poetic animals and it is in taking care to verify, each person for themselves, this shared poetic ability that they can establish a community of equals between them.'³² We see here that the quest for truth (*vérité*) is pushed aside in favour of a need for *verification*. Some people claim to know and pretend to be able to deliver explanations and ultimately reveal truths. But anyone is able to refigure and reconfigure sentences and gestures. It is, in Rancière's works, a recurrent movement of thinking to put particular verification where general Truth used to stand. Not *La Vérité* once and for all, but recurring acts of *verification*.³³

How is it possible to check and what does it mean to verify? Returning to Joseph Jacotot, whose experiments he wrote about in *The Ignorant Schoolmaster*, Rancière asks all of us to be attentive to the signs left by other people and to translate them into something new for others:

> It is essential to set out, to act like a researcher, to be attentive to all the signs a hand has traced or to all of the surrounding words, and like an artist, to strive to arrange in one's own way all the signs suitable for speaking to another intelligent being. [...] This equality exists only if it is always in action, held between one word and the next, one voice and another voice, one intelligent being and another intelligent being.³⁴

Equality does not exist by itself, in a mysterious place that should be discovered. Equality is an action in the world fuelled by chains of equivalences produced by anyone who is attentive to signs.

We can use the example of the news item: a story of something happening that is the locus of surprise and singularity but still has the power of exemplifying other events of life. What is fascinating in the news item is that it breaks from the causal linking of everyday life. Its singularity is certainly appealing. It is not reduced to a pure fragment of life, however; it is always possible for anyone attentive to gestures of thought to connect it with another news item, another moment, or a new meaning. It does not automatically lead to a totality of signification, but it is a carrier of a potential totality: 'It's the act that comes down to itself, that escapes causal chains [...] But is also the act that, for this very reason, opens up to a new type of narration and interpretation [...] a reticular system where each moment is in a way a bearer of the power of all.'[35] This is why we need narrators and translators: in order to keep open an entire reticular activating system.

Modern beauty and its aesthetics offer us a good way to figure this reticular system. Reading a detail, as Rancière so often does, in Baudelaire's *Spleen de Paris*, he shows the modern use of windows, since 'the window, firstly, should only open onto a world of other windows [...] Modern beauty is also this: this way not of inventing stories featuring characters who resemble us, but of dis-resembling by inventing lives that could be real, seen behind an interface.'[36] With the invention of photography in the nineteenth century, windows are often used as a way to frame the possible and organise the gaze. Here they are not only stagings but systems of unlikeness (*dissemblance*). Contrary to what Alberti said about painting, where a picture is supposed to be a window opened onto history, modern figuration is a window opened onto a world of other windows, so that the story is less about verisimilitude and likelihood than unlikeness and disparity. Figuration and translation turn on likelihood and unlikeness, arousing fear in those in power who would like windows to open onto the same world, and bringing hope to the people who are not supposed to know, speak and act, but who nevertheless can open windows onto other windows and invent new lives, even their own.

To come back to our opening remark, reading is not a side issue for Jacques Rancière. Maybe that is the true Althusserian lesson, which was at the beginning of his long quest. *Lire le Capital* was above all an experience of what reading could be. True, the content and manner of the Althusserian reading was, for Jacques Rancière, an excellent example of so-called demystifying reading, typical of any hermeneutical procedure. Despite the good intention, pretending to emancipate people by reading signs in their place and showing how to interpret them was an exercise of power and a wrong move politically. To read is to be sensitive to the textures of signs and to offer translations to other translators, since

There are a thousand ways of approaching a book – of reading it and appropriating it: as a pastime and as an object of worship; as a rigorous demonstration or as a fabulous story; [. . .] by believing it or by not believing it; by not believing it and believing it. The use of a book is made up of the variable combination of these choices that can also be stripped of their alternative character. In this way one inserts something of one's own life into writing, like in the re-figuration of a communal distribution of the sensible.[37]

Such is the goal of reading. Reading is a way of writing one's life in the figurative texture of a shared 'sensible', not as a blessed consensus, or as a revealed truth, or even as the flux of differences, but as a movement of reconfiguration, which implies both likelihood and unlikeness. The locus of figurality appears then to be heterotopy: far from any utopian phantasmagoria, it designates the political positioning where something other than what is expected may appear. As Renaud Pasquier claims about Rancière's conception of heterotopy, 'we also risk a double definition of the *other* that it implies: like the other of consensus that comes to scramble its foregone conclusions, but also perhaps like the other it addresses, towards which it stretches.'[38]

This gives us another reason for stepping outside the discipline of philosophy. As Jean-Luc Nancy remarks, 'philosophy is at odds with its "form," that is, with its "style," which is to say, finally, with its address. How does thinking address itself to itself (which also means: how does thinking address itself to everyone [. . .])?'[39] Indeed, Nancy is one of the few philosophers who tries to give to the question of the address an ontological status with his metaphysics founded on a 'being-with'. But moreover the question of the address should be addressed with a political agenda in mind. It is not enough to quickly shift from the traditional reflexive mode of thinking addressing itself to the political issue of addressing everyone, all the more so since everyone is not yet anyone.

'I must verify the reason of my thought, the humanity of my feelings, but I can do this only by having them venture forth into this forest of signs, which by themselves have no correspondence with this thought or that feeling.'[40] This quotation from *The Ignorant Schoolmaster* which constituted our little window onto Jacques Rancière's works is now more understandable. Not that I pretend to have given an explanation, but a simple tacking of pieces. I have tried to translate the quotation in different reflections and case studies opened by Jacques Rancière. It is not by chance that we find the very same image again in a recent figuration of an emancipated community. Here is what could also be a daydream: 'An unprecedented community of individuals searching for the means to connect through the forest of signs and its forms, a community constituted at the risk of journeys and multiple encounters under the sign of equality.'[41]

Notes

1. I would like to thank Bronwyn Haslam for her help with the English.
2. Jacques Rancière, *The Ignorant Schoolmaster: Five Lessons in Intellectual Emancipation*, trans. Kristin Ross (Stanford: Stanford University Press, 1991), 67; *Le Maître ignorant, cinq leçons sur l'émancipation intellectuelle* (Paris: Fayard, 1987), 114–15.
3. See Rancière, *Le Fil perdu. Essais sur la fiction moderne* (Paris: La Fabrique, 2014), 10–12.
4. Jacques Rancière and Jon Roffe (trans.), 'Thinking Between Disciplines: An Aesthetics of Knowledge', *Parrhesia*, 1 (2006), 9.
5. 'Jacques Rancière and Indisciplinarity: An Interview', <www.artandresearch.org.uk/v2n1/jrinterview.html> (last accessed 15 September 2015).
6. 'L'amateurisme est aussi une position théorique et politique, celle qui récuse l'autorité des spécialistes en réexaminant la manière dont les frontières de leurs domaines se tracent à la croisée des expériences et des savoirs.' Rancière, *Les Écarts du cinéma* (Paris: La Fabrique, 2011), 14.
7. 'The Janus-Face of Politicized Art: Jacques Rancière in Interview with Gabriel Rockhill', in Rancière, *The Politics of Aesthetics: The Distribution of the Sensible*, trans. with intro. by Gabriel Rockhill (New York: Continuum, 2006), 50.
8. Rancière, *The Emancipated Spectator*, trans. Gregory Elliott (London and New York: Verso, 2009), 22.
9. Immanuel Kant, *Critique of Judgment*, trans. W. S. Pluhar (Indianapolis: Hackett, 1987), §49, 5:314; 182.
10. Rancière, *The Emancipated Spectator*, 131.
11. See also Rancière, *La Fable cinématographique* (Paris: Seuil, 2001).
12. 'In order for the mechanical arts to be able to confer visibility on the masses, or rather on anonymous individuals, they first need to be recognized as arts. That is to say that they first need to be put into practice and recognized as something other than techniques of repro-

duction or transmission [...] it is because the anonymous become the subject matter of art that the act of recording such a subject matter can be an art.' Rancière, *The Politics of Aesthetics*, 32.
13. See my chapter, 'La pensivité du médium', in Adnen Jday (ed.), *Politiques de l'image. Questions pour Jacques Rancière* (Brussels: Éditions La Lettre volée, 2013), 53–70. Media refers here not only to mass communication, but to an institutionalised medium.
14. Rancière, *The Politics of Aesthetics*, 44.
15. 'Il y a une vertu subversive dans le fait de ne pas agir ou plutôt de rendre l'action inactive et l'inaction active.' Rancière, *Le Fil perdu*, 80.
16. 'The process of emancipation is the verification of the equality of any speaking being with any other speaking being [...] enacted in the name of a category denied either the principle or the consequences of that equality: workers, women, people of color, or others. But the enactment of equality is not [...] the enactment of the self, of the attributes or properties of the community in question. The name of a community that invokes its rights is always the name of the anonym, the name of anyone.' Rancière, 'Politics, Identification and Subjectivation', *October*, 61 (Summer 1992), 59–60.
17. See Sudeep Dasgupta, 'Words, Bodies, Times: Queer Theory before and after Itself', *Borderlands*, 8:2 (2009), <http://dare.uva.nl/document/2/73154> (last accessed 15 September 2015); and Rancière, *La Leçon d'Althusser* (Paris: Gallimard, 1974).
18. Donna J. Haraway, *Modest_Witness@Second_Millennium: Feminism and Technoscience* (New York and London: Routledge, 1997), 11.
19. See Rancière, *Le Fil perdu*, 12–13.
20. Ibid., 24–5.
21. Ibid., 104–5.
22. Ibid., 101.
23. See Carol Gilligan, *In a Different Voice: Psychological Theory and Women's Development* (Cambridge, MA: Harvard University Press, 1982); Joan C. Tronto, *Caring Democracy: Markets, Equality, and Justice* (New York: New York University Press, 2013).
24. See Rancière, *The Emancipated Spectator*, first chapter.
25. Ibid., 22.
26. 'J'aurai passé ma vie à chercher des mots qui me faisaient défaut. Qu'est-ce qu'un littéraire? Celui pour qui les mots défaillent, bondissent, fuient, perdent sens. Ils tremblent toujours un peu sous la forme étrange qu'ils finissent pourtant par habiter. Ils ne disent ni

ne cachent: ils font signe sans repos.' Pascal Quignard, *La Barque silencieuse* (Paris: Gallimard, 2009), 9.
27. Julien Gracq, *Reading Writing*, trans. Jeanine Herman (New York: Turtle Point Press, 2006), 150.
28. Rancière, *The Politics of Aesthetics*, 43–4. See also the excellent remarks proposed by translator Rockhill on the very question of translation.
29. Rancière, *The Politics of Aesthetics*, 43.
30. 'Every word, when once it is written, is bandied about, alike among those who understand and those who have no interest in it, and it knows not to whom to speak or not to speak; when ill-treated or unjustly reviled it always needs its father to help it; for it has no power to protect or help itself.' Plato, *Phaedrus*, 275 d, in John M. Cooper and D. S. Hutchinson (eds), *Plato: Complete Works* (Indianapolis: Hackett Publishing, 1997), 552.
31. Rancière and Roffe, 'Thinking Between Disciplines', 3.
32. 'Les hommes sont des animaux politiques parce qu'ils sont des animaux poétiques et c'est en s'appliquant à vérifier, chacun pour son compte, cette capacité poétique partagée qu'ils peuvent instaurer entre eux une communauté d'égaux.' Rancière, *Le Fil perdu*, 89.
33. On the act of verifying, see for example *Le Maître ignorant*, 68; *Aux bords du politique* (Paris: Osiris, 1990), 88, 115–16.
34. 'L'essentiel est de se mettre en marche, de se comporter en chercheur, attentif à tous les signes qu'une main a tracés ou à toutes les paroles environnantes, et en artiste, appliqué à disposer à son tour les signes propres à parler à une autre intelligence. [. . .] Cette égalité n'existe en effet que si elle est toujours en acte, tendue entre un mot et le suivant, une voix et une autre voix, un être intelligent et un autre être intelligent.' Rancière, *Le Fil perdu*, 88. We may see here a proximity to François Jullien's conception of translation and betweenness: translating is to 'open-produce the "between" between languages, between source and target. The translator is the one who does not stay on one side or the other [. . .] but who cannot count either on a meta- or third language. [. . .] No. The translator's characteristic is to be able to keep oneself, for as long as one can hold it, on the breach of between-languages, the modest hero of this reciprocal depropriation.' ('[O]uvrir-produire de l'"entre" entre les langues, de départ et d'arrivée. Le traducteur est celui qui ne reste ni d'un côté ni de l'autre [. . .] mais qui ne peut pas non plus compter sur une méta- ou troisième langue. [. . .] Non, le propre du traducteur est de se maintenir aussi longtemps qu'il pourra "tenir" sur la brèche de

l'entre-langues, héros modeste de cette dépropriation réciproque.')
François Jullien, *L'Écart et l'entre. Leçon inaugurale de la Chaire sur l'altérité* (Paris: Galilée, 2012), 63.

35. 'C'est l'acte qui se réduit à lui-même, se soustrait aux chaînes causales [. . .] Mais c'est aussi l'acte qui, pour cela même, s'ouvre à un type nouveau de narration et d'interprétation [. . .], un système réticulaire où chaque moment est en quelque sorte porteur de la puissance du tout.' Rancière, *Le Fil perdu*, 124.

36. 'À la fenêtre d'abord il importe de ne s'ouvrir que sur un monde d'autres fenêtres [. . .] La beauté moderne, c'est aussi cela, cette manière non plus d'inventer des histoires mettant en scène des personnages qui nous ressemblent, mais de se dissembler en inventant les vies possibles d'être réels perçus derrière une croisée.' Rancière, *Le Fil perdu*, 109.

37. 'Il y a mille manières de traiter un livre – de le lire et de se l'approprier: comme passe-temps et comme objet de culte; comme démonstration rigoureuse ou comme histoire fabuleuse; [. . .] en y croyant ou en n'y croyant pas; en n'y croyant pas *et* en y croyant. L'usage d'un livre est fait de la combinaison variable de ces choix qui peuvent aussi se dépouiller de leur caractère alternatif. C'est de cette manière qu'on l'insère dans l'écriture de sa propre vie comme dans la refiguration d'un partage commun du sensible.' Rancière, 'Sens et usages de l'utopie', in Michèle Riot-Sarcey (ed.), *L'Utopie en questions, La philosophie hors de soi* (Saint-Denis: Presses universitaires de Vincennes, 2001), 77.

38. 'On risquera aussi une double définition de l'*autre* qu'elle implique: comme autre du consensus, qui vient brouiller ses évidences; mais peut-être aussi comme l'autre à qui elle s'adresse, vers qui elle tend.' Renaud Pasquier, 'Politiques de la lecture', *Labyrinthe*, 17:1 (2004), <http://labyrinthe.revues.org/172> (last accessed 15 September 2015).

39. Jean-Luc Nancy, *Being Singular Plural*, trans. Robert D. Richardson and Anne E. O'Byrne (Stanford: Stanford University Press, 2000), xv.

40. Rancière, *Le Maître ignorant*, 114–15.

41. 'Une communauté inédite d'individus cherchant les moyens de se joindre à travers la forêt des signes et des formes, une communauté constituée au risque de trajets et de rencontres multiples sous le signe de l'égalité.' Rancière, *Le Fil perdu*, 93.

3

Rancière and Tragedy
Oliver Feltham

Tragedy as missing object: genre, spectacle or history

For some philosophers tragedy furnishes a key to modernity: the death of tragedy forms the backdrop against which modernity is defined; or tragedy plays the role of first critique of modernity; or modernity is characterised by the impossibility of writing tragedy.[1] Such speculations seem quite foreign to Rancière's approach to literary modernity, in which the novel takes pride of place, blurring the lines between art and life, scavenging amongst commerce and law for its words and objects, foregrounding the mundane micro-events of everyday life, slowly undoing social hierarchies, rendering obsolete any distinction between sacred and profane, noble and vulgar, high and low. His champions are not Hölderlin and Hegel but Balzac and Flaubert. 'What careful pacing of episodes in a drama,' he asks, rhetorically, 'what tragic hero's internal strife will ever equal the power of language present in the shambles of the Galeries de Bois, but also, and every bit as much, in cousin Pons' hat and spencer?'[2] His heroic anti-heroic crusade continues: 'the democracy of mute things [...] talk[s] better than any prince of tragedy.' Elsewhere he simply notes 'We no longer do tragedies' with regard to the dissolution of the system of genres favoured in the eighteenth century.[3] Not only that but Rancière also criticises the pertinence of the term 'modernity', preferring to replace it with a set of competing regimes for the identification of art: the ethical, the representational and the aesthetic, with the aesthetic gaining the upper hand from the mid eighteenth century onwards.[4]

When Rancière does mention tragedy it is to refer to another thinker's conception of it. For instance in the early essay 'The People's Theatre', he dismisses Michelet's use of the term to designate an ideal communion of the people with itself through theatrical representation. This is an ideal, Rancière claims, that the subsequent history of popular theatre reveals to be unreachable and misguided. In *The Emancipated Spectator* he repeats this point, dismissing the concept of tragic spectacle as vehicle of the city-state's self-presence as an obsolete error, a negative backdrop to the history of critical thinking about theatre.[5] But this is a different kind of dismissal, with different stakes, since what is at stake in this 'philosophical concept' is not tragedy as a literary genre but rather tragedy as a kind of spectacle.[6]

To tease out the stakes of Rancière's multiple dismissals of tragedy as genre or tragedy as spectacle-communion, we should briefly examine a third instance of a missed encounter with tragedy. Again it occurs indirectly, with reference to another philosopher's concept of tragedy. In *The Philosopher and His Poor* there is a passage on Marx's critical review of Hans Daumer's work *Religion in the New Era*. In Rancière's reading, Marx's framework opposes 'two theatrical figures of history: the tragic, an authentic expression of the struggle between the ancient and the new world; and the comic, a ridiculous repetition of a history already performed and of dead values'.[7] Rancière folds this framework back onto Marx's own relation to history and argues that the impossible challenge for Marx, faced with actual historical events which go against his own division of labour, is to 'attain the tragic dimension of the revolution'.[8]

In conclusion, in Rancière's work there are traces of three missed encounters with tragedy: tragedy as literary genre is obsolete under the aesthetic regime, tragedy as spectacle-communion is a mistaken ideal, and tragedy as a form of history in which philosophy bears witness to the creative and destructive struggle between the ancient and the new. Rather than examine the reasons for these missed encounters, this chapter will investigate the pertinence of a fourth concept of tragedy: tragedy as a structure of action, or, to be more precise, tragedy as a mode of the presentation of action. My argument is that the concept of tragic action is quite pertinent to Rancière's work, and that it can be used to articulate and elucidate Rancière's strategy faced with the most persistent obstacles to his thinking.

The ancient matrix: philosophy and its division of labour

One of the most central themes in Rancière's oeuvre from *The Philosopher and His Poor* (1982) to *On the Shores of Politics* (1991) to *Disagreement* (1995) is the idea of a fundamental and inegalitarian distortion in the sharing out of roles in the city as the basis for all political philosophy, political economy and political judgement. There is a miscount of the kinds of people who make up the political body in every division of labour that philosophy carries out, right from the outset in the ur-texts Plato's *Republic* and Aristotle's *Politics*. Rancière's arguments are well known; what is important here is the conclusion. In *The Philosopher and His Poor* he states that Plato's concept of 'justice' as each and everyone to his or her place and function is in fact a simple 'hierarchy of functions and virtues' that has been naturalised by means of faulty arguments.[9] In *Disagreement* he argues that when philosophy attempts to resolve the problems of politics by assigning places and functions to types of people, it always carries out a 'fundamental miscount' of parts, which could be 'the constitutive wrong of the political itself'.[10] The structure of the miscount is that one part of the people, the poor, suffers a dissymmetry in its definition by a supposedly distinguishing characteristic. Each part is defined by a characteristic: the few (*oligoi*) by their wealth, the nobles (*aristoi*) by their excellence and the poor (*demoi*) by their liberty.[11] The problem is that liberty is not actually a positive property but simply the fact that each male individual born in Athens is counted as a citizen. For this reason it is not particular to the *demos*, since the wealthy and the nobles are also free. The part of the people thus oscillates between having no proper identity, and identifying with the entirety of the political community.[12] This is the 'fundamental wrong' for Rancière.

This diagnosis has consequences not just for the social division of labour and its justifications, but also for the discipline of philosophy. For Rancière philosophy has instituted itself and guaranteed itself a proper place within the city-state precisely by means of such a miscount. This is not to say that without an explicitly theorised division of labour there would be no practice of philosophy – before Plato wrote the *Republic* Socrates and the pre-Socratics had no trouble engaging in their nomadic and interstitial practice without a systematic justification of its existence. Indeed, in the

Apology Socrates places the philosopher in regard to the city – as gadfly, as ideal statesman and public servant – without engaging in any detailed division of labour. Rather this is to say that once the division of labour is laid out in order to ground a concept of justice and civil peace, philosophy arrogates for itself a superior position: 'Philosophy posits itself by positing its other. The order of discourse is defined by tracing a circle that excludes those who earn their living working with their hands from the right to think.'[13]

Rancière sees 'paradoxical inheritances' of the structure of the miscount everywhere, in modern and contemporary philosophers, activists, politicians, sociologists and Marxists of all stripes. Rancière delights in showing how the very attempt to escape the prejudices and injustices of ancient philosophy has often led to a mere reshuffling of its terms, and to a reinstallation of its structures. For example, in *The Philosopher and His Poor* he shows how Marx's, Sartre's and Bourdieu's treatment of the modern proletariat simply inverts Plato's treatment, with philosophy now becoming the reason or truth of the knowledge of the poor. Sartre is said to install a 'new guardianship', save that the new guardians (the proletarian activists) 'who took over from the philosophers [as subject of history] are actually not at their post'. The reason is exactly the same as in Book II of the *Republic*: these activists 'do not have the leisure to perform this function'.[14] Again the workers are said to not have sufficient free time for politics.

To show that the structure of the miscount is at work in contemporary philosophy, even in conscious attempts to transcend the limits, is to reveal the existence of an ancient conceptual matrix. A matrix is a structure whose terms can undergo permutations without any change to the overall structure: it thus induces the repetition of the Same despite the appearance of alterity. The existence of an ancient or foundational matrix is a leitmotif in Rancière's writings. For the sake of economy I shall mention just five instances:

- In the 1988 essay opening *Aux bords de la politique*, Rancière takes an apparently contemporary theme, that of the 'end of politics', and shows how Aristotle had already developed a concept of the art of politics as precisely that art that put an end to politics.[15]
- In *The Philosopher and His Poor* when Cabet and the 'Icarien' activists attempted to think and practise a community of equals

in the early nineteenth century, their enquiry ended up oscillating between two historically predetermined models, that of a community of masters (Plato's guardians) and that of a community of slaves (Christian monks).[16]
- In the 1991 essay 'Politique, identification, subjectivation', Rancière engages in a diagnosis: 'The current impasse of political action and reflection is due, in my opinion, to the identification of the political with the manifestation of the proper identity of a community.'[17] The scope of the diagnosis is vast: it embraces all kinds of political activity and its aetiology designates a malady that stretches back to Plato and Aristotle.
- In his early essays on the paradoxes and dead-ends of popular theatre, Rancière formulates the idea of the matrix in the following terms: 'This does not mean that all cats are grey in the dark, but rather that roles and significations are distributed at an early stage according to an autonomous logic, forming a finished ensemble of alternative solutions to which the most dominant theoretical and political novelties cannot help bending.'[18]
- Three decades later the terminology has changed but the matrix remains; the task of the essay 'The Emancipated Spectator' is set out as follows: 'We need to map the set of suppositions that place the question of the spectator at the centre of the discussion of the relations between arts and politics. We need to outline the global model of rationality that lies behind our habits in judging the political consequences of theatre as show.'[19]

There are two fundamental characteristics of this ancient foundational matrix that immediately identify it with tragedy as a structure of action. First, it is all-swallowing: for instance, modern philosophy as repository of the truth of the knowledge of the poor is found everywhere, 'populating our theories, our politics, our social sciences'.[20] Rancière sees 'paradoxical inheritance[s]' everywhere.[21] Second, these ubiquitous matrices are traps: in the essay on 1970s French cultural politics, 'The Cultural Historic Compromise', Rancière characterises the matrix as a 'finished ensemble of alternative solutions' and then asks, 'How then is the circle formed that traps the desire for an activist culture into a demand on the state?'[22] The totalisation of a trap is what identifies the structure of these matrices as tragic. Any attempt to escape the trap is included within the totality, by definition, and thus leads one to simply embrace another one of the matrices' permutations, falsely believing it to be emancipatory.[23] This is the case whether the matrix concerns the creation of a community of equals, an authentic people's theatre, or the relation between the philosopher and the poor.

In conclusion, tragedy as literary genre may not be one of the central objects of Rancière's philosophy, but it certainly names one of its logics. The matrix of philosophy reproduces the dialectical structure of tragic action: the act that saves destroys. The action intended to secure freedom is precisely what brings about destruction and entrapment. To attempt to avoid fate is to ensure its inexorable advance. There is a tragedy at the heart of our thinking of politics and political theatre in the form of all-swallowing matrices. What is to be done?

The tragic theatricality of Rancière's discourse and its limits

There is a light held out to us by Rancière. If we are critical and sufficiently vigilant then we may just step around these fatal traps. But does the ruthless denunciation of the repetition of the Same underneath apparently different discourses lead to emancipation itself? Is not Rancière's discourse itself trapped by these foundational matrices doomed to retrace their logic forever? The irony is that Rancière is well aware of the limitations of critique.[24] His very first publication in the famous anthology *Reading Capital* focused on the nature of 'critique' in Marx's critique of political economy. In *The Philosopher and His Poor* Rancière cites Marx in *The Holy Family* stating 'the critical critic produces nothing; the worker produces everything'.[25]

It may appear at this point of our investigation that we have strayed far from the topic of tragedy as a form of theatre, but nothing could be further from the truth. Tragedy as literary genre is certainly not an object of Rancière's theory, but we have discovered how Rancière's own discourse is intimately bound up with tragedy as a structure of action. That structure is a dialectical fusion between salvation and destruction, emancipation and imprisonment, novelty and tradition: the act that saves destroys. The presence of this tragic structure in some of Rancière's writings is not without consequence. The question of how to dissolve philosophy's ancient division of labour is not merely a logical problem that confronts the assiduous exegete. Rancière's discourse has a powerful referential field in its embrace of overlapping fields of aesthetics, history and politics: it projects an entire world and interpellates its readers, placing them in that world. When Rancière sees 'paradoxical inheritances' everywhere, how are we not positioned as heirs of those paradoxes? If we spend enough time reading Rancière, that world remains with us, and becomes a stratum of our imagination – we start to filter cultural and political phenomena through its schemata, we begin to ask Rancière's questions. These schemata can in turn receive reinforcement and 'thicken' through accumulated overlaps with the schemata of other projected worlds, worlds encountered through other readings and diverse cognitive experiences. Moreover, when a discourse is inhabited by a particular structure of action, so is its projected world. The tragic structure of action is very simple and easy to reproduce: it captures the imagination. That structure is also present in many discourses that a reader of Rancière might encounter in her life. So we might plausibly speculate that within the overlapping referential worlds that we inhabit, one could find a sedimented schema of tragic action. No one discourse alone is responsible for its existence, but each contributes to its reproduction.

There is an additional link between Rancière's projection of a world and tragedy: not just as a structure of action but also as theatrical spectacle. Critical theory and philosophy often project their worlds in a theatrical mode; they populate their environment with protagonists, named 'capitalism' or 'the state' or 'the metaphysics of presence', 'truth' or 'the trace' or 'the event', and they stage grand dramas between these protagonists. In such theatricality the protagonists are not just individuals, but regions of a world that behave like factions, treating themselves as metonymies, taking their part as the whole. As Rancière recognises in his analysis of the division of labour, philosophy typically sets up grand hierarchies between types of actor, whether the actors be kinds of discourse, institutions or types of people. These hierarchies of value are reflected in the capacity of agents to enter into transformative interactions with other agents. For example, Marx's *Capital* projects a world in which parliament is assigned a low value in the project of arresting the immiseration of the working class since its reforms are continually bypassed by capital. The theatrical mode of Rancière's writings on political philosophy and popular culture is tragic. Tragedy, Aristotle tells us, always imitates the action of a noble protagonist. In Rancière's diagnosis of ancient matrices, the sole protagonist who is capable of action is given all its titles of nobility: philosophy. As Rancière recounts the failure of Cabet to found a community of equals: 'The real reason escapes [Cabet]: the logical gap involved in the simple inference from work as measure to the working community as realisation of justice. More an orator than a philosopher, he cannot see that in the end it is old Plato who takes his revenge here.'[26] In this projected world activists and founders of communities have a lesser capacity to win through with their actions than 'old Plato'.

Whether it is on the restricted stage of a playhouse or on the generalised stage of a projected world, theatricality brings together words, bodies and places. It institutes very particular relationships between discourses, mobile agents and contexts, both temporal and spatial. Rancière's own tragic theatricality has limitations in the way it articulates these elements: totalisation as idealism, lack of orientation, and a Manichaean understanding of technique. First, the identification of these foundational matrices requires a gesture of totalisation. To unearth the foundations of political thinking in just two ur-texts – Plato's *Republic* and Aristotle's *Politics* – is massively to simplify the emergence of thought, sidelining any exogamous influences. Totality is a category of idealism whereas a materialist approach is marked by infinite investigations and no definitive pronunciations as to the nature of a field. Second, the problem with the stance of the critical critic, the great demystifier, is that it leads to a lack of orientation. As Lacan pointed out in the title for a seminar that he never gave, *Les non-dupes errent*. Homonym for *les noms du père* ('the names of the father'), the phrase translates as 'those who are nobody's dupe are condemned to wander without direction'. If every kind of political thinking is trapped in the philosophical matrix of the division of labour, then the question 'what is to be done?' goes without response. The good, individual or common, can no longer be named. But then what task is Rancière's own discourse carrying out? One sign of lack of orientation is the absence of a clear and lasting name for Rancière's own discourse. The occasional names he adopts are negative, such as 'another thinking of democratic facticity', and are not accompanied with a set of projects or tasks.[27]

The third limitation to the tragic theatricality of some of Rancière's writings is that, faced with totality and their own lack of orientation, they end up adopting a melancholy Manichaeism. This occurs in the following manner: given the all-swallowing embrace of philosophy's division of labour, there is one orientation Rancière can adopt and that is the irruption of the negative. Rancière celebrates the emergence of dissensus as the authentic moment of politics: 'It is the power of inconsistent and forever re-enacted division that tears the political away from the various figures of animality.'[28] In the essay 'Good Times or Pleasure at the Barricades', he sponsors theatre's powers of subversion.[29] He champions the improper nature of the poor against any order of places that would privilege the rich and the nobles.[30] Indeed, any irruption of disorder is taken as a moment of freedom.[31] Like many philosophers labouring in the shadow of Hegel, Rancière gives his colours to the work of the negative on the sole condition that its effect will be not 'work' but disruption alone. It is difficult to see how he can avoid awarding the position of agent of history to dissensus.

The Manichaeism lies in the stark opposition between order and disorder, consensus and dissensus. The melancholy is an after-effect of the all-swallowing matrices: disorder will never give rise to a positive social or political work that could be celebrated. Indeed, all art that could give rise to such a work is structured by the domination and domestication of negativity. Technique can only ever be the doomed attempt to paper over contradictions. Indeed, to suppress negativity and disorder in Rancière's eyes is to paradoxically attempt to erase technique's own existential condition: 'to depoliticize is the oldest trick of the art of politics'.[32] Philosophy itself becomes one of these techniques, embroiled in a permanent drama of mastery as its regulative ideal versus non-mastery as its actual condition.[33]

At this point our own conclusion appears evident: in his tragic theatricality, championing subversion and disorder alone, Rancière remains caught in the machinations of the matrix he himself reveals. As a critical critic Rancière is condemned to a melancholy Manichaeism, tarrying with the negative but not being able to count beyond two. The question that will seal his fate is whether all of his writings engage in this tragic theatricality. It just so happens that there is another set of writings in Rancière's oeuvre, just as established as his work on philosophy and cultural politics, consisting of investigations into the archives of workers and their various experiences in the nineteenth century. Our task will be to determine whether or not these writings give rise to an alternative kind of theatricality.

Emancipation through the archive: an open theatricality

In 1987 Rancière published the work translated as *The Ignorant Schoolmaster*.[34] Therein he recounts the practice and arguments of Joseph Jacotot, a revolutionary pedagogue. Jacotot showed how it was possible for anyone whatsoever to teach a language to anyone else without prior knowledge of that language, simply using a text as support, checking the reoccurrence of written words against their oral pronunciation, word by word, sentence by sentence. The principle at work in this practice is that of the equality of intelligences: the teacher is not positioned as a superior intelligence, possessor of a knowledge to be transmitted. Rather, the teacher is a fellow companion in a journey of slow discovery.

Jacotot himself theorises this procedure as a practice of intellectual emancipation. Following Rancière's commentaries, the following steps may be identified in such practice. First, there is always a localising verification, step by step, of the equality of any person whatsoever with any other person whatsoever.[35] Second, the drawing of such equivalences is not so much a form of identification as the assertion of a form of anonymity through the undoing of hierarchical social identities. The first such identities to be undone are those of teacher and student, who are rendered equivalent, fellow voyagers in an enquiry. The process of verification of the equality of intelligences is carried out text by text, passage by passage. Equality is both the presupposition of this pedagogy and also its concrete result each step of the way. In no way is equality placed as a goal of the process. This practice of verification is thus a demonstration and a form of consequentialism: equality will present itself in this social situation precisely as what it turns out to have been.[36] As teacher and student learn a new language together, these sequential verifications of equality make it impossible to identify them according to the ancient hierarchy of teacher as subject of knowledge and student as lacking knowledge. The positive version of this point is that the process launches what Rancière terms a paratactic logic of 'and x and y' in the description of identity. Each individual is both teacher and student, and someone else, or more, besides.

This is all very well, but it is not clear what kind of theatricality emerges from Rancière's commentary on this pedagogy. To pursue this question we must look at how Rancière tries to generalise the shape and logic of this practice of emancipation.[37] He makes his initial moves in *The Ignorant Schoolmaster* itself, before repeating them in an essay of the same year, 'The Community of Equals'. The first move is to identify a *social* form of the verification of equality in the historical event of the Roman Senator Menenius Agrippa deciding to speak to the plebeians who in 494 BC had seceded from the city, withdrawing to the southernmost of its seven hills, Mont Aventino, in an ancient equivalent to a general strike. Rancière argues that the very fact of recounting a fable to the plebs – the famous 'Apology of the Belly and the Members' – presupposes an equality of intelligence between two social strata, patricians and plebs.[38] The second move is to analyse this event as a rectification or overturning of the original miscount of the police. In such an event an excluded part of society 'name themselves, and let it be heard that they too are speaking beings to whom it is appropriate to come and speak [. . .] This effraction [. . .] renders visible the invisible, gives a name to the anonymous.'[39] Rancière also sees such action as 'giving a common measure to the incommensurable', that is, to the previously incommensurable social orders, and thus installing a polemical space. His second historical example makes this point clearer: in 1833 the stonemasons went on strike. In his declarations their leader, Mr Schwartz, cited the Preamble to the 1830 Constitutional Charter in order to develop a revolutionary syllogism: the Preamble says that all French men are equal before the law, yet our demands and reasons are being dismissed without a hearing, therefore we are not being treated as equal before the law. This form of argumentation exposes the incommensurability between the letter of the law and actual social practice. At the same time it establishes a common measure by demanding the application of the law to this social practice, and it also opens up a space for polemic around whether and how a strike can be dealt with in line with the Preamble.

In this generalisation of the Jacotot procedure of emancipation we can begin to glimpse elements of a different theatricality. Rather than the grand hierarchies of tragedy we have the assertion of an unprecedented equality across a social space characterised by chasms of inequality. There is also the emergence of a new voice

– that of the strikers – and the public appearance of a new kind of discourse that links up previously disparate texts and practices such as constitutions and strike demands. Rancière develops two concepts that help solidify these intuitions: the treatment of a tort, and modes of subjectification.[40]

The treatment of a tort is an action that exposes an unjust or harmful structure that excludes part of the people – proletarians, plebs, women – from participating in the realm of politics.[41] A 'tort' is thus another name for the miscount which assigns people to places or non-places within society and its political institutions. In *La Mésentente* Rancière identifies two logics operating in politics: that of the police, which assigns hierarchised places to types of people, and the logic of equality.[42] Since a tort is constitutive of the order of the police, and the latter is incommensurable with the logic of equality, a tort cannot be resolved through negotiation, dialogue or compromise.[43] However, a tort can be 'treated'. For example, in the stonemasons' strike, Schwartz's declaration verified the equality of all French citizens. Schwartz publicly demonstrated that striking workers could be understood under the terms of the Preamble and thus were to be treated as equal before the law. Such a treatment can subsequently have an effect on the police as distribution of social roles. It does so by reconfiguring what Rancière calls 'the sensible', the distribution of who is visible and who is invisible, who is heard or unheard. Such a demonstration also develops new articulations of social activities and texts, showing what elements can be put together and seen together (64). Thus to treat a tort is not simply to redress a wrong, but it is a public demonstration that builds new articulations between ways of doing and saying things.

A mode of subjectification, on the other hand, is the emergence of a new voice, a new political identity that upsets the 'police' as order of who speaks and who remains silent in the business of politics.[44] As such, a mode of subjectification is a denial of an identity imposed by the police, and at the same time the affirmation of an improper or impossible identity.[45]

These concepts of a tort and subjectification evidently lend substance to our hypothesis of a different theatricality to the tragic, a theatricality we shall simply term 'open'. At this moment our enquiry switches modes, from the interpretation of Rancière's philosophy to speculative invention on its basis. The open theatricality of Rancière's writings on Menenius Agrippa, the stonemasons' strike and others consists of four elements: a pluralised place, composite actions, the emergence of new agents, and an expanded public.

First of all, these social procedures of emancipation occur within a disunified or split space rather than a unified totality. This is not just a matter of dramatising the difference between social classes – that much is the classic material of comedy. Rather, the treatment of a tort exposes a disjunction between two 'heterogeneous logics', that of the police and that of equality.[46] These logics are shown to be clashing and thus they are brought into a relationship. However, this relationship does not occur within a unified space but rather across disparate places: indeed, each of these logics, police and equality, inhabits and structures a different kind of place. In other words, the treatment of a tort opens up plural scenes, and not in chronological succession, as in classic narratological sequence, but rather simultaneously. In the terms of political philosophy, the pluralisation of scenes introduces a thinking of justice that does not begin in the assumption of unity – a unity of right, reason, nature or history – but in the assumption of antagonism.

The second theatricalising element is the public appearance of a very particular form of action. As in tragedy, there is always a deep conflict at stake in the treatment of a tort: the clash between the logic of the police and the logic of equality. However, the action that drives this conflict is not tragic: there is no unity of salvation and destruction programmed by a unified totality. Take Schwartz's syllogism again; it is a composite action in two senses. It joins together elements of society that were previously held apart, such as workplace injustice and the letter of the constitution. It also brings about an encounter between the artificiality of social order and a legally founded claim for justice. A composite action concentrates and exposes the entirely different reception and consequences it has within the separate contexts in which it occurs.

The third element is a direct consequence of the concept of modes of subjectification: the emergence of a new voice immediately changes the configuration of who can speak and act in the space of politics. Different words and a different kind of speech emerge into the public space and start to reconfigure relationships between types of people, thus ultimately leading to a different perception of public space and what it allows. In contrast to tragedy as a historical pattern, it is a question not of repetition but of novelty, and not of a fake novelty that is supposed to save any subject, but a genuine novelty without any normative guarantee.

Finally, the fourth element of this open theatricality is its configuration of the people. In contrast to Michelet's concept of tragic spectacle-as-communion, here we have a conflict that presents the political body to itself as other-than-itself, or as multiple and incomplete. There is no communion here, but rather the uncomfortable and cognitively dissonant experience of the city being 'out of joint'. A citizen's perception of the order and identity of his or her own political body is upset by the treatment of a tort since suddenly they are led to hear people speak who usually do not speak, and whose discourse seems at first unreasonable and unacceptable. In *Aesthetics and its Discontents*, Rancière phrases this idea in terms of what is 'common':

> Politics [. . .] is not the exercise of power and the struggle for power. It is the configuration of a particular sphere of experience, of objects posited as common, and belonging to a common decision, of subjects recognized as capable of designating them and arguing about them. Elsewhere I have tried to show how politics is the very conflict over the existence of this space [. . .] over the designation of subjects having the capacity of common speech.[47]

Thus in the treatment of a tort the very nature of what counts as 'common' is up for contestation and no longer taken for granted. Consequently, in open theatricality the 'public' is multiplied outside itself and beyond itself precisely through the discovery of parts of itself that had remained hitherto concealed. The public is subject to an expansionary process which paradoxically also involves internal exploration of its own basements and attics, its refugee camps and squats.

In short, the open theatricality of Rancière's writings on emancipation projects a world in which some kind of commensurability is possible between 'regional powers'. Far from the logic of the exception and the totality, or of good versus bad, or of salvation versus destruction, an open staging sets in place a logic in which contrasting protagonists find themselves, all of a sudden, endowed with comparable power and entering into an unpredictable interaction that ends up by undoing all hard and fast distinctions, and bringing all disjoint parts together.

Conclusion

During this enquiry into Rancière and tragedy it initially appeared that tragedy was not so much a missing object as an obsolete object, relegated to the past, subject of outdated philosophical fantasies of lost community. Yet once it had been distinguished from a literary genre, or a structure of history, or a rite for the self-presentation of community, and thought rather as a certain structure of action, it turned out that tragedy was central to Rancière's thinking, specifically to his critique of philosophy and its division of labour. A tragic matrix captured and rendered impotent every alternative philosophy of politics, dooming it from the beginning to repeat the same errors of distributing a population into fixed roles of mastery and subordination. Rancière's own critique struggles to escape the force field of this all-swallowing matrix, and it projected a world condemned to a tragic theatricality. Fortunately there has always been another strand to Rancière's writings, in which he explores the archives of nineteenth-century worker experience. In his discovery of Joseph Jacotot's method of intellectual emancipation he takes a step beyond philosophical critique and its tragic theatricality, inventing a generalised model of social emancipation and identifying its mechanisms at work in various historical episodes. At this point a different kind of world is projected with a different spatiality and historicity to that of the tragic, a world characterised by an open theatricality.

It just so happens that this concept of open theatricality has a few parallels with Rancière's own prescriptions for contemporary theatre in *The Emancipated Spectator*. In this text he places theatre centre-stage in his Schillerian aesthetic regime: 'Theatre has been, more than any other art, associated with the romantic idea of an aesthetic revolution, changing [...] the sensuous forms of human life.'[48] Once he rids this theatrical project of any Platonic presuppositions, Rancière re-articulates it in his own terms, identifying three conditions for intellectual emancipation at the theatre: first, the radical distance between two supposed conditions (master and student, actor and spectator) must be cancelled out; second, the distribution of appropriate places for types of body must be annulled; and finally, any frontiers between territories must be erased.[49] These antidotes for critical theatre and its Platonism, which has bothered him since the 1970s, are in fact drawn directly in the text from Jacotot's project of intellectual emancipation.

Moreover, in quite a rare move for Rancière, in this essay he comes close to naming the good: 'new intellectual adventures'.⁵⁰

The stakes for Rancière's generalisation of Jacotot's thinking of emancipation are quite high: if it doesn't work we are condemned to wander amongst the apparent alternatives of an ancient matrix programmed by philosophy. Not only are the stakes high, but they also happen to be theatrical. In both the original 1987 text and a 1991 essay, he recognises Jacotot's own Manichaeism between individuals and the collective as an obstacle. If a practice of emancipation can only occur between individual intelligences, and if all human collectivity is irredeemably hierarchical and stupefying, then there will be *'no political scene'*.⁵¹ In other words, if the logics of the police and the political remain incommensurable, then no one – including Marx, as Rancière notes in *The Philosopher and His Poor* – will accede to the properly theatrical dimension of history, where a struggle between old and new might just give rise to something new.

From the open theatricality of Rancière's thinking of political emancipation, let us finish with the actual praxis of a theatrical troupe. However temporary its existence might be, and however basic its resources, the troupe's work is polyvalent and cooperative. Dismissing any division of labour, we all become part-time literary critics, acrobats, dancers, psychologists, carpenters, marketers and seamstresses. When we put on a play together we all roll up our sleeves and become, for the time of a rehearsal, Marx's worker under communism, or Rancière's millennial peasant, jack of all trades, prisoner of none.

Notes

1. George Steiner, *The Death of Tragedy* (London: Faber & Faber, 1961); Terry Eagleton, *Sweet Violence* (Oxford: Blackwell, 2003); Philippe Lacoue-Labarthe, 'The Caesura of the Speculative', in *Typography: Mimesis, Philosophy, Politics* (Cambridge, MA: Harvard University Press, 1989), 220–1.
2. Jacques Rancière, 'The Politics of Literature', in *The Politics of Literature*, trans. Julie Rose (London: Polity, 2011), 19.
3. Rancière, *La Parole muette* (Paris: Hachette, 1998), 28.
4. Rancière, *Malaise dans l'esthétique* (Paris: Galilée, 2004), 43–4.
5. Rancière, *Le Spectateur émancipé* (Paris: La Fabrique, 2008), 12, 61. Another gesture with regard to theatre that occurs in Rancière's work

is to relegate it to the past. For instance, when he refers to debates over democracy and museum space that require a new articulation of art and politics, he dismisses theatre; 'debates today [...] no longer [involve] crowds gathering around theatrical action.' *Malaise dans l'esthétique*, 40.
6. In another context Rancière himself recognises the distinction between literature and spectacle: responding to Gérard Genette's classification of Racine's *Brittanicus* as belonging to literature. Rancière objects, 'The evidence of this deduction is deceptive, since there is no criterion either universal or historic which founds the inclusion of the genre "theatre" within the "genre" literature. Theatre is a genre of spectacle, not of literature.' See Rancière, *La Parole muette*, 7.
7. Rancière, *Le Philosophe et ses pauvres* (Paris: Flammarion, 1982), 99; cf. 90–118, and in particular 104–5, 131, 133, 140.
8. Ibid., 133.
9. Ibid., 31, 47.
10. Rancière, *La Mésentente: Politique et philosophie* (Paris: Galilée, 1995), 25.
11. Ibid., 25.
12. Ibid., 27.
13. Rancière, *Le Philosophe et ses pauvres*, 289.
14. Ibid., 201.
15. Rancière, *Aux bords de la politique* (Paris: Folio Essais, 2004), 34, 47.
16. Rancière, *Le Philosophe et ses pauvres*, 145.
17. Rancière, *Aux bords de la politique*, 114.
18. Rancière, *The Intellectual and His People: Staging the People Volume 2*, trans. David Fernbach (London: Verso, 2012), 3.
19. Rancière, *Le Spectateur émancipé*, 8.
20. Rancière, *Le Philosophe et ses pauvres*, 193.
21. Rancière, *Aux bords de la politique*, 100.
22. Rancière, *The Intellectual and His People*, 59.
23. Rancière, *Aux bords de la politique*, 81.
24. See also 'Les mésaventures de la pensée critique' in *Le Spectateur émancipé*.
25. Rancière, *Le Philosophe et ses pauvres*, 112.
26. Rancière, *Aux bords de la politique*, 155.
27. Ibid., 72.
28. Ibid., 68.
29. Rancière, 'Good Times or Pleasure at the Barricades', trans. John Moore, in Adrian Rifkin and Roger Thomas (eds), *Voices of the*

People: The Social Life of 'La Sociale' at the End of the Second Empire (London: Routledge and Kegan Paul, 1988), 38.
30. Rancière, *Le Philosophe et ses pauvres*, 38.
31. Rancière, *Le Spectateur émancipé*, 26.
32. Rancière, *Aux bords de la politique*, 47.
33. Ibid., 62.
34. *Le Maître ignorant, cinq leçons sur l'émancipation intellectuelle* (Paris: Fayard, 1987).
35. Rancière, *Aux bords de la politique*, 116–18.
36. Ibid., 116, 124. There is an interesting parallel to explore with Alain Badiou's concept of political, artistic, scientific and amorous praxis as a 'generic truth procedure' which proceeds through local enquiries verifying the consequences of the occurrence of an anomalous event.
37. To confirm the ever-present danger of Manichaeism, note that Rancière met with an obstacle in generalising Jacotot's thinking to more political processes of emancipation. The obstacle was Jacotot's own refusal of any collectivisation or institutionalisation of his techniques. Rancière characterises this limit in the following terms in *La Mésentente*: 'This forever singular act of equality cannot consist in any form of social bond. Equality transforms into its contrary as soon as it assigns itself a place within social and state organization' (58). One-to-one emancipation versus collective enslavement: in Jacotot at least the opposition is absolute.
38. Rancière, *Le Maître ignorant*, 162–6.
39. Rancière, *Aux bords de la politique*, 164. On Menenius Agrippa see also *La Mésentente*, 47–9.
40. These concepts are developed in the 1991 essay 'Politique, identification, subjectification' and taken up again and systematised in the 1995 work *La Mésentente*.
41. Rancière, *Aux bords de la politique*, 117; *La Mésentente*, 63.
42. Rancière, *La Mésentente*, 63.
43. Ibid.
44. Ibid., 59–60, 65.
45. Rancière, *Aux bords de la politique*, 119–22.
46. Rancière, *La Mésentente*, 63.
47. Rancière, *Malaise dans l'esthétique*, 37.
48. Rancière, *Le Spectateur émancipé*, 13.
49. Ibid., 24–5.
50. Ibid., 22.
51. Rancière, *Aux bords de la politique*, 113, my italics.

4

Rancière Lost: On John Milton and Aesthetics

Justin Clemens

> The ideas of eternity and infinity are among the most affecting we have; and yet perhaps there is nothing of which we really understand so little, as of infinity and eternity.
>
> Edmund Burke

The Argument

England falsifies France; or, English falsifies French. The English Revolution of the mid seventeenth century accomplished, well over a century before the American and French Revolutions, the legal execution of a monarch and the installation of a new form of republic. John Milton, radical puritan, polemicist and poet, was instrumental in that (qualified) English success. Proselytiser for divorce, new kinds of education, the extrication of religion from the state, and epic poet, Milton produced work which at once exemplifies many of the theses proffered by Jacques Rancière regarding politics, education and aesthetics – as he exceeds and falsifies them. This chapter will discuss a late pamphlet of John Milton titled *Of True Religion*, in order to suggest how Milton confronts and rebukes Rancière's theories of disagreement, ignorant masters and the distributions of the sensible, not only by contravening many of the latter's demonstrations and arguments, but in anticipating them. The key points of the exposition will hinge on Milton's doctrines of indiscernibility, infinity and decision. In doing so, this chapter shows how Rancière's three regimes seem unable to account for a fourth modality, transversal to his own.

Distributions of the sensible

Rancière opens his brilliant book *Aisthesis* (2011) with a reiteration of his by-now well-known position. 'For two centuries in the West', Rancière asserts, '"aesthetics" has been the name for the category designating the sensible fabric and intelligible form of what we call "Art" [...] Art as a notion designating a form of specific experience has only existed in the West since the end of the eighteenth century.'[1] Rancière's historicisation, dating 'aesthetics' proper to the late eighteenth or early nineteenth century, is in itself quite uncontroversial, corresponding to revolutionary, industrial, Romantic bourgeois modernity. Thinkers as different as Alain Badiou, Jürgen Habermas and Niklas Luhmann would also agree, with the requisite nuances.[2]

Indeed, the term 'aesthetics' is itself of perhaps surprisingly recent coinage. First deployed by Alexander Baumgarten in his treatises on *Metaphysics* (1739) and *Aesthetica* (1750), the term derives from the Greek *aisthanesthai*, 'to perceive', *aesthesis*, 'perception', and *aisthetikos*, 'capable of perception'.[3] The modern philosophy of aesthetics is thereby born and borne on the basis of a Germanic Latin Attic etymologising, as at once act, fact and capacity of a subject – if not necessarily that of a *human* subject, as we shall see. What is striking in this context is that Baumgarten, the coiner of the neologism, directs it towards an end in which the perfection of sense cognition is to be identified with beauty.

Immanuel Kant in the *Critique of Pure Reason* remarks that Baumgarten, in replacing with 'aesthetics' what other European theorists had previously simply called 'taste', had thereby hoped to be able to bring aesthetics under a rational principle. 'The Germans are the only ones who now employ the word "aesthetics" to designate that which others call the critique of taste,' Kant writes, immediately adding: 'The ground for this is a failed hope, held by the excellent analyst Baumgarten, of bringing the critical estimation of the beautiful under principles of reason, and elevating its rules to a science.'[4] At the very inception of Kant's own critical project, then, is the diagnosis of such a 'failed hope' as an occasion which licenses a new, stringent and purified division of reason. The first *Critique* notoriously takes up Baumgarten's term in order to give it an entirely different destiny, in the form of the transcendental aesthetic: space and time are no longer empirical concepts drawn from experience, but the pure and empty forms of possible experience in general, 'the pure forms of all sensible intuition', which 'thereby make possible synthetic *a priori* propositions'.[5] The transcendental aesthetic is key to Kant's rearticulation of the metaphysical relation between spontaneity and receptivity in the first *Critique*.

Yet Kant, as we know, cannot remain happy with his own radical de-rationalisation of the aesthetic condition. By 1790, he has significantly altered his position, which involves yet another re-uptake of Baumgarten's proposals. For the Kant of the *Critique of the Power of Judgment*, a return to 'aesthetics' requires a revaluation of the domination of cognitive operations, above all the requirement of determinative judgement. If only the understanding is 'capable of affording constitutive *a priori* principles of knowledge', it cannot be the case that judgement is absolutely foreign to concepts. Reflective judgement works rather with particulars, from which it moves upwards towards universality; in doing so, it requires a non-empirical principle, which can be given only as a law to and by means of itself. Such legislation, Kant remarks, is properly '*heautonomous*', 'since the power of judgment [...] is not a faculty for producing concepts of objects, but only for comparing present cases to others'.[6] As such, 'aesthetics' now has a double destiny in Kant: at once the condition of possibility of any phenomenon in general, and also the name for that which is 'purely subjective in the representation of an object', that is, the affect of pleasure or displeasure connected with the form of such an object.[7]

But it is precisely the logic of such a metaphysical splitting that Rancière will shatter. The aesthetic symptom is legible in this split between a transcendental operation constitutionally foreign to concepts and a self-reflexivity which passes through yet exceeds any conceptual capture. If Rancière's historicisation of the emergence of aesthetics is unremarkable in itself, one cannot say the same for his singular conception of the organisation and operations of the aesthetic as such. As he points out, precisely in regard to Baumgarten and Kant, 'It is only in the context of Romanticism and post-Kantian idealism [...] that aesthetics comes to designate the thought of art, even as the inappropriateness of the term is constantly remarked.'[8] For Rancière, then, aesthetics designates a regime of treating art that considers 'confused knowledge is no longer a lesser form of knowledge but properly *the thought of that which does not think*'.[9] Aesthetics undermines every received hierarchy of knowledge by displacing the process of real thinking into and onto phenomena that have no acceptable essence in themselves.

It is this paradox that helps to differentiate the properly distinct regimes in which 'art' has been treated in the West. In *Aesthetics and its Discontents*, Rancière identifies three different philosophical distributions of the arts. The first, 'Platonic' or 'ethical', separates 'the application of forms of knowledge founded on the imitation of models' from their simulacra; in this modality, what is at stake is not 'art' per se, but the problematic of a philosophical education.[10] In the Aristotelian regime, by contrast, the criteria for art are delivered by the *mimesis/poiesis* distinction: imitation at once picks out a specific class within the arts, functions as a normative principle which evaluates whether imitations are in fact art, and enables comparisons between different kinds of imitation. This is what Rancière will also call the 'representative regime of the arts'. Finally, there is the aesthetic realm proper. In this realm, mimesis no longer hinges on resemblance but serves to separate art from non-art according to a novel paradox:

> all the new, *aesthetic* definitions of art that affirm its autonomy in one way or another say the same thing, affirm the same paradox: that art is henceforth recognizable by its lack of any distinguishing characteristics – by its indistinction. Its products perceptibly manifest a quality of a thing that is *made* that is identical with the *not made*, a *known* thing identical to the *unknown*, a *willed* thing identical with the *unwilled*. With this, art at last positively comes within the ambit of truth.[11]

In the aesthetic regime, we no longer have proper or improper subjects as such. On the contrary, anything whatsoever can be represented (in a certain sense, at least), and beyond the dominion of any particular form, genre or judgement.

If Rancière's local interpretations of nineteenth- and twentieth-century artworks, education and political action are usually strikingly persuasive in themselves – a feature that even hostile commentators seem chary of not mentioning – so too are his criticisms of contemporaneous philosophers of aesthetics. Not only can he write with an extraordinary eye for detail with regard to Wordsworth, Balzac, Rimbaud and Proust, not to mention Loïe Fuller, Dziga Vertov and Peter Behrens, but he identifies, with extreme incisiveness, the weak points and inconsistencies, the unjustifiable or contradictory presuppositions of thinkers such as

Jean-François Lyotard, Gilles Deleuze, Alain Badiou and Louis Althusser. With regard to rival thinkers of the arts, he tends to do this precisely by pinpointing their adherence to a distribution of the sensible that is not up to, that refuses, or that poorly comprehends the radicality of the aesthetic regime. Hence Lyotard will be shown to misunderstand the stakes of the unrepresentable, or Badiou will be shown to reinject illicitly the Platonic stakes of education into his account of art.[12] Rancière sums up the global context of what he calls 'the ethical turn': 'the subsumption of all forms of discourse and practice beneath the same indistinct point of view.'[13] The rejection of aesthetics in the name of ethics is therefore not at all a salvific arrival, as its adherents claim, but, à la Lyotard, a transubstantiation of trauma into a new theology of time. Where 'ethics' indiscriminates all presentations with reference to an alleged *arché* that exempts itself globally from appearances, the works of aesthetics locally present an indiscrimination of sense and sensibility in their trans-formal apparition.

That there is something exorbitantly democratic about the creations of an aesthetic regime should be evident from Rancière's close readings not only of aesthetic works proper but of political action proper. As he puts it in 'Ten Theses on Politics', after having separated the practice of politics proper from the exercise or even pursuit of power, as a rupture with the police, and the subject of politics as a participation in contraries: '*Democracy is not a political regime. As a rupture in the logic of the arkhê, that is, of the anticipation of ruling in its disposition, it is the very regime of politics itself as a form of relationship that defines a specific subject.*'[14] For Rancière, then, it is the emergence of 'dissensus' as a 'deviation' or 'anomaly' that manifests the originary dehiscence of the social order itself that is 'the essence of politics'.

Jean-Luc Nancy summarises Rancière's doctrine of the relation of art and politics:

> His conjunction of the two carefully avoids subsuming one into the other. Art is articulated as the representation of assemblages according to which the sensible is distributed, and politics is the reworking of these assemblages by means of litigation or disagreements that open up, in the (in principle) egalitarian community, the inequality of the community or the 'people' within itself. Art and politics are joined and distributed as two orders of 'fictions': one is a representation of the distribution, and the other is its reworking.[15]

Although Rancière's work on education is not the focus of Nancy's attention here, its implications should nonetheless be underlined in such a context. Indeed, the former's commitment to equality is such that the slightest traces of hierarchy must be pursued to their most insidious asylum and alibi: that education is impossible without at least a mandatory detour through the asymmetries of a master-pupil dialectic, in which the master is, as Jacques Lacan might say, the subject-supposed-to-know. But it is the supposition of a transfer of knowledge as the ineluctable modality of the pedagogical that Rancière rejects. As Rancière puts it in the extraordinary text that is *The Ignorant Schoolmaster*: when the revolutionary pedagogue Joseph Jacotot realises the '*enforced stultification*' of the 'explicative system' of education, '*emancipation*' emerges when he unlocks 'the act of an intelligence obeying only itself even while the will obeys another will'.[16]

As Alain Badiou has phrased the questions that emerge from this aspect of Rancière's work, 'what is the new figure of the master that results if one excludes all the validation of institutional authority? Are there masters outside of the institution? Are there masters at all?'[17] Rancière's response to this limit educational conundrum – that equality induces mastery to become a shared non-mastery of experimental ignorance – is also the intellectual operator that enables him to characterise education as precisely a mode of linking dissensual-politics-as-emancipation and aesthetic-creation-as-egalitarian. Yet Rancière does not relate these three 'themes' according to the teleologies inscribed in representative or ethical regimes, or according to a stabilised or ordered set of relations. On the contrary, this triplet is precisely radically unstable and destabilising. Politics-Education-Aesthetics: this is Rancière's own, utterly atheistic version of Trinity.

The finitude of aesthetics

If Rancière's account of the modern aesthetic regime is persuasive and singular, it nonetheless shares, in addition to its periodisations, one other very significant feature with the tradition with which it otherwise breaks. This feature is one underlined and valorised by Martin Heidegger, and subsequently underlined and repudiated by Badiou: its finitude.[18] One can easily illustrate this apparently essential aspect of all talk of aesthetics by adverting again to Kant. What is perhaps not always sufficiently emphasised about the third *Critique* is the peculiar status that it assigns to aesthetic phenomena, whether of beauty or of sublimity. In a word, they are *inexistent*. Why? Because they are the consequences of forms-of-representation, without being forms of representation. Strictly speaking, neither phenomena nor noumena, the alleged 'forms' about which we make attributions of beauty, are in fact the unmarked markings of the subjective activity of the faculties, the spontaneous operators of mind that invariably disappear themselves in and as an essential part of their operations. But, as such, they must be inherently bound to finitude, just as Heidegger has emphasised, if here with a different inflection.

But this is also something that Rancière has to accept alongside the recuperation of the radicality of aesthetics: that it is simultaneously necessarily a question of finitude. An 'artwork' – if that name is still legitimate for the productions of the aesthetic regime – is exemplarily finite. This has consequences for its canonical status. Whereas his presentation of two other major regimes of the distribution of the sensible are indexed to the most ancient philosophical authorities, those of Plato and Aristotle, the sponsors of the aesthetic regime are at once anonymous and polynymous. As I have already noted, Rancière ensures that, whatever its links to Baumgarten and Kant, those names are by no means determining for the constitution of what he means by aesthetics. Rather, it is following the Romantic revisions of German Idealism that aesthetics is established. Nor does this happen quite as is proposed by Jean-Luc Nancy and Philippe Lacoue-Labarthe in their *The Literary Absolute*, in which the birth of modern literature must be conceived of as the bastard love-child of philosophy and literary criticism.[19] On the contrary, the aesthetic distribution Rancière outlines precisely cannot be reduced to a novel *literary* compact with the *philosophical*, although it remains the case that Rancière does give literature a certain priority in this regard.

Moreover, Rancière at once gives a rough temporal order of emergence to his three distributions – the ethical preceding the representative preceding the aesthetic – as he shows their competitive, coterminous tendencies. So modernism becomes an attempt to curb and counteract the aesthetic regime from within, reinjecting ethical elements into the disorderly house of aesthetics. As such, Rancière's approach is neither strictly epochal nor topological, but investigates the supple ceaseless interweaving of the immanent struggles concerning sensorial practices at the level of distribution.

But this is, again, to insist on the absolute finitude of such practices even in their aesthetic delimitations.

If there is evidently more to be said about this feature of finitude, one significant aspect in the present context goes directly back to the origin of the nomination of aesthetics as such. Baumgarten's project expressly arises as a *response* to the radical developments of seventeenth-century philosophy, to that of Descartes, Spinoza and especially Leibniz. These thinkers had precisely introduced the category of the infinite into rationalist philosophy in what we might too-briefly name a post-religious and post-theological sense. What Descartes or Spinoza nominate, for example, as the 'infinity' of God no longer has very much to do with their theological predecessors.[20] Aesthetics as a philosophical category was thus born *after* the intrusion of the infinite into thought. One might certainly see a reaction-formation in this coinage: against the infinite of thought, philosophy comes to inject the limiting *aesthesis* of the body. But one might just as well see a continuity or exacerbation of the demands of the infinite: aesthetics as the name for the consequences of the intrusion of the thought of infinity into the body itself. If, as Paul de Man suggests, aesthetics was ubiquitous before finitude, its very ubiquity entailing that it went unnamed as such, it could only be *as* finitude that the term 'aesthetics' could emerge. This may further suggest that the moment of the nomination of aesthetics was the moment of its decisive restriction, if not its disappearance.[21] This would have the appearance of a paradox: aesthetics appears as such, is only or can only be named as such, at the moment it is no longer itself. Modern aesthetics would be the mere remainder of itself, a finite residue of its own foreclosed infinity.

So if, at the very historical moment prior to the nomination of aesthetics as such, the infinite had explicitly entered thought as counter-theological strike, this is surely one of the critical consequences of the Copernican Revolution. But this thought – Descartes, Spinoza, Leibniz – was also, as Badiou notes in the *Handbook of Inaesthetics*, absolutely disinterested in thinking what we would now call art, and a fortiori the study of art qua aesthetics. Is there, then, at this moment, a form of rationalist thought that at once incorporates infinity *and* thinks 'aesthetically'? I believe there is: an exemplary variant can be found in the work of the great English poet and political writer John Milton. In the present context, I want to suggest that a certain attention to Milton's work can demonstrate the effective actuality of a thinking of art that does not conform to Rancière's historical or conceptual division of regimes.

The paradox of Milton

To my knowledge, Rancière never discusses the writings of John Milton directly. In fact, his only mentions of Milton come up in the course of separating two senses of what it means to be 'unrepresentable':

> To declare that a given subject is unrepresentable by artistic means is in fact to say several things at once. It can mean that the specific means of art, or of such-and-such an art, are not adequate to represent a particular subject's singularity. This is the sense in which Burke once declared that Milton's description of Lucifer in *Paradise Lost* was unrepresentable in painting. The reason was that its sublime aspect depended upon the duplicitous play of words that do not really let us see what they pretend to show us.[22]

Salient as this remark is in the context – Rancière is arguing against the confused 'ethical' deployment of motifs of the 'unrepresentable' as forms of theological transcendence – it does raise two or three points that need to be marked. First of all, the issue that Burke raises seems to concern the specific presentational powers of different materials and media, along lines that would later be concretised by theorists such as Clement Greenberg. One might therefore propose that Greenberg is a belated and disavowed Burkean. However, as Rancière notes elsewhere, explicitly comparing Schiller to Greenberg, the former's position 'proves to be somewhat more complicated than the modernist paradigm, which seeks to emphasize the work's material autonomy'.[23] As ever, Rancière insists on rebuking all attempts to reduce the aesthetic work to ethics or representation, however close they may otherwise seem to be. Second, Rancière's invocation of Burke here doesn't make it quite clear – unlike in Schiller's case – whether Burke is a Classicist or a Romantic, a representative of the representative regime or the aesthetic regime. It is, however, clear, third, that Rancière is not really speaking about Milton or his poetry as such, but about Burke's remarks about Milton. This indifference to Milton 'himself' is confirmed a few pages on when Rancière remarks:

The film *Shoah* is therefore not to be opposed to the televised *Holocaust* in the way that an art of the unrepresentable is to an art of representation. The rupture with the classical order of representation does not translate into the advent of an art of the unrepresentable. On the contrary, it is a freeing up with regard to the norms that prohibited the representation of Laocoön's suffering and the sublime aspect of Milton's Lucifer. These norms of representation defined the unrepresentable.[24]

Am I mistaken to discern a certain slippage in Rancière's argument? From a citation of Burke's remarks on Milton, Rancière has reiterated his doctrine of partial supersession of regimes by taking Burke's comments as at once true of Milton and as revealing Burke's own adherence to classicism. The representational regime that Rancière believes dominated the seventeenth century or classical age – and thus, if we are to take strict contemporaneity seriously, Milton's work too – is displaced by the aesthetic regime, which no longer in principle or practice prohibits the re-uptake of the sublimity of Lucifer (rather: Satan) into the sphere of visual representation.[25] Yet the struggles against aesthetics by its rivals continue to the present, embodied in works of art themselves, such that one work exhibits its solidarity with an ethical outlook, another its participation in aesthetics proper.

Yet one of the many odd things about these remarks of Rancière's is that Milton's great epic poem *Paradise Lost* is notorious for itself bringing into the ambit of representation the most extraordinarily diverse and surprising subjects, not just in its depictions of Lucifer (or Satan) himself, but in those of Satan's daughter/paramour Sin and his son/grandson Death, not to mention God's disquisitions in heaven with his Son, as well as any number of other unexpected themes, including the length of Adam and Eve's hair in Paradise, proper attitudes to gardening, and various forms of sexual congress.[26] This in itself might seem to make *Paradise Lost* a rather unexpected candidate for inclusion in the classical or representative regime, not least because it would immediately seem to rupture with all that regime's hallmarks. There is a constant experimental commingling of genres, from the prose arguments that were inserted before each book of blank verse in the poem, whose metre is an expressly poetico-political rebellion against the supposed 'bondage of rhyme', to the astonishing constant shift between incorporated allegories, lyrics, soliloquys and so on.[27]

There is a motivated assault upon all received divisions between 'high' and 'low', 'sacred' and 'profane', and so on.

In *The Aesthetic Unconscious*, Rancière examines Corneille's *Oedipus* of 1659 and Voltaire's *Lettres sur Oedipe* of 1719. For Rancière, what is significant about both writers – despite their temperamental, stylistic and chronological differences – is their incapacity not to tamper with the Sophoclean model. 'For Corneille and Voltaire', Rancière writes,

> this scenario established a defective relation between what is seen and what is said, between what is said and what is understood. Too much is shown to the spectator. This excess, moreover, is not merely a question of the disgusting spectacle of the gouged-out eyes; it concerns the mark of thought upon the body more generally. Above all, the scenario allows too much to be understood.[28]

Corneille's and Voltaire's attitudes are certainly in solidarity with Dr Johnson's notorious reservations about *Paradise Lost*; he offers almost exactly the same reasons for such reservations.[29] But there is a very significant difference: Milton was not an ancient Greek, but an almost-exact contemporary of Corneille.

Then again, nor was Milton French; nor was he a Catholic; nor was he a playwright. He was a radical puritan English political pamphleteer and poet. But these denominations don't just place Milton in a different national, linguistic, political, religious or literary space that nonetheless might still be seen as continuous with what Rancière describes as the representative regime. Rather, they should force the acknowledgement that another kind of work is under way, one that already substantially conforms to the criteria Rancière gives to the aesthetic, yet is not quite exhausted by them. Certainly, 'English exceptionality' is widely accepted in the study of the seventeenth century, whether one considers England as the home of the first true modern nationalists or the first modern revolutionaries or the first modern literary figures as such.[30] But rather than make general claims for the English exception, I want only to focus on a single aspect of Milton's work in this context. Let me take several moments from his political pamphleteering, which at once show how close his own theory and practice are to Rancière's, with some crucial differences.

Take the minor late pamphlet by Milton entitled *Of True Religion, Heresy, Schism, Toleration; and What Best Means May*

Be Used Against the Growth of Popery, his last prose intervention into public discourse in early 1673, the year before his death.[31] As Oliver Cromwell's Secretary for Foreign Tongues, and the man who had written *the* Commonwealth's propaganda justifications for Charles I's execution, there is still some mystery as to how Milton survived the Stuart Restoration of 1660, which saw the return of Charles II from exile. Milton, who was by that stage physically blind, was fined, imprisoned and excluded from public office. It was not until 1667, with the publication of the first ten-book version of *Paradise Lost*, that his name began to recirculate in ways that were not simply condemnatory. For Milton to enter once again into explicitly political and religious controversy was a bold move.

There are a number of interesting features about this little political sally, whose immediate occasional cause was the attempt by Charles II to issue a 'Declaration of Indulgence' in March 1672 to suspend the ecclesiastical penal laws against non-conformists. As Elizabeth Sauer comments, 'unacceptable for its indulgence of Catholics, the Declaration was voted down by the Cavalier Parliament, which persisted in debating questions of accommodating nonconforming Protestants.'[32] In fact, *Of True Religion* functions not only as a topical response to the proposed Declaration, but – in line with Milton's own long-term commitments – as a rational argument about the proper uses of reason.

What is a pamphlet, after all? It is a new thing in the context of Protestantism generally but given a decisive new inflection in the English pamphlet wars of the 1630s and 1640s, which both preceded and accompanied the uproar of the Civil War. Who do such pamphlets address? They no longer address anybody in particular; they are not written to or for a prince, a friend, or indeed any stable grouping of persons. If such pamphlets address anybody, it is a collective – in this case, the 'English people' or 'nation' – whose referent is by definition divided, undecided and mutable. Such pamphlets address the divisions of a collective. They aim, moreover, at a topical event or theme: here, now, this! Pamphlets are precisely occasional, partial. They enter into a polemical field of discourse, of other pamphlets, other competitors. They are linked to cheap, fast printing technologies and to the expansion of literacy. Pamphlets don't aim primarily to educate, but to sway, to convince. They take their chances. The issue is not simply propaganda, although there is evidently a propagandistic element in play; rather, such pamphlets do not emerge from a stable institution, but from and into an unstable extra-institutional zone. This is a zone of noise, of the multiple, of erratic vectors.

So Milton's pamphlet needs to be understood as interventional, linked to a specific political event. But this also is to emphasise its exacerbation of divisiveness in a situation of properly political division. It is clearly partisan, taking the threat of Catholicism as its titular motivation. It is universalising in its address, in that it addresses everybody – even, as we shall see, Catholics – insofar as they are rational creatures. Yet it is also meta-interpretative, in that it suggests how it can be reread beyond its immediate context. As the title announces, the pamphlet takes the distinction between 'heresy' and 'error' as one of its key operators, terms which are identified here with, respectively, the religious phenomena of Catholicism and Protestantism. Yet it is also linked with positions around succession, nation and, at another level, to the volatile relationships between 'obedience' and 'toleration'.

The thread that I will briefly follow in this pamphlet concerns its argument for toleration in 'true religion'. Its argument involves accepting the necessity, even desirability, of schism and error in religious matters, and the concomitant separation of state from church. It rationally demands arguing, preaching, pamphleteering and press liberty from and for (almost) all – in line with some long-standing arguments of Milton's which date back to at least the 1640s, including the arguments of *Areopagitica* for no pre-publication censorship, the toleration of dissent, and the doctrine that 'reason is but choosing'.[33] This doctrine – which is in fact axiomatic for Milton – is functionally equivalent to what Rancière calls 'the equivalence of intelligences'. It recurs throughout Milton's oeuvre, often in nearly-verbatim forms when it is not palpably implicit, including in *Paradise Lost* itself: 'reason also is choice' (III 108). Note, too, that Milton himself is intervening into contemporary political translations of the etymology of heresy from the Greek *haeresis*, 'choice'.[34] Because of the Fall, however, reason cannot insure itself against error; reason must rationally know it might always be in error; therefore reason must constantly reinterrogate its own choices and reasons for choosing in order to continue to be reason.

Although commentators have exhausted themselves trying to explain (justify, affirm, reject, vitiate, etc.) what has often been seen as Milton's unjustifiable exclusion of Catholics from toleration, it seems to me his arguments are at once clear, precise and, on his own terms, incontrovertible.³⁵ Because to be a Catholic requires obedience to the dogmas of the Church, one cannot genuinely be a Catholic and truly follow God's Word. Why not? Because the pope is only a man; if he is a man, he must be fallible; if he claims otherwise, he must be a liar or a hypocrite; if he admits to being just a man, then his word cannot be taken for God's; if one is a true Catholic, then one must assent to the pope's doctrines; to do so is to give over one's own reason to another man. To have chosen Rome is to have chosen the refusal to keep choosing. And to refuse choice is to choose tyranny. Even if it turns out at Judgement Day that the pope's reading of the Bible was absolutely correct, you would still have been an idolator to follow him blindly. With Catholicism for Milton, we find a triple abomination of idolatry: one man has elected himself above other men; that man has claimed a special relationship to God; to the extent that one follows him, then one has killed reason in oneself by worshipping an idol that separates reason from freedom from obedience. To obey God is to have to keep exerting your reason; to obey the pope is to have abandoned reason. As Milton puts it:

> But here the Papist will angrily demand, what! Are Lutherans, Calvinists, Anabaptists, Socinians, Arminians, no Hereticks? I answer, all these may have some errors, but are no Hereticks. Heresie is in the Will and choice profestly against Scripture; error is against the Will, in misunderstanding the Scripture after all sincere endeavours to understand it rightly: Hence it was said well by one of the Ancients, *Err I may, but a Heretick I will not be*.³⁶

So one can take only the language of the Bible, not any reliable connection with God, as the basis for true religion. Instead of the uninterpretable clarity and command of the divine Word, we have the fallen necessity of incommensurable interpretations. This is part of the work of reason for Milton: the necessity for interpretation under irremediable conditions of non-knowing. This doctrine of Milton's should be reapplied to the very genre of the pamphlets which freight it, which themselves present both a problem and an opportunity: reason, as the trait of the divine in man, must govern the chaotic space of unreasoned print; and this must be done by the very means of print by which chaos promulgates itself; this is to be reflected upon within the pamphlet, as well as its own necessary partiality and potential error to the extent that it is rational. Rationality and conflict are essentially bound together by Milton, but with an eye towards the construction of a properly political mode of conflict: neither war nor rebellion but ongoing irreducible dissensus is the sign of freedom.

Certainly, the Protestantism remains paramount: Scripture is the only authority. Nonetheless, Scripture does not speak clearly or self-evidently to men; it can appear piecemeal, obscure, even contradictory; yet it also speaks of precisely this situation, of our irreducible fallen partiality before the word, of our temptations to repeat the worst precisely insofar as we are unable to take responsibility for the possibility that the other is right, that we have gone astray. And yet we should not retreat into scepticism and doubt, that is, into despair; our struggles must be prosecuted sincerely and without hypocrisy; the truth must be absolute, or it must not be. The apparent paradox – how can we act with absolute conviction about the knowledge we know we cannot know? – is resolved by the injunction to continually reread one's own convictions in the light of others'.

It is here that Milton's political pamphleteering – which proselytises for endless dissensus as the model of liberty itself – rejoins his aesthetic works. And they rejoin each other according to another, related doctrine of Milton's that accords with Rancière's diagnosis of the aesthetic regime as 'welcoming images, objects and performances that seemed most opposed to the idea of fine art' and in which art is 'constantly merging its own reasons with those belonging to other spheres of experience'.[37] This emerges in Milton through what we could call his 'doctrine of the two blanks'. In *Areopagitica*, he famously announced:

> I cannot praise a fugitive and cloistered virtue unexercised, and unbreathed, that never sallies out and sees her adversary, but slinks out of the race, where that immortal garland is to be run for, not without dust and heat. Assuredly we bring not innocence into the world, we bring impurity much rather; that which purifies us is trial, and trial is by what is contrary. That virtue therefore which is but a youngling in the contemplation of evil, and knows not the utmost that vice promises to her followers, and rejects it, is but a blank virtue, not a pure; her whiteness is but an excremental whiteness.[38]

Here, as elsewhere, Milton insists that conflict is fundamental for virtue; such virtue requires engagement with its contraries;

yet such contraries may precisely appear in the world as indistinguishable. In fact, two different forms of virtue – the ignorant and the achieved – may themselves appear as indiscernible. It is the task of every human to work to turn the one into the other, without any guarantees, by taking risks and with the cost of error, by engaging in a world that is itself composed of imperceptible antitheses. Just as Rancière also comes to hold, Milton's politics is a politics of participation in contraries. In such a situation, there are no certain markings to tell the true from the false, the good from evil. Under such a description, too, even the topical pamphlet shows its solidarity and shares its essence with the most ambitious works of art.

Moreover, it is at this point that the infinite returns to supplement the putative finitude of aesthetics and politics. If, for Milton, the necessity and urgency for a decision under conditions of not-knowing is the very emblem of finitude, insofar as it is structured by precisely not-knowing, and insofar as such a decision reduces to choosing between indiscernibles, the ultimate rationale for such a decision depends on the binding of reason's acts to the contingent infinity of grace: 'Thy sovereign sentence, that man should find grace' (*Paradise Lost*, III 145). Milton's poetry proliferates operations designed – as this chapter's epigraph from Burke explicitly states – to give a sense of the 'immutable, immortal, infinite' (*Paradise Lost*, III 373).

Conclusion

Very simply, Milton's work does not conform to the tripartite elaboration of regimes offered by Rancière. Milton, however, might be considered much closer to the aesthetic regime than to the ethical or representative regimes, in his introduction of confused knowledge into the realm of perception, in his paradoxes of activity and passivity, in his displacement of hierarchies of genre, of sight and sense, and of the relations between showing and understanding. Yet if Milton is also clearly Platonic in his doctrine of the two blanks – which emphasises the primacy of ethical education coupled with the necessity to split the real from its simulacra – he does this precisely aesthetically as well as propositionally, in the very non-Platonic genre that is vernacular epic poetry. In doing so, finally, art is to be practically reconnected with the infinite.

In fact, when one starts to discern exceptions to Rancière's rules, others start to turn up, often in unexpected places. In *Remnants of Auschwitz*, Giorgio Agamben notes the utter horror of the 'grey zone' exemplified by a notorious soccer match between the SS and Sonderkommando. Commenting on this passage, Rancière makes the claim that, for Agamben, in conformity with what Rancière sees as a broader logic of 'the ethical turn', 'All differences simply disappear in the law of a global situation.'[39] The point of falsification here is in Rancière's 'All'. (And possibly, too, in the modifier 'simply'.) Why? Because it is that *certain* received conceptions of significant political differences are erased by the fact of the concentration camps, not *all* such differences. Part of the situation that Agamben wants to analyse is the disappearance of any substantial friend/enemy distinction in a contemporary political frame as an operative category for action. Indeed, Agamben's analysis of such motivated occlusions is directed to reopening the question regarding the status of action after Auschwitz, and precisely not according to received, identifiable or recognised differences. Yet these 'messianic' differences are indiscernible within the current situation; they need to be squirrelled out in the course of a process that itself has to decide the indiscernible from the point of the undecidable (to invoke here the terms of Badiou's doctrine of the subject). And it is at such points that Rancière fudges: Agamben can no more be assimilated to an ethical turn than Milton can be assimilated to the representative regime.

Badiou himself notes the 'melancholy' of Rancière's position on art, in which the dreams of cobblers and the people have been separated by the failures of history: 'The circumstantial failures of history should not invoke melancholy but should rather activate the deployment of the idea in the tension of its future.'[40] In other words, Milton, Agamben and Badiou, by contrast with Rancière himself, are eminently concerned with a kind of eternity that is not theological. Milton finished the bulk of *Paradise Lost* when blind, impoverished and abominated, and in the wake of the near-complete collapse of all his hopes for the English Republic. But the work of the poem is not melancholic but messianic, in its rewriting of the Protestant rewriting of the Catholic doctrine of *felix culpa*: the first creation was God making something out of nothing; the second, more marvellous still, was Christ making good out of evil; the third, making art from disparity, the infinite prosaic-politico-philosophical-poem of human reason. To say this, however, is to engage in a literary-political practice that is not ethical, representative, nor aesthetic.

Notes

1. Jacques Rancière, *Aisthesis: Scenes from the Aesthetic Regime of Art*, trans. Zakir Paul (London and New York: Verso, 2013), ix.
2. See Alain Badiou, *Handbook of Inaesthetics*, trans. Alberto Toscano (Stanford: Stanford University Press, 2005); Jürgen Habermas, *The Structural Transformation of the Public Sphere*, trans. Thomas Burger with Frederick Lawrence (Cambridge, MA: MIT, 1989); Niklas Luhmann, *Art as a Social System*, trans. Eva M. Knodt (Stanford: Stanford University Press, 2000).
3. See Alexander Baumgarten, *Metaphysics: A Critical Translation with Kant's Elucidations, Selected Notes, and Related Materials*, ed. and trans. Courtney D. Fugate and John Hymers (London: Bloomsbury, 2013) and *Aesthetica* (Hildesheim: Georg Olms Verlag, 1986). 'Aesthetics', Baumgarten asserts at the very beginning of his preface, 'is the science of sense cognition.' See Mary J. Gregor, 'Baumgarten's "Aesthetica"', *The Review of Metaphysics*, 37:2 (1983), 357–85. Gregor argues, against the prevalent views that Baumgarten was seeking a correlate for perception analogous to that which logic does for intellectual cognition or, alternatively, something like an inductive logic, that Baumgarten wishes 'to carve out a sphere in which perception will enjoy a certain autonomy' (360).
4. Immanuel Kant, *Critique of Pure Reason*, ed. and trans. Paul Guyer and Allen W. Wood (Cambridge: Cambridge University Press, 1998), A21/B35, 156.
5. Ibid., A39/B56, 183.
6. Kant, *Critique of the Power of Judgment*, ed. Paul Guyer, trans. Paul Guyer and Eric Matthews (Cambridge: Cambridge University Press, 2002), 28.
7. Ibid., 75.
8. Rancière, *The Aesthetic Unconscious*, trans. Debra Keates and James Swenson (Cambridge: Polity, 2009), 6.
9. Ibid., 5.
10. Rancière, *Aesthetics and its Discontents*, trans. Steven Corcoran (Cambridge: Polity, 2009), 64.
11. Ibid., 66.
12. See, for example, the essays he dedicates to these thinkers in *Aesthetics and its Discontents*.

13. Ibid., 110.
14. Rancière, *Dissensus: On Politics and Aesthetics*, ed. and trans. Steven Corcoran (London and New York: Continuum, 2010), 31. Italics in original.
15. Jean-Luc Nancy, 'Jacques Rancière and Metaphysics', in Gabriel Rockhill and Philip Watts (eds), *Jacques Rancière: History, Politics, Aesthetics* (Durham, NC, and London: Duke University Press, 2009), 88.
16. Rancière, *The Ignorant Schoolmaster: Five Lessons in Intellectual Emancipation*, trans. with intro. by Kristin Ross (Stanford: Stanford University Press, 1991), 13. Italics in original.
17. Badiou, 'The Lessons of Jacques Rancière', in Rockhill and Watts, *Jacques Rancière*, 34.
18. See Martin Heidegger, *Kant and the Problem of Metaphysics*, 5th edn, trans. Richard Taft (Bloomington and Indianapolis: Indianapolis University Press, 1997).
19. See Nancy and Philippe Lacoue-Labarthe, *The Literary Absolute: The Theory of Literature in German Romanticism*, trans. Philip Barnard and Cheryl Lester (Albany: SUNY Press, 1988). See also my *The Romanticism of Contemporary Theory* (Aldershot: Ashgate, 2003) for another account of the import of romanticism in this regard.
20. It is worth reiterating here the impact of the so-called 'Copernican Revolution' upon the thought of God's infinity as guarantor of immanence. This 'event' has consequences for aesthetics and politics that I don't believe have yet been satisfactorily analysed, except in the loosest fashion. No doubt this is partially because of the rift that the new sciences of the seventeenth century introduce into knowledge more generally. As Jean-Claude Milner usefully remarks, however, noting a 'dyschronia' in the de facto separation of God from transcendent and ungraspable infinity: 'When mathematized physics started to reflect on the infinite universe, mathematicians had only a vague, fuzzy notion of infinity [. . .] It's paradoxical that physics became mathematized and, in so doing, opened the possibility for an infinite universe, and yet it didn't know, in mathematical terms, what the infinite was.' Badiou and Jean-Claude Milner with Philippe Petit, *Controversies: A Dialogue on the Politics and Philosophy of our Time*, trans. Susan Spitzer (Cambridge: Polity, 2014), 72.
21. See Paul de Man, *Aesthetic Ideology*, ed. with intro. by Andrzej Warminski (Minneapolis: University of Minnesota Press, 1996), 92.

22. Rancière, *Aesthetics and its Discontents*, 123.
23. Ibid., 27.
24. Ibid., 126.
25. Indeed, what makes me suspect that Rancière has not actually read Milton or *Paradise Lost* in this context and, as a result, misses something about Burke as well is, first, that Rancière refers to 'Lucifer' rather than to 'Satan', when the poem concerns itself primarily and explicitly with the *fallen* angel; second, that the remarks of Burke regarding unrepresentability in the poem primarily concern not only Satan himself but either the non-figure of Death or Milton's language per se. See Edmund Burke, *A Philosophical Inquiry into the Origin of our Ideas of The Sublime and Beautiful* (London: George Bell and Sons, 1889), 42. See *passim*, e.g. 44 (this is clearly the reference upon which Rancière is commenting), 131–2. Why Rancière even invokes 'Lucifer' at all is a little enigmatic to me; Chateaubriand's French translation, for example, correctly provides the appellation 'Lucifer' in accordance with the original, e.g. '*palais du grand Lucifer*'/'The palace of great Lucifer' (*Paradise Lost*, V 760), but the rarity of this nomination is precisely of the highest significance in and for the poem, e.g. 'Known then, that after Lucifer from heaven / (So call him, brighter once amidst the host / Of angels, than that star the stars among)'/'*Sache donc: après que Lucifer (ainsi appelé parce qu'il brillait autrefois dans l'armée des anges plus que cette étoile parmi les étoiles)*' (*Paradise Lost*, VII 131–3).
26. For the best possible introduction to the reception history of *Paradise Lost*, which goes far beyond the issues at stake here, see John Leonard, *Faithful Labourers: A Reception History of Paradise Lost, 1667–1970*, 2 vols (Oxford: Oxford University Press, 2013).
27. In this regard, see above all Barbara Kiefer Lewalski, *'Paradise Lost' and the Rhetoric of Literary Forms* (Princeton: Princeton University Press, 1985), and her 'The Genres of *Paradise Lost*', in Dennis Danielson (ed.), *The Cambridge Companion to Milton* (Cambridge: Cambridge University Press, 1989), 79–95.
28. Rancière, *The Aesthetic Unconscious*, 16.
29. For example, 'Another inconvenience of Milton's design is, that it requires the description of what cannot be described, the agency of spirits. He saw that immateriality supplied no images, and that he could not shew angels acting but by instruments of action; he therefore invested them with form and matter' and 'The confusion of spirit and matter, which pervades the whole narration of the war of heaven, fills it with incongruity; and the book in which it is related is,

I believe, the favourite of children, and gradually neglected as knowledge is increased.' Samuel Johnson, *The Lives of the Most Eminent English Poets, with Critical Observations on their Works* (London: J. Fergusson, 1819), 130/131. One could suggest that Milton's aesthetic radicality was such that even the greatest commentators could only attempt to re-classicise in their judgements upon him.

30. See Liah Greenfield, *Nationalism: Five Roads to Modernity* (Cambridge, MA: Harvard University Press, 1992) for its account of England as the 'first nation'; the radically different accounts of Christopher Hill, *The Century of Revolution 1603–1714* (London: Routledge, 2002) and Oliver Feltham, *Anatomy of Failure: Philosophy and Political Action* (London: Bloomsbury, 2013) for different takes on the singularity of the revolution ('Civil War') that precedes the Glorious Revolution of 1688 and the American or French Revolutions late in the following century; and literary critics as different as Franco Moretti, *Signs Taken For Wonders*, trans. Susan Fischer et al. (London: Verso, 1983) and Stephen Greenblatt, *Shakespearean Negotiations* (Berkeley and Los Angeles: University of California Press, 1988) for various indications of the exceptional transformations of the literary-political spheres associated with the synecdoche 'Shakespeare' (or 'Elizabethan and Jacobean theatre').

31. John Milton, *Of True Religion*, in *Complete Prose Works of John Milton, Vol. 8: 1666–1682*, ed. Maurice Kelley (New Haven and London: Yale University Press, 1982), 408–40. Note that Milton's title picks up on the writings of the Church Fathers on precisely the sense of this syntagm. For a recent examination of the situational nuances of the phrase 'true religion', see Peter Harrison, *The Territories of Science and Religion* (Chicago: Chicago University Press, 2015). In my opinion, Milton is alluding above all to Augustine's *De vera religione*, which he is contradicting and modifying, e.g. 'This Catholic Church, strongly and widely spread throughout the world, makes use of all who err, to correct them if they are willing to be aroused, and to assist its own progress. It makes use of the nations as material for its operations, of heretics to try its own doctrine, of schismatics to prove its stability, of the Jews as a foil to its own beauty. Some it invites, others it excludes, some it leaves behind, others it leads'; also, 'Its own carnal members, i.e., those whose lives or opinions are carnal, it tolerates as chaff by which the corn is protected on the floor until it is separated from its covering. On this floor everyone voluntarily makes himself either corn or chaff. Therefore every man's sin or error is tolerated until he finds

an accuser or defends his wicked opinion with pertinacious animosity.' *Augustine: Earlier Writings*, ed. J. H. S. Burleigh (Louisville: Westminster John Knox Press, 2006), 231.
32. Elizabeth Sauer, 'Milton's *Of True Religion*, Protestant Nationhood, and the Negotiation of Liberty', *Milton Quarterly*, 40:1 (2006), 5.
33. See Milton, *Areopagitica*, in *Complete Prose Works of John Milton, Vol. 2: 1643–1648*, ed. Ernest Sirluck (New Haven and London: Yale University Press, 1959), 480–570.
34. The *OED* gives the following etymology:

> < Old French *eresie, heresie* (12th cent.), modern French *hérésie*, < Latin type **heresia* (whence also Italian *eresia*, Portuguese *heresia*), for Latin *hæresis* school of thought, philosophical sect, in eccl. writers, theological heresy, < Greek αἵρεσις taking, choosing, choice, course taken, course of action or thought, 'school' of thought, philosophic principle or set of principles, philosophical or religious sect; < αἱρεῖν to take, middle voice αἱρῖσϑαι to take for oneself, choose. The Greek word occurs several times in the N.T., viz. Acts. v. 17, xv. 5, xxiv. 5, xxvi. 5, xxviii. 22, where English versions from Tyndale render 'sect' (i.e. of the Sadducees, Pharisees, Nazarenes or Christians, considered as sects of the Jews); Acts xxiv. 14, where all versions from Wyclif to 1611 have 'heresy', R.V. 'a sect (or heresy)'; in 1 Cor. xi. 19 Wyclif, Geneva, Rhemish, and 1611 have 'heresies', Tyndale and Cranmer 'sectes', R.V. 'heresies (or factions)'; in Gal. v. 20, Wyclif, Tyndale, Cranmer, Rhemish have 'sectes', Geneva and 1611 'heresies', R.V. 'heresies (or parties)'; in 2 Peter ii. 1 Wyclif, Tyndale, Cranmer, Rhemish have 'sectes', Geneva and 1611 'heresies', R.V. 'heresies (or sects)'. The earlier sense-development from 'religious sect, party, or faction' to 'doctrine at variance with the catholic faith', lies outside English.

35. Take the almost-panicky identification of 'an intolerant Milton' in the introduction to Sharon Achinstein and Elizabeth Sauer (eds), *Milton and Toleration* (Oxford: Oxford University Press, 2007), e.g. 'While Milton at times surrendered to a knee-jerk anti-popery fear, he saw in popery not simply Roman Catholicism, but all forms of servitude, dependence, and alienation of reason' (7). Such remarks seem to me to miss the fundamental rigour of Milton's axiom that 'reason is but choosing', for reasons I will elaborate upon. It is also surprising that this book has no index listing for 'Augustine', although he is briefly mentioned in Nigel Smith's very useful chapter 'Milton and the European Contexts of Toleration', 37.
36. Milton, *Of True Religion*, 423.

37. Rancière, *Aisthesis*, x/xi.
38. Milton, *Areopagitica*, 515.
39. Rancière, *Aesthetics and its Discontents*, 120.
40. Badiou, 'The Lessons of Jacques Rancière', 53.

5

'A New Mode of the Existence of Truth': Rancière and the Beginnings of Modernity 1780–1830[1]

Andrew Gibson

There is something curious and intriguing about the place of the period 1780–1830 in Rancière's work. He has written a great deal about it, if often in a rather piecemeal fashion, and its most prominent intellectual figures repeatedly loom large in his historical panoramas, though sometimes fleetingly: Kant and Hegel, Goethe and Schiller, Schelling and the Schlegels, Hugo and Chateaubriand, Wordsworth, Byron and Keats. He repeatedly refers back to the period as apparently in some sense decisive for modern politics and, above all, modern aesthetics. Phrases like 'depuis deux siècles' and 'depuis le XVIIIe siècle' recur in his work.[2] Yet, since Rancière aims to break with what he calls 'the standard intelligibility of history',[3] he turns out to be distrustful, sometimes deeply distrustful, of concepts frequently associated with the period: the birth of modernity, the beginning of the democratic revolution, the inception of the modern will to liberation, the inauguration of the modern progressivisms, the emergence of the modern narratives of progress. Rancière urges the need to resist a conception of any politics as being 'tied to a determined historical project', like that supposedly engendered by the emancipatory drive of the French Revolution (PA, 51). He is adamant in his refusal to confer the status of a transcendental on any specific concept, like justice or equality, that would appear to underwrite such a project. He is likewise sceptical of explanatory historical systems that too crudely map historical and cultural phenomena on to allegedly coherent historical contexts thought of as totalities, and opposes all ideas of 'grand historical master-signifiers' which might appear to govern epochs, like modernity, as mere carryovers from onto-theology (TP, 207–8). He has been explicitly dismissive of Alain Badiou's grand theory of the event and what he takes to be its insistence on the 'rupture exemplaire' (TP, 207),

99

the absolute break with the historically given. Indeed, he has on occasions sounded almost intemperate on the theme ('ce sont des choses que je ne peux absolument pas partager'; TP, 353–4). There is a Rancièrian thought of the event. But here the event is not only rare, as Badiou also suggests, but tends to be modest, small-scale and even minimal. If politics does occasionally appear 'in its purity', as an egalitarian politics that an irrecoverable, inexplicable event releases from the 'ambiguities' of social existence, then it does so only fleetingly and locally.[4]

In fact, Rancière both repeatedly resorts to a concept of modernity and repeatedly fights shy of it. This suggests that, for him, 1780–1830 might indeed be the crucible of a certain modernity, but a modernity that in some degree was and has remained limited, suspended, quiescent, intermittent, dispersed or adulterate, ambivalent. The period in question witnesses the birth of a modernity 'under erasure' that has in fact long been ours and is the one we might know by now we have to work with. I want briefly to explore this modernity here – this modernity, as distinct from the one Rancière takes to task – not least, by setting it alongside certain other conceptions of the period, conceptions that are, like Rancière's, historical, philosophical or theoretical and aesthetically focused together, and that allow us further to specify this particular content within his thought.

Firstly, then, the affirmative concept of the period as of world-historical importance, as in Eric Hobsbawm's *The Age of Revolution: 1789–1848*: Hobsbawm's period of the 'dual revolutions', French and British (or Industrial), is one of 'qualitative and fundamental transformation' that is 'constant, rapid and up to the present limitless'.[5] The initial transformations take place abruptly and with violence, in a 'sudden, sharp, almost vertical turn upwards which marks the "take-off"' (AR, 44). Note how the technological metaphor (so much of its time, in England) makes the historical process seem peremptorily modern and modern from the start. Here, with all the explosive power of a missile or jet engine, revolution launches history into a blue-sky future. This future is a universal one. Hobsbawm's period sees rampant new energies swirling out of France and Britain and tearing down obsolete and moribund structures across Europe, from feudalism to the Holy Roman Empire to the Italian city-states to the German free cities. The vast surge of the Industrial Revolution in Britain has consequences worldwide. The French Revolution sends liberal and radical-democratic politics spinning round the globe from Latin America to Bengal. The revolutions colonise all space. Their effects spread everywhere, 'by spontaneous contagion' (AR, 138). Modernity's drive, in other words, is towards a totality, which the arts and indeed the sciences and historiography reflect, 'echo[ing] the thunder of the earthquakes' which are shaking 'all humanity' (AR, 312). 'No-one could fail to observe', writes Hobsbawm, 'that the world was transformed more radically than ever before in this era. [. . .] No thinking person could fail to be awed, shaken, and mentally stimulated by these convulsions and transformations' (AR, 353).

At almost the opposite pole to Hobsbawm stands what we might call the catastrophic vision of 1780–1830. The Carl Schmitt of *Political Romanticism* thinks of the period, and with it, in effect, the emergence of modernity, as a catastrophe. For Schmitt, the period is characterised above all by an individualist, irrationalist, romantic disintegration of the concept. This disintegration has its major origins in 1789, but occurs whether romanticism takes on a revolutionary hue, as in France, or a reactionary one, as in Germany. The disintegration of the concept, the schism Kant opens up between thought and being, as contrasted with, say, the Hobbesian will to hold them together via 'systematic rationality', has several consequences, notably, perhaps, ungroundedness.[6] The disintegration of the concept leaves the romantic rootless or unmoored in that he or she is no longer capable of holding fast 'to an important idea on the basis of a free decision', and can no longer find any 'inner resistance to the most powerful and immediate impressions that prevail at the time' (PR, 51). This means that the political romantic or fledgling modern is always frail, vulnerable to betrayal and self-betrayal. It also means that he or she gives over to subjectivism and accepts no objective imperatives: as Schmitt puts matters, 'in the struggle of the deities', the political romantic 'does not commit himself and his subjective personality' (PR, 64). Furthermore, absolute subjectivity breeds absolute creativity or 'productivity'. The historical and political worlds, the moral and legal spheres, are of interest above all for what the subject can make of them, as his or her products. Or, as Friedrich Schlegel put matters, the real beloved is only the occasion of a 'marvellous flower of [the] imagination' (PR, 84).

But this can also breed disenchantment, disillusionment, despair, since any return to 'limited reality' itself is likely to mean contact with the dullness and futility that, in Schmitt's phrase, 'a lottery ticket has after the drawing' (PR, 69). Out of this logic springs another consequence of subjectivism and the self-reflection that goes with it, romantic irony. The concept – with its limits, its clarity and definition – perishes in the hands of Rousseau and the romantics. Romantic irony appears in its wake, taking the supposed inadequacy of reality as its target, as an absolute way of seeing, and, in doing so, once again promoting the 'suspension of every decision' (PR, 56). Romantic irony, but also possibility: bereft of foundations, which always fix certain limits, the political romantic abandons him- or herself to his or her own possibilities, to plans ('plan upon plan unfolds,' says Goethe's Faust),[7] to promises and prospects, and in doing so also to an unbounded future, limitlessness. (From this springs the romantic cult of the child, imagined as the locus of 'innumerable possibilities'; PR, 69.) Because the limit has disappeared, all categories in the Kantian sense, all pure concepts of the understanding, break down. Revolutionary attachments shade or mutate into reactionary ones, revolutionary positions bleed into or depend on reactionary positions, and vice versa, interminably. At the far end of this tendency stands an 'emotional pantheism', the appreciation of 'everything and its opposite' together (PR, 128). The logical conclusion of all this is an affirmation or prioritisation of aesthetic and, above all, literary experience in its sublime indeterminacy or open-endedness. But this is a lure which should not take us in, since what it indicates is that the political romantic 'does not want to be bothered' by questions of choice, determined activity, 'the constraints of objectivity', 'the task of a concrete realization' (PR, 71–2).

Schmitt is by no means a foe of irony per se. Indeed, he welcomes self-irony, precisely because he deplores the lack of its objectifying force in the romantic mind. It is only seldom, however – as is also the case with Hobsbawm – that he fastens on irony within his subject matter. Though there are moments when both see irony glittering within modernity, irony never threatens to usurp their perspectives. Yet beyond the world-historical and affirmative view of the emergence of modernity, and the catastrophic and negative one, one might wonder whether another view of modernity has not been slowly but steadily evolving and gaining weight. This is the conception of modernity as from the start an ironical historical phenomenon, one afflicted with historical irony, constantly bogging down in its own counter-valences. Ironical modernity:

this is an idea, for example, that we may happen upon in Marshall Berman's *All That Is Solid Melts into Air*, which articulates some major aspects of it. Berman sees that Marx understood modern life as 'radically contradictory at its base' (ATS, 19), that Nietzsche like Marx perceived the currents of modern history as ironic, that a thread of irony runs right the way through two centuries of modernism (recalling that Rousseau is the source of the term). Berman knows that 'modern irony repeatedly animates great works of [modern] art and thought' (ATS, 14). What's more, he traces modern irony precisely back to 1780–1830, supremely, in the case of a work whose composition more than that of any other, even *The Prelude*, spans the whole period from beginning to end: Goethe's *Faust*.

What Berman grasps as quintessentially and unsurpassably modern in *Faust* is perhaps this: Faust's vast drives are both creative and destructive; they are also creative and destructive at the same time, at once, and this, their immediately paradoxical constitution, is irreducible and inescapable. In other words, modernity is not to be extricated or separated out from havoc and monstrosity. One way of putting the point is that Goethe understands proleptically that Stalin (a name Berman introduces) is part of modernity, that it is impossible to filter modernity out from what the name of Stalin represents. With every modern advance, the evidence of gross, unwarranted suffering will 'pierce the night', in Goethe's phrase (ATS, 64). Benjamin supposed this, too, in his concept of 'catastrophe in permanence' or satanic modernity.[8] In Derrida's great formulation, 'there is a holocaust for every [modern] date, and somewhere in the world at every hour'.[9] Faust's extraordinary development of human powers is also a pact with the devil, and there is no way out of or beyond this double-bind, whether in sexual relations (as with Gretchen) or political and social ones (as in Acts IV and V of *Faust* Part Two). The logic of modernity, a logic that Goethe grasps at its beginning and with preternatural acuity, is a logic of explosion and implosion together, or what Berman calls 'the tragedy of development' (ATS, 37–86), which we continue with, at one and the same time, inexorably and with unacceptably high costs. Furthermore, the logic of modernity afflicts Marxism and progressivism indifferently with capitalism. The desire to eliminate tragedy incessantly produces more tragedy. So long as we remain modern, Goethe's Philemon and Baucis endlessly go to the wall.

Yet for all Berman's shrewd grasp of modern irony, his discourse is in some degree lacking in it. Again and again, like Hobsbawm in this respect, he himself is caught up in his own equivalent of what he glosses as Marx's excitement at the onset of modernity, even in the act of admitting its devastating consequences. Indeed, here Berman is effectively paradigmatic. Understanding ironical modernity is not the same as thinking or writing it. For Berman, working within Marxist tradition as he is, irony repeatedly shades into dialectics, and indeed he repeatedly pairs the two words in his book. To push them further apart, we may turn to the second aspect of ironical modernity. Published in 1925, Karl Mannheim's *Conservatism: A Contribution to the Sociology of Knowledge* suggests that we can properly understand modernity only by placing within it what is habitually conceived of as anti-modernity, recognising that anti-modernity is modern too, expanding the meaning of modernity to encompass anti-modernity and thereby, again, charging it with irony. The most obvious and well-known example of this is the emergence of conservatism, which arrives in 1790, the year after the beginning of the French Revolution, with Burke's *Reflections on the Revolution in France* – though so startlingly new is the conservative phenomenon, so distinct from the traditionalism that preceded it, that it finds a name only nearly twenty years later, with the foundation of Chateaubriand's journal *Le Conservateur*, and the word 'conservative' enters the English language only in 1830. (Similarly, 'reaction' in its recent sense dates back to Constant's *Des reactions politiques* of 1797.) Conservatism turns out to be more modern than modernity. Think the logic of that through to its obvious consequence, and modernity appears as the revelation of groundlessness and the immediate restitution of grounds. Or, as Alain Badiou puts the point in his *Second manifeste pour la philosophie*, though Badiou is hardly an ironist, what we think of as modern and what Badiou calls 'reactive' forms of subjectivity are both 'new figures' determined as such by modernity.[10] Thus, for example, Christianity after the Enlightenment is a new Christianity, indeed a series of new Christianities, marked by the very historicity that their insistence on eternal truth ought logically to debar. Thus the event of the new requires that the 'reactive' subject not merely resuscitate but refashion old forms.

Mannheim particularly demonstrates this with reference to the post-revolutionary traditions of a new thought, piquantly known as German *Altconservatismus*, 'old conservatism', as exemplified in Möser, Muller, Savigny, Stahl, Gustav Hugo and many others. The beginning of the nineteenth century sees the culmination of a process whereby *'the political element'* has increasingly become *'the point around which all of the currents in the ideological universe crystallize'*.¹¹ Thus 'we are no longer concerned with a unified, though internally variegated world-view; from now on, in accordance with the plurality of strata in the social whole [. . .] worlds confront one another' (C, 52). The French Revolution spawns two disjoined traditions of thought, one which, in all its diversity, we might loosely call progressive, the other conservative, each of which has its own immanent logic. Certainly, 'the conservative element' is always secondary; that is, 'it is not the bearer of events, authentically creative, but rather "reactive" [Badiou's word again], in the sense that it first becomes aware of itself as antithesis' (C, 53). But this does not make it less of 'a specifically historical and modern phenomenon' (C, 72), and we ignore the insistence with which antithesis shadows thesis at our peril.

Furthermore, the two traditions often share the same 'formal assumptions'. Both rely on a concept of '"what lies behind us"', whether that which is antecedent in time, or 'the "germ," the seed which has yet to unfold. Both tend towards an intuition of totality. Both expand upon the particular.' Both think in terms of historical substrata, whether supposedly laid down by past generations or as classes or relations of production. Both repeatedly exchange terms, like *Volksgeist* and freedom, adapting their meanings as they proceed (C, 37). Nor are they necessarily identifiable with individual subjects: 'it is frequently not at all clear whether an individual is to be taken as conservative, or as progressive' (C, 47; easy enough to show: Byron's, Chateaubriand's and Kleist's various tergiversations, mutations and shifts of position all readily come to mind as examples). 'Something which is progressive today' may quite readily take on 'the function of conservatism tomorrow' (C, 81). Finally, indeed, conservatism during this period gives 'shape', like revolutionism, 'to an entirely new way of thinking', one 'capable of interpreting the world in a new way' (C, 101). Unlike traditionalism, modern conservatism cannot merely assume that things remain the same. It must reflect on that which it wishes to maintain.

Albert O. Hirschman's *The Rhetoric of Reaction: Perversity, Futility, Jeopardy* provides a certain additional sophistication to

Mannheim's case. Right from the start, conservative modernity developed a new set of rhetorical strategies, as if, in Mannheim's terms, it knew that it had to leave traditionalism's automatic assumption of continuity behind; as though it knew it had to cover the void that modernity and revolution had opened up. If, with the French Revolution, modernity embarks on a 'protracted and perilous seesawing of action and reaction', precisely in keeping with its tacit recognition of the void, reaction requires rhetorics.[12] But Hirschman also finally shows that radicals, progressives and liberals themselves learn from and co-opt those rhetorics, that there is osmosis between the two sides. Here again modernity shows itself to be ironical, in that the two sides both foster what Hirschman calls *'rhetorics of intransigence'* (RR, 168) and, in the very ferocity of their discursive antagonisms, seem all the closer to each other. Hirschman is a liberal, and one suspects that his position relative to these rhetorics is finally a liberal one, involving a plea for a Berlinian *modus vivendi*, or at least a mitigation of intransigence. But there have of course been other ways of thinking the problem through. Rancière's is a distinctive and important one.

ஐ

The logical consequence of the emergence of Mannheim's two modes of thought were Hegel, and indeed historically he belongs precisely here – Mannheim's last words in the manuscript of *Conservatism* are 'We now turn to Hegel, and his attempt at a synthesis which somehow works its way through all the problems of the time' (C, 188) – and, after Hegel, Marx. Indeed, one way of thinking of the emergence of Hegel and Marx by this time is as involved in an admirably courageous if doomed attempt at *Überwindung*, the overcoming of ironical modernity. But Rancière is working at the end of this great project. Like Badiou, he is in some degree conscious of thinking his way through the twilight years of French Hegelianism. At the same time, however, he is certainly not a historical ironist. We might think of him partly as manoeuvring delicately between the world-historical and the ironical conceptions of modernity, whilst close to Schmitt in some of his insights, if not his conclusions; but also as in some degree recasting the whole problematic of modernity, pitching it at a lower key, and as doing so precisely because of what one might express as a cardinal Rancièrian injunction (though Rancière himself would not). This is surely the gist of *La Haine de la démocratie*: do not lose sight of or renounce your identification with the people, or, perhaps better, your membership of the masses. Do not mistake the people, any more than Brecht mistook the German workers still doggedly toiling on in the munitions factories in 1945.[13] But do not fail to keep thinking from within the purview of Plato's 'untameable democratic ass'.[14] To do otherwise is to break with the modern democratic ethos, if in a manner all too familiar in the modern theorist, and cannot but be at the very least unhelpful for modern politics, aesthetics and thought. Do not replicate the error of the philosophers (as recounted in *Le Philosophe et ses pauvres*) – say, of the Sartre of the *Critique of Dialectical Reason*, looking down from the height of his apartment window at the bus queue outside[15] – which is to separate oneself off from the people, or to speak of and for them, but from another place than theirs, from a position of abstract mastery equivalent to that of government. If Hobsbawm suggests that '[n]o thinking person could fail to be awed, shaken, and mentally stimulated by [the] convulsions [of 1780–1830]', there is an extent to which the author of *La Nuit des prolétaires* seems closer to Agamben. What of all those, the innumerable masses, who were not fortunate enough to get as far as thought, or only rarely did so? *La Nuit des prolétaires* provides the answer, but it hardly fits with Hobsbawmian ebullience. This, coupled with the characteristically Rancièrian modesty, a nuancing of thought in itself, allows him to rethink the meaning of 1780–1830 in terms quite different to Hobsbawm's, Schmitt's, Berman's or Mannheim's, even whilst repeatedly coinciding with one or other of them. Finally, Rancière allows us not exactly to get beyond the irony of modernity – that would be to relapse into Hegelianism – but rather to start rearranging its proportions, in a way that makes it seem less imposing or threatening, and less of a blind alley.

In some degree, the Hobsbawmian conception of 1780–1830, the world-historical conception, does lie behind Rancière's, and perhaps, given the Marxist tradition from which Rancière emerges and to which Hobsbawm belongs, it could hardly not do so. Rancière seems happy, for example, to use precisely Hobsbawm's term the 'age of revolutions' in describing the emergence of a 'new sensibility' (specifically with regard to Keats).[16] Yet at the same time the notion of the period as world-historical does not loom large in Rancière's thought, and does not serve as a determining context within it. The French Revolution – unlike Hobsbawm,

Rancière has comparatively little to say about the eighteenth- and nineteenth-century British one, though rather more about the English Revolution of 1640–60 – is rather one manifestation of a historical movement that is in some degree anonymous, processual, dispersed; less a volcanic upheaval than a broken set of uneven but cumulative tectonic shifts; less a historical watershed or an unheralded and unprecedented historical dynamism, less Hobsbawm's space rocket or jet engine than an unpredictable rhizomatic propagation that is lateral as well as linear. Above all, there is no totalising drive in Rancière's concept of modernity, which makes it a more various phenomenon than it is in Hobsbawm's description of it, but also a sparser one.

Let us look firstly at three familiar Rancièrian themes that he roots in the period 1780–1830. Firstly, there is transposition, the 'court voyage', as in *Courts voyages au pays du peuple*, the 'short voyage' into the realm of the people of a figure not commonly deemed to belong there. Passing through France in July 1790, Wordsworth unexpectedly finds himself caught up in events decisive for his life and career, in carnival, the celebrations of the people.[17] In doing so, he encounters 'a new mode of the existence of truth' (CV, 24). Others are encountering it too, notably, perhaps, Wordsworth's friend Michel Beaupuy, who appears in Book IX of *The Prelude* and who has deserted his 'noble caste' without abandoning his 'aristocratic virtues', bringing them into a new world for which he hopes they may serve partly as a principle (CV, 233). There is more than one vector of transposition. As one of the 'children of the people seized by the power of words' and by the adventure of a thought and a writing to which 'neither their birth nor their education' seemed to destine them (FP, 75), Keats launches himself into a poetic career in which he will maintain a concept of poetry as 'not first and foremost a manner of writing but a manner of reading, and of transforming what one has read into a way of life' (FP, 78).

Rancière's concern, here, would seem to be with relations, and it is multiple. In his taking hold of a world not supposed to be his, emerging in the wake of the Revolution, Keats recasts a variety of seemingly pre-ordained relations, like that between work and rest, doing and doing nothing, an important theme, not only in Keats but in Winckelmann, Rousseau, Kant et al. In pursuing it, Keats imagines appropriating a feature of a supposedly privileged mode of life which has traditionally excluded his like. So, too, joiners, printers, seamstresses, cobblers and weavers 'with polite manners and dreaming minds' are beginning to imagine another destiny for themselves, that of 'men [and women] of the written word'.[18] The possibility of recasting relations in general is the real meaning of the famous Keatsian '"negative capability"' (FP, 79–80). The period 1780–1830 emerges as one in which all kinds of relations come into question and are radically opened to question, to negotiation and transformation, as not before.

This is not merely, nor even of necessity principally, a matter of social, economic or class relations. An age-long order of things is sagging or giving way, and what this makes possible is, the second familiar theme, redistributions or new distributions of the *visible* and *sensible*:[19] this is precisely a phenomenon Rancière traces to the period, if not thinks of as originating in it. The redistributions are many and various; indeed, it would be possible to establish a typology of them on the basis of Rancière's work. Recounting his experience in France, for example, Wordsworth sees, literally sees, 'humanity renewed' by nature,[20] and both records the new invention of a political landscape and invents one himself, turning July into springtime, offering 'a new benediction to the world' (CV, 25). Less immediately concerned with historical events, Hazlitt asserts that poetry exists before words, that it is present in 'the movement of a wave' and 'the unfolding of a flower [. . .] the games of a child' and a peasant gazing at a rainbow. This poetics of the visible in effect both reconfigures it and points towards a new 'mode' of *communication sensible* which poetry can project as 'a possible relationship between human beings' (FP, 77–8).

Thirdly, there is the Rancièrian theme of the simultaneous autonomy and heteronomy of the artwork, which appears particularly clearly in his account of Schiller's *Letters on the Aesthetic Education of Man* (in *Malaise dans l'esthétique*). The *Letters on Aesthetic Education* radicalise the 'double negative' in Kant's concept of aesthetic judgement. For Schiller, 'aesthetic judgment is neither subject to the law of understanding that imposes conceptual determinations on experience nor to the law of sensation which imposes upon us an object of desire';[21] that is, it is neither merely idealist nor merely empiricist. It rather suspends both laws on each other. Their relation becomes one of a conflict of faculties, or, to introduce another familiar Rancièrian term, dissensus, in which imagination and understanding are pitted against one another, and this puts aesthetics at the very heart of an incipient modernity.

Modern art both confirms things in place – or, better, confirms them as in place – and disputes the place itself, because that is now how understanding on the one hand and imagination on the other respectively construe the world. A given work of art will both seduce us through its charm and distance us through its self-sufficiency, and in that lies precisely the experience of its heteronomy and its autonomy, together. Here art matches and reflects a world in which there has been a political promise that has been *sensible* if unfulfilled, but which it would not be possible for art to retrench on, even if or when it wished to. Equally, modern art adumbrates a community; not, however, the community towards which Kant points, one founded on reconciliation, the *sens commun* which will unite the refinement of the elites with the natural simplicity of the people, but rather a *sens commun dissensuel* which will incessantly raise the question of the world supposedly available to the common senses, who really shares it, and how. But modern art does not offer us an equivalent of the Revolution in politics. For it keeps the question of dissensus open and in play, as the Revolution failed to (as indeed did those which followed it), and with it the question of the forms of the future, the forms that have yet to arrive, as virtualities within the actuality to which the work of art is nonetheless also tied.

In effect, for Rancière, the mode of existence of the work of art is indeed both virtual and real together. This is evident in what he takes to be its condition of 'suspension', which also designates a 'limit' (*échec*) beyond which art cannot go (PM, 98). With the inauguration of an ambivalent modernity, art may represent any subject and correlate it with any other subject whatsoever. The old aesthetic dividing-lines are disintegrating. This is a gain, most notably perhaps for realism; yet, at the same time, art bends back on itself, on its own reality or, better, materiality, becomes radically more conscious of itself as language or writing. For the world in which all dividing-lines are thrown into question or disappear remains comprehensively unavailable. For all the level, democratic openness of Byron's reconfigured Europe in *Don Juan* (to give my own example), perhaps above all in its treatment of sexuality, we will never encounter it. Its contours will never be visible. This world, so very present, so historically rooted in the battle of Ismail, as it might be, or the court of Catherine the Great, is also definitively remote from us, not just in time, but because, as a literary representation, it is at once deprived of any material or sensory concreteness. This limit is decisive and cannot be broken or transcended. At a certain point, it decrees that literature is not and can never be anything more than a linguistic assemblage forever incapable of merging with the material world, other than as words.

What becomes evident with modernity is that the world of literature is that of *sensation insensible* or the 'quasi-corporeal' (CM, *passim*), and that literary worlds exist in a mode whose order is that of a promise, since in reality those worlds will continue indefinitely to anticipate their embodiment (it is less surprising than it might seem that one of Rancière's more contemporary reference points is Blanchot). Literary worlds forever await their actualisation, as after 1830 Rancière's isolated workers will await an indeterminately remote embodiment of their political dream. For Benjamin, Leskov offers the paradigm of the storyteller for whom storytelling is still 'rooted in experience', a link broken by 'the new technological age and the traumatic experience of the First World War' (PL, 159).[22] But from the beginning of modernity onwards, says Rancière, literature is '*already* itself the loss of this experience', this form 'of continuity between words and life' (ibid.). Modernity makes literature of cardinal political importance as it had not been before. Indeed, Rancière states very clearly that 'man is a political animal *because* he is a literary animal, because he lets himself be deflected from his "natural" destination by the power of words' (italics mine).[23] In this respect, we might add, the many 'political' literary theorists and critics of the '70s, '80s and '90s were pointing in the right direction, but their assumption that literature required a political hermeneutics or had to be 'framed' by politics was not: if anything, the reverse. The politics of literature and art is *sui generis*, a politics of suspension, of ghostly bodies that have yet to take on flesh.

☙

With the onset of modernity, then, things no longer stay still. There is a *franchissement des frontières*,[24] movement across boundaries, slippage or osmosis between categories and classes. No limit is anything other than provisional. This is precisely what Schmitt sees as the origin of the modern catastrophe: the borders that define, establish and maintain the categories break down. Rancière's understanding of modernity is at times very close to Schmitt's – there are moments when they cite more or less the same pages – but he has no appetite for Schmitt's absolute prioritisation of the decision, and his valuation of what he finds is almost antithetical to Schmitt's. Rancière quotes approvingly a passage from the *Letters on the Aesthetic Education of Man*: 'nothing is more hostile to beauty than the desire to give the spirit a determined tendency' (FP, 80). This assertion would appal Schmitt. But for Rancière, it is not an indication of a perilous foundering into unresolved or indeterminate subjectivity. Nor, he says, is it a mere assertion of the apolitical nature of pure beauty. Schiller is asserting 'a new "art of life" which is an education of each and everyone', an art, we might note, that works as does Joseph Jacotot's educational practice as described in *Le Maître ignorant*. Rancière actually puts Jacotot and Keats together, as two very different figures both intent on opening up the world of literature, learning, writing, to *l'un quelconque* or *n'importe qui* ('no matter whom'; FP, 88). He also recasts the Romantic commitment to the principle of infinity within the finite subject that Schmitt finds so repellent. Certainly, for Fichte (one of Schmitt's most egregious false prophets), writes Rancière, 'the "I" of transcendental subjectivity already contains the unity of the subjective and the objective, the finite and the infinite'. But it does so as a testament to the capacity of pure subjectivity working 'towards a common world' as part of 'the process of a life in formation' (PM, 58–60).

For Rancière, there is in the end a clear logic to the emergence of modernity, but it is undramatic, not a logic that begins with a Hobsbawmian explosion. It is probably most evident in aesthetics and above all literature as described in the introduction and the first two parts of *La Parole muette*. This is the period when the hierarchies founder, notably the 'old hierarchies' of the *beaux arts* (PM, 8). The 'normative system' of aesthetic, generic and rhetorical rules, of vraisemblance as a question of observing proprieties, of the necessary relations between discourse and character, words and action, disintegrates (PM, 13). Literature becomes something different, 'includes forgotten continents', expels the glories of yesteryear (PM, 12). Literary language is the modern 'parole muette', an 'orphan language' that is deprived of the power of living language and begins to roll 'haphazardly' in different directions, increasingly available, in more ways than one, to *n'importe qui*, whoever comes along (PM, 81–2). This creates new democratisations of the literary, proclaims new forms of literary equality and new regimes of the visible and *sensible* within literature. So much is above all the case with the novel, the anarchic genre, the genre that knows no generic limits, and for which the adulteries of a Norman peasant's daughter will be as interesting as the loves of a Carthaginian princess and require no specific mode of expression given as an a priori.

But, as we have seen, literature now also retreats into and declares its own literariness, the literariness of its language. In so doing, it declares its democratisations unrealised and indefinitely unrealisable. In this respect, the new literature and new conceptions of literature are statements of the uncompleted project that is modern politics, that is, of political virtualities. 'All is seed,' wrote Novalis in a notebook.[25] With the beginnings of modernity, literature and art proliferate democratic potentials that their producers hope may find some actual form in a more or less distant future. But there is no logic according to which this must or will happen or actual forms will ever appear corresponding to the potentials. The point nonetheless is that, as in France after the Restoration of 1814, there is still equality to be had, but irregularly, so, too, modern literature becomes a dispersed set of generative possibilities – or fragments, since the Romantic fragment as elaborated by Novalis or Schlegel is not a ruin of something gone but in fact the token of a promise. The fragment is a fragment of a future.

There can be no timeline for modernity. The reasons for this are perhaps particularly clear in *Les Noms de l'histoire*. According to the third chapter, 'L'excès des mots', the time of the French Revolution is both recursive and proleptic. It is recursive in that it defines itself against, and thus remains tied to, what preceded it. It also commits itself to re-elaboration of past forms, saying things again, but differently. At the same time, it introduces a modern anticipation of the *pas encore*, that which has yet to arrive but, as such, remains nebulous, unclear. The Revolution does indeed produce a new temporality, but it is not the time of the French republican calendar. It is a time in which a present overlaps with indefinite presentiment and interrogative retrospection, together, and within which relations in a world which no longer exists are connected with others that have recently appeared or have yet to come into being. In its 'paradoxical novelty', anachronism or untimeliness, this temporality is precisely the one we will increasingly experience as deeply modern. Far from, say, the concatenations of Marxist historiography, which connects past to present to future in distinctly bounded segments according to a logic in which the future explains and justifies the past and present, modern time consists of temporal ambiguities, splits, fissures, internal differences in time, a kind of eddying of time, a swirl or 'confusion of times'.[26] There is not necessarily any perceptible development within it, and it looks forward to no quick or ascertainable completion (FP, 89). Furthermore, for all the abundant clusters of examples of modernity in Rancière's work, notably perhaps in *Aisthesis*, it is clear that, for him – *La Nuit des prolétaires* is evidently the crucial litmus test of it – modernity does not happen very much, and only mistaken presumptions regarding the historical process on the one hand and the meaning of democracy on the other can lead us to suppose that it does. Modernity takes place here and there, and now and again. Hence the series of precise but discrete and unconnected dates attached to the separate chapters of *Aisthesis*. That does not mean that there are not 'filiations', subterranean runnels and channels, growths, hookings and graftings that link the separate emergences of modernity together. But these emergences nonetheless remain distinct, and sporadic.

This is of a piece with Rancière's being very much at ease with the contradictions within modernity which so trouble the historical ironists and leave Schmitt aghast. La Harpe, who announces the disintegration of the hierarchies of the *beaux arts*, was by turns a revolutionary, a Montagnard, a Thermidorean and proselytiser for the restoration of Catholicism. It was the *counter-revolutionaries* who, cast 'outside time and the language of opinion' by revolutionary upheaval, as often as not were the bearers of the new literature (PM, 47–8). Hegel is likewise an ambivalent figure. In his *Lectures on Aesthetics* of 1828, on the one hand, he rejoices in Murillo's paintings of the 'little gods of the street', the urban beggars and their indifference to all exteriority. Such paintings impose the idea of art as 'the property of a people, the expression of its form of life' (AI, 43). Hegel also persists with the universalising poetics of the Romantics, the unity it asserts between the poetic image and 'the movement of the forms of life'. Yet, on the other hand, because he insists on seeing its correlative as historicisation, he ends up finding in Homeric epic '"the originally poetic state of the world"' (PM, 68), thus turning romantic poetics back on itself, and against its theorists. For Hegel, their 'programme for the future thus becomes an interpretation of the past. And this interpretation of the past shows in turn that their programme for the future is without a future' (PM, 65). So, too, the very men of letters who are opening up new relations between previously unrelated spheres of life and culture, like Charles Nodier, Eugène Lerminier and Victor Hugo, often react quite strongly against the novelty of the joiners, printers, cobblers and weavers who aspire to enter theirs, describing them as 'lost children and perverted labourers' (PM, 77–8). They thus restate the golden rule of the Platonic republic, that there are some to whom it is given to think and to write, and others to whom it is not. The modern lyric poem involves 'a new political experience of the *sensible*' that is 'liberated from the iron collar of the genres' (CM, 20, 33), a different kind of personal speaking that invokes a different kind of experience of being a citizen. But this does not commit the poet to being either revolutionary or counter-revolutionary; he or she may be either, or from time to time both.

It is important to note that Rancière says of the haphazard career of the 'parole muette' that it rolls equally 'to right and left' (PM, 81). This is no accident. There is no 'scene reserved' for democratic language (PM, 82), which is heedless of the positions of both its origin and its recipient. Rancière tends to break down any concept of the properly modern subject. There are occasions of modernity, but modernity is not to be identified with subjects, who may stray through a variety of modern and anti-modern positions without coming to rest. Here one has an intuition of why it is, not only that Rancière claims to be closer to Foucault than to any other of his contemporaries or near-contemporaries, but also that, seemingly rather oddly, he has intermittently shown an explicit interest in Deleuze. It would be going too far to seek to identify a 'Deleuzian strain' in or 'Deleuzian influence' on Rancière's thought. But the Rancièrian conception of a desubjectified 'confusion of times' from the French Revolution onwards is thinkable by way of analogy with Deleuzian molecularity, and therefore by way of what Rancière himself calls a metaphysics. For '[t]here is a metaphysics of literature', Rancière writes, and its metaphysical regime is precisely that of the '*sensation insensible*' (CM, 185). In grasping this regime as having a virtual and an actual dimension, we are not very far away from Deleuze. Rancière even revivifies Deleuzian philosophy, precisely in giving it material point and plausibility whilst not merely 'making it material'. At all events, his Deleuzian affiliations are evident enough in his conception of literature and, for Rancière, literature is central to any adequate idea of what modernity has been about.

Yet, piquantly, Rancière's most compelling version of Deleuzian molecularity does not exactly find its paradigm in Deleuze at all. In his readings of Kafka, Proust, Dostoevsky and American literature, notably Melville and above all 'Bartleby', says Rancière, Deleuze limits, blocks or obscures the scope of his concept of molecularity by understanding it in the context of either fraternity or the figure of the 'hero' as subject. Deleuze can see that the modern literary text is material and produced by a 'material operation' (CM, 179). He knows that this operation disorganises the 'causal order' imposed by representation, and thereby 'disorganizes a certain life' (CM, 170). In this respect, the modern text includes an indefinite anticipation: Kafka's *Metamorphosis*, for instance, enacts 'the power of indetermination or metamorphoses' (CM, 188), which is a power of molecular multiplicity, desubjectified individuation. But in fact, sooner or later, Deleuze always centres his analysis on a hero (Myshkin, Charlus, Ahab, Gregor Samsa). This is due to a flaw in his aesthetics. He is concerned to privilege 'the antinarrative powers of becomings' (CM, 191). But in writing story out of the equation, he writes character in. He cannot quite see how literature *practises* indetermination, so the 'hero' himself becomes an incarnation of the molecular 'puissance de dé-liaison' or power of undoing (CM, 192). In this respect, particularly in American writing, he also represents a 'grand fraternal hope' or a new 'fraternal people', a community of equals that will succeed by opposing the Oedipus, achieving its victory over the 'paternal community' (CM, 195, 197).

Here, says Rancière, Deleuze ignores the politics intrinsic and special to literature, and the quite different meaning of equality in literature. Rancière's great example is Flaubert, above all the Flaubert of *The Temptation of St. Anthony*, but, crucially in this context, a Flaubert who has his roots in Schelling, Schlegel and an early nineteenth-century Spinozism (of which Deleuze is a late inheritor)[27] – in other words, in the revolutionary period. What is this incipiently modern Spinozism we find in Flaubert? It involves a break with the norms and hierarchies of classical mimesis, an abandonment of its modes of representation, causality and inference, the presentation of individuals and their relations and the invention of new ones. In this new order of literature, there is always the void or groundless ground, in relation to which everything is placed, and therefore no element counts for more than another any longer: this is what Flaubert meant when he declared that style is an absolute way of seeing things. Style now ushers in a principle of indetermination and, its corollary, one of indifferent equality. This condition of equality is the singular gift of modern literature, one that modern politics and political thought have been unable to match. Flaubertian Spinozism

> is the politics inherent in the metaphysics of literature. This politics appeals from the equality of individual human beings in society to a greater equality that only holds sway beneath it, at the molecular level – an equality that is truer and more profound than that claimed by the poor or the workers. (CM, 194)

In modern literature, thought itself breaks into atoms commensurate with the atomic being of the material world. Furthermore, the separate and equal elements form new figures and generate new intensities. New *liaisons* connect them. New fluxes and flows establish unprecedented relations between elements, or lines of flight from one to another, catching them up in local turbulences, making possible new percepts, affects, speeds, 'traits of expression' (CM, 184). This is the manner in which modern literature thinks and articulates the 'natural' world. It is surely what underlies Rancière's assertion that equality is a hypothesis in some sense there from the start, 'an axiom, a presupposition' (TP, 152). But the mode of modern literature also seems peculiarly close to Rancière's way of thinking the modern historical process.

The problem for the historical ironists and equally the Schmittian problem with modernity remain such only so long as we place the subject at the centre of modernity, as Rancière does not. They also depend on a presumption of historical totality, whereas for Rancière modernity appears occasionally and intermittently. Molar schemes may break open to reveal the molecularity that 'holds sway beneath' them (CM, 186), but they also close over and reabsorb it (as in Deleuze's aesthetics). It is precisely the consciousness of this insistent reabsorption as the power against which one wagers that allows Rancière's work to stand as a model of a certain kind of isolation of what matters and persistence with it. There is no disappointment in Rancière of the kind Hirschman talks about, the dismay, for example, of finding de Maistre still alive in 1971 in the high-tech language of the anti-social welfare polemics of Jay W. Forrester. Frankly aware that the young Wordsworth who made the short journey to the realm of the people later became a rebarbative old Tory, Rancière nonetheless remains much more concerned with how the ageing poet keeps on revisiting his early experience and his youthful account of it, continually working on and re-appraising its meaning. It is a mistake to be overly exercised by the regularity with which the moderns convert to anti-modernity, even by the prevalence, the rampancy or current triumphalism of anti-modernity. What matters is the inextinguishability of modernity, the insistent and various if sporadic character of its occurrences, the preservation of its spirit, irrespective of the denials, unconscious compromises, equivocations and retreats of (some of) those who, for a while, function as its representatives and spokespersons.

But finally: why should modernity be inextinguishable? Why should molar schemes not simply close over it and hold fast? The answer to this question occurs again in 'L'excès des mots' (and elsewhere in *Les Noms de l'histoire*) and again refers us back to 1780–1830. With the French Revolution, words are no longer contemporary with what they seek to name. They must therefore take on new meanings, and new words must be found. Actually, this process had already begun with the English Revolution. But from Hobbes to Burke, what Rancière calls the royal-empirical tradition – a tradition currently reinvigorated by the decline of Marxism – sought to pacify the threat posed by the destabilisation of the language, insisting that words must 'mean what they say' and be used 'properly'. (Hobbes asserts, for example, that the word 'tyrant' cannot and must not be used of a king.) From the French Revolution onwards, however, a 'new disorder and arbitrariness' disturb the old 'objective rigours' (NH, 21). No given and incontestable harmony between words and things seems possible any longer. People confront the historical contingency of names. Floating signifiers appear which seem to designate no real property or clear and distinct idea. From now on, there is abundantly diverse speech, and there are abundantly diverse speakers who may be indifferent to demonstrating or guaranteeing the referential value of the words they use. Equally, people take old texts and give them daring and unforeseen meanings. This is the historical dimension to Rancière's concept of dissensus, and his understanding of modernity is inseparable from that concept.

The logic of the case for an ironical view of modernity that we derived from Berman, Mannheim and Hirschman is that the onset of modernity inaugurates a seemingly interminable struggle over power and naming, in which both sides are inexorably caught up in very much the same game. The event of the new requires that both modern and 'reactive' writers and speakers resuscitate and rework old names and invent new ones (like 'conservatism'). If, certainly, it is impossible securely to replace 'right' names with 'wrong' ones, equally it is no longer possible securely to insist on the rightness of 'right' names. But merely to formulate this condition as ironical is to ignore that it also always represents a democratic opportunity in a democratic epoch. It means that anyone, anyone at all out of the people now arriving on the scene, *n'importe qui, le premier venu* or *la première venue*, can take possession of language and use it in his or her own fashion and for his or her own purposes. Now *l'un* (or *l'une*) *quelconque* can tell his or her own story, for example, in his or her own singular fashion, resorting to his or her own singular lexicon. There may be no modern subjects, thought of as coherent, self-same wholes. But there have been, are and will continue to be singular instances of modern subjectification. From the late eighteenth century, the crucial 'modern revolution' (Rancière's term) is 'the revolution of the children of the Book' (NH, 54). Rancière is right: there is no modernity, if we think of modernity as 'a grand or global signifier' (TP, 208). Yet at the same time the modern genie is out of the bottle, and will not be crammed back in.

Notes

1. A first draft of this essay was presented as a lecture to the Program in Critical Theory at the University of Berkeley. I am grateful to all those in the audience who listened and responded and thereby helped me substantially to improve it. Translations are my own except where otherwise specified.
2. Jacques Rancière, *Et tant pis pour les gens fatigués: Entretiens* (Paris: Amsterdam, 2009), 210; and *Aisthesis: Scènes du regime esthétique de l'art* (Paris: Galilée, 2011), 9. Hereafter cited as TP and AI respectively.

3. Rancière, *The Politics of Aesthetics*, trans. with intro. by Gabriel Rockhill, afterword by Slavoj Žižek (London: Continuum, 2004), 65. Hereafter cited as PA.
4. Rancière, *La Mésentente: Politique et philosophie* (Paris: Galilée, 1995), 9.
5. Eric Hobsbawm, *The Age of Revolution: 1789–1848* (London: Abacus, 1977 [1962]), 43–4. Hereafter cited as AR.
6. Carl Schmitt, *Political Romanticism*, trans. Guy Oakes (Cambridge, MA: MIT Press, 1986 [1925]), 52, 56. Hereafter cited as PR.
7. Quoted in Marshall Berman, *All That Is Solid Melts into Air: The Experience of Modernity* (London: Verso, 2010 [1982]), 62. Hereafter cited as ATS.
8. See Walter Benjamin, *Selected Writings, Vol. 4: 1938–40*, ed. Howard Eiland and Michael W. Jennings, trans. Edmund Jephcott et al. (Cambridge, MA, and London: Harvard University Press, 2002), 164. For a singularly brilliant account of Benjamin that emphasises both terms, see Françoise Proust, *L'Histoire à contretemps: Le temps historique chez Walter Benjamin* (Paris: Cerf, 1994), *passim*.
9. Jacques Derrida, *Shibboleth: For Paul Celan*, trans. Joshua Wilner, in Aris Fioretos (ed.), *Word Traces: Readings of Paul Celan* (Baltimore: Johns Hopkins University Press, 1994), 50.
10. See Alain Badiou, *Second manifeste pour la philosophie* (Paris: Fayard, 2009), 106.
11. Karl Mannheim, *Conservatism: A Contribution to the Sociology of Knowledge*, trans. David Keller, Volker Meja and Nico Stehr (London: Routledge and Kegan Paul, 1982 [1925]), 51. Hereafter cited as C.
12. Albert O. Hirschman, *The Rhetoric of Reaction* (Cambridge, MA: Belknap, 1991), 3. Hereafter cited as RR.
13. See Rancière's superbly austere 'Le Gai savoir de Bertolt Brecht', in *Politique de la littérature* (Paris: Galilée, 2007), 113–43, especially 132. Hereafter cited as PL.
14. Rancière, *La Haine de la démocratie* (Paris: La Fabrique, 2005), 41.
15. See Jean-Paul Sartre, *Critique of Dialectical Reason, Vol. 1: Theory of Practical Ensembles*, trans. Alan Sheridan-Smith (London: Verso, 1976), 256–69.
16. Rancière, *Le Fil perdu. Essais sur la fiction moderne* (Paris: La Fabrique, 2014), 77. Hereafter cited as FP.
17. Rancière, *Courts voyages au pays du peuple* (Paris: Seuil, 1981), 17. Hereafter cited as CV.

18. Rancière, *La Parole muette: Essais sur les contradictions de la littérature* (Paris: Hachette, 1998), 76. Hereafter cited as PM.
19. The word *sensible* is in italics throughout the essay, marking it as French and properly untranslatable, or translatable only with (too much) wordage.
20. Rancière, *La Chair des mots: Politiques de l'écriture* (Paris: Galilée, 1998), 25. Hereafter cited as CM.
21. Rancière, *Malaise dans l'esthétique* (Paris: Galilée, 2004), 130.
22. Cf. Benjamin, *Illuminations*, ed. with intro. by Hannah Arendt, trans. Harry Zohn (London: Fontana/Collins, 1979), 83–109.
23. Rancière, *Le Partage sensible: Esthétique et politique* (Paris: La Fabrique, 2000), 63.
24. See FP, 87 for an expression of what I mean.
25. Quoted in Violet Plincke, 'Novalis: A Sketch', *Anthroposophy: A Quarterly Review of Spiritual Science*, 3:3 (Michaelmas 1928), 1.
26. Rancière, *Les Noms de l'histoire* (Paris: Seuil, 1994), 54–5. Hereafter cited as NH.
27. On this tradition of Spinozism, see also TP, 275.

II Realisms

6

The Novelist and Her Poor: Nineteenth-Century Character Dynamics
Elaine Freedgood

Elizabeth Gaskell's 1848 novel *Mary Barton* is full of poetry, but not where the characters can see it. In the epigraphs and footnotes, for the eyes of readers and narrators only, Samuel Coleridge's 'Christabel', John Keats's 'Hyperion', Edmund Spenser's *The Faerie Queene*, Dante's *The Divine Comedy*, John Donne's 'Second Anniversary', Robert Burns's 'Mary Morison', Walter Savage Landor's 'The Mermaid', Tennyson's 'Mariana' (which Gaskell misquotes), bits of Geoffrey Chaucer, John Wycliffe, Ben Jonson, Shakespeare and Thomas Carlyle – all mark out the common culture of the readers of this novel, who are not the same as its characters. The epigraphs were added at the suggestion of Gaskell's publisher, Chapman and Hall, for reasons I will discuss below, and the footnotes were added by her husband, Peter Gaskell, and are 'translations' of Manchester dialect that often use medieval and early modern literary sources as examples.

The reading that the characters do, or the textual matter that they hear (literacy being a complicated matter), is represented in a handful of documents, including a Manchester song, 'The Oldham Weaver', which the seamstress Margaret Jennings sings and the lyrics of which the narrator transcribes for us – except that she leaves out one problematic stanza in which conflict emerges between weaver and master, thus softening the song's 'note of rebelliousness';[1] the People's Charter, which Parliament refuses to read but of which the Chartist characters in the novel have probably read, or heard, a significant part; 'an old copy of the *Northern Star*', a Chartist newspaper the narrator tells us John Barton has 'borrowed from a public-house',[2] a typical source of periodicals for the poor in the period; the Bible; and a poem by Samuel Bamford, 'the working class radical',[3] that Job Legh, Margaret's autodidactic grandfather, recites and that Mary Barton then copies down, at her father's request. The apparent homogeneity of this list – all of the reading by the poor seems to concern the poor – is deceptive and relies on the middle-class reader, from 1848 to the present, having very little idea of the complexity of Chartism as a political movement and of the variety and cosmopolitanism of a radical paper like the *Northern Star*.

Mary copies the Bamford poem on to the blank part of a valentine sent to her by Jem Wilson in a typical nineteenth-century reuse of paper, the kind from which we get the expression 'reading between the lines'. John Barton will use half of this valentine as wadding for the gun he uses to kill Harry Carson – the son of the mill owner for whom he works – and Jem Wilson, Mary's sometime lover and future husband, will be arrested for the murder. Even the (apparently) limited reading material of the poor leads them astray. The Chartist newspaper, the (redacted) sentimental song, the sympathetic poem, the material on which it is written, and the problem of litter as a findable kind of evidence suggest that reading and writing are activities that require careful guidance – the kind a narrator can provide in some cases, a philosopher in others, in the arguments of Jacques Rancière.[4] The poor of the novelist, I will argue, are both the literally and subjectively poor characters of *Mary Barton* – fictional characters in the history of the novel more generally who must, for generic logistical reasons, be subjectively poorer than their narrators – and readers, who require all kinds of narrators, in the novel and outside it, to help them (us) navigate the world and its texts. The 'poor' of the novelist are physically, materially, intellectually and emotionally less than their narrators, and their poverty limits their experiences in ways that fictions of certain kinds have made predictable. This chapter considers the industrial poor of nineteenth-century Britain and alludes to other kinds of poverty in later novels about other kinds of 'poor' characters.

Inventing a culture for the poor

John Barton kills Harry Carson, the mill owner's son, because during a meeting of masters and men, Harry draws caricatures of the men, which he throws at the fire but which are not burned. The labouring men pick up the drawings (they think their children will enjoy them) and are deeply hurt by the pictures – they recognise themselves immediately in the sad details of their ragged clothing.

They declare that they could take a joke as well as the next person if they and their families were not starving, or, as Manchester dialect has it, 'clemming' – a frequent topic in the novel. Starving men, the novel tells us, cannot abide satire. Not because they cannot understand it but because they are in too much pain to laugh at themselves. And in fact the details are painfully unfunny: 'that's me, by G_d,' an anonymous mill worker exclaims; 'it's the very way I'm obligated to pin my waistcoat up, to hide that I've getten no shirt. That is a shame, and I'll not stand it' (247). The poor, this scene suggests, require a kind of literal and respectful realism. Hence the reading of the novel's characters itemised above: an apparently simple diet of items that are immediately for and about them.

An even more constrictive subjective effect of poverty is constructed by Gaskell in her imagining of John Barton's pilgrimage to London to present the People's Charter to Parliament. Barton is represented during his trip to London as an uncomprehending non-citizen of modernity: he thinks naked statues are signs for tailors' shops and all carriages with feathers are hearses (as Methodist hearses were so styled). 'I were like a child,' he says, and so we as readers think too: he is literal-minded and incapable of what one might call interpretation (146–7). Everything is based very strictly on his own experience; he cannot imagine the idea of an ornamental statue or a carriage – even though the novel is regularly punctuated with painful encounters of starving workers watching the wives of mill owners coming out of shops laden with purchases, often getting into what must be similar carriages.

Still, Barton cannot partake of even the most concrete items of what Rancière calls the 'common culture'. The Bamford poem that Mary copies between the lines of the valentine is untitled, but it might be called 'God Help the Poor', since that phrase is repeated in the first and last lines of all five stanzas, and 'God help' is repeated many times in between. Poverty is described realistically in the poem but in a grammar more affecting than the prose of *Mary Barton* and in a regular rhyme scheme, which also makes it more mentally portable than any prose could be. The poem explores the experience of cold and hunger repeatedly:

God help the poor! Behold yon famished lad,
No shoes, nor hose, his wounded feet protect;
With limping gait, and looks so dreamy sad,

> He wanders onward, stopping to inspect
> Each window, stored with articles of food. (158)

The lad is not simply a barefoot boy: he has been abandoned by both shoes and socks – he is doubly deprived of the two things that might protect his feet, which are wounded like those of Christ. And indeed shoes and hose are the subject of the clause, his feet the passive, helpless, wounded object. He limps because of these wounds, and possibly others, and looks in shop windows at food, which is lavishly and, for the famished lad, cruelly displayed behind the newly mass-produced plate glass windows that changed shops and shopping in the mid nineteenth century. His 'sad'-ness is a weak rhyme for the 'food' that he will not eat. His condition could, of course, be readily improved by someone other than God. Bandages, hose, shoes and food would help him enormously.

The characters empathising with the famished lad can do very little to alleviate the misery of those like him. The novel shows them doing whatever they can for their own starving friends and neighbours, pawning their very small 'superfluities' in order to buy food and coal, but the mill owners, who might provide substantial help, refuse responsibility for the suffering of their workers, insisting that workers, along with everyone else, accept market downturns. 'It [the demand for labour] depends on events which God alone can control,' as John Carson, the mill owner, puts it (471). The poem inside the novel suggests to middle-class readers that they ought to be moved, as the poor are moved, by simple descriptions of poverty: the middle class is immersed in the 'culture' of the poor that the novel invents. It also suggests that the poor are limited in their intellectual pursuits by their immiseration: they do not, in the confines of this novel, read material that does not concern their immediate needs and problems.

If, as Rancière argues in *The Philosopher and His Poor*, for Plato, Karl Marx, Jean-Paul Sartre and Pierre Bourdieu the poor are consumed by poverty and cannot think beyond it, in this novel of poverty, the reader cannot do anything other than be consumed by the idea that poverty is subjectively crushing; Sartre's description of the function of exhaustion seems ineluctable:

> At first sight there is not in principle the least difficulty in an unskilled worker's making an excellent militant: the only serious obstacle would seem vulgar and circumstantial: it is fatigue. Only there it is: this

fatigue is not an accident; it accumulates without melting, like the eternal snows, and it makes the unskilled worker.[5]

A novel like *Mary Barton* convinces us of this apparent truth once again. This is perhaps why Chapman and Hall, Gaskell's publisher, insisted that she add the epigraphs: to keep the two nations literally on the page, in their separate textual spaces.

Two nations, two cultures

Again and again over the past sixty or so years, scholars have had to assert and reassert labouring-class traditions of autodidacticism; students of the radical press must produce evidence of the reprinting of Milton, Southey, Byron, Shelley, Wordsworth and Dickens in various papers and pamphlets as evidence of the intellectual life of that class, 'because literary historians', Gregory Vargo argues, 'have too readily accepted middle-class writers' descriptions of the gulf separating "the two nations"', in which the middle class was isolated from the radical press and the working class was isolated from the 'polite' press. 'The cultural reality of social division was different, characterized on both sides by argument, contest, parody and appropriation rather than by separation and ignorance.'[6] Mike Sanders argues that 'with determination and a degree of good fortune, the [labouring-class] autodidact could complete a course of reading which would stand comparison with many a contemporary undergraduate syllabus.'[7] Chartists, for example, were active educators, poets and publishers. Ian Haywood suggests that Chartists believed that 'in order to prove themselves worthy of political representation, it was a vital task to conquer the realm of symbolic representation'.[8] In this they were well-attuned to the liberal cultural critics of the mid-century, including George Eliot, who firmly believed that the representation of the labouring class ought to occur in the novel and not in the state: like Matthew Arnold, she worried that they could not see beyond the interests of 'their own order'.[9]

The subjectively and physically impoverished fictional population of Gaskell's 'Tale of Manchester Life' is in conversation with what Haywood describes as the proliferating 'didactic and agitational fiction in both radical and polite periodicals [which] constituted a highly politicised literary subculture'.[10] Industrial novels like *Mary Barton* were influenced by the fiction published in the radical press and, in part, tried to answer or modify it. Vargo argues that fiction like Gaskell's was profoundly influenced by Chartist fiction in particular and that this 'secret history' of the mid-Victorian novel needs to be understood, as does its occlusion, as an effacement of the agency and influence of Chartist cultural energy.[11]

Gaskell knew many Manchester mill workers in her capacity as a minister's wife in that city. She also knew the autodidact and prolific writer Bamford quite well and thus had an example of the kind of labouring-class person whose reading was quite similar to her own and who exemplifies the autodidact tradition studied by Martha Vicinus, Mike Sanders, David Vincent and Jonathan Rose, among others. Bamford was a great reader and reciter of Tennyson and through Gaskell's intervention received a signed copy of Tennyson's works for his seventieth birthday. In the note he writes to thank Tennyson, he says that Tennyson's language 'is almost unlimitedly expressive. This language of ours, what can it not be made to say? What height, what depth filled with all glorious hues, terrible glooms, and vivid flashes does it not combine and your poems exhibit all?'[12] 'This language of ours,' Bamford writes, claiming a common tongue with Tennyson. Indeed, Gaskell is having her characters speak a dialect that she frequently footnotes for clarification, as if she and they and we were not speaking a common language at all, and yet the examples used (by Peter Gaskell) are from the works of a 'great' English lineage, including Chaucer, Wycliffe, Spenser, Jonson, Shakespeare and John Skelton, suggesting that it is the middle class who may not be speaking the finest – or what for Gaskell would have been the most expressive – English. Gordon Bigelow argues that 'the text makes an argument that the poor remain closer to an original English linguistic heritage, while a more mobile middle class becomes increasingly distant from it.'[13] It is undergoing, as the language of the professionals at Jem's trial suggests, 'a pitiless standardization' (149). Gaskell thus creates a portrait, a culture and a set of characters that cannot seem to settle down entirely into the world she creates. Indeed, two worlds seem to come in and out of focus: first, a robust, working-class culture with strong regional and historical linguistic usages, profound political affiliations, and extraordinary loyalty to one another. In another world that frequently eclipses this one, the poor can only be poor.

John Barton may like Bamford's poem, but it is doubtful that an actual Chartist would have wanted a copy of it. Bamford was a radical only through the Peterloo riot and massacre; that is, up to the 1820s. He becomes an opponent of Chartism in the 1830s, at one point becoming a constable in order to help put down a demonstration.[14] He also becomes a writer of poetry for several middle-class newspapers in London rather than for any of the many radical papers being published in the period. His poetry bewails the condition of the poor, but it does so without offering a political programme to remedy it. Gaskell gives her radical characters a radical poet who no longer is one; she represents as radical poetry that which has become as sentimental as her own ideas about easing the suffering of the labouring class.

Letters and litter

Mary Barton's plot turns on the dangerous instability and circulation of refunctioned paper, a kind of literalisation of Rancière's 'errant letter', the emblem of the literary in his thinking, derived from Plato's critique of writing: '[T]he art of writing in which the writer is anyone at all and the reader is anyone at all. [. . .] it circulates [. . .] without a master to accompany it.'[15] The valentine/poem/wadding has three 'writers': Jem as valentine writer and Bamford the poet via Mary as transcriber, and it has for its readers Mary, John Barton, Esther and then Mary again. The wadding similarly circulates randomly, as a poem in John Barton's pocket, as mere paper that comes to hand to fill a gun, and then as waste paper that catches the observant eye of Mary's Aunt Esther, who is trained to see well at night by her career as a prostitute and who brings it to Mary – to keep the secret and destroy it at the same time. We have here the kind of chronic Victorian miniature archival crisis described by Priyanka A. Jacob in which both saving and throwing away various kinds of text might prove disastrous and in whose history the pigeonhole, the memo, the filing cabinet, the paper shredder and the forensic and hygienic problems of litter have all had consequential roles.[16]

The vicissitudes of rubbish versus text are difficult to predict as a piece of paper moves among various writers, readers, hands, pockets, streets and courts. These errant letters lose their way, they lose their authors, and they lose their connection to the authors of the crime with which they are associated. The letters cross paths with the characters in the novel, drawing the lines of the plot as they go. Gaskell waxes Platonic in her concern for the fate of human characters caught up in the agency of the typographic characters that circulate among them, between them, and around them, creating circumstances that only the novelist can finally organise or undo: no reading, no interpretation – by characters or extradiegetic readers – can put the valentine back in the right pocket or the gun in the right hand. We are all – fictional characters and actual persons – dependent on our author and narrator to explain the speech, and the feeling, behind the letters and their various destinations. We all need someone to talk to rather than something to read. And the narrator is the 'function' of the novel that speaks to readers, the one whose adumbration of the speech of others may be trusted.

Rancière's democratic vision of the literary relies on the idea of the errant letter: the novel is the text that is written for no particular audience; it can go anywhere and be read by anyone. This is not quite true of a novel like *Mary Barton*, which was published in two expensive volumes by Chapman and Hall and would have been, like most Victorian novels, beyond the reach of the poor represented in it. What the Bartons and the Wilsons could have afforded to read would have been penny dreadfuls, cheap pamphlets and the productions of the radical press. So the errancy of the letter is practically, economically circumscribed. Novelists at this juncture in the nineteenth century had some knowledge of who was going to read their work. This is why Gaskell can represent John Barton's theory of value uncontested and why she can represent Chartism, strikes, trade unions and murders of masters. Indeed, Gaskell, if she were worried about her contemporary audience, might not have written this novel at all.

The democratic novel and democratic narration

In his introduction to *The Philosopher and His Poor*, Andrew Parker describes Rancière's project as asking if 'philosophy [can] ever refrain from thinking for' the poor.[17] If we ask the same question about the novelist, the answer is obviously and obdurately no: the job of the novelist is to invent characters and thus their thoughts and then to narrate them through direct and indirect discourse. In the preface to *Mary Barton*, Gaskell describes her subjects: 'The more I reflected on this unhappy state of things between those so bound to each other by common interests, as the employers and the employed must ever be, the more anxious I became to give some utterance to the agony which, from time to time, convulses this dumb people' (30). In this same preface, Gaskell insists that she is not writing a novel of 'Political Economy or the theories of trade' (30); her decision about the 'dumbness' of the Manchester 'employed' is an eminently political decision, in Rancière's definition: '[A]ll political activity is a conflict aimed at deciding what is speech or mere growl; in other words, aimed at retracing the perceptible boundaries by means of which political capacity is demonstrated.'[18] Gaskell decides, before the novel begins, that her characters have no political capacity: they are growling and she is translating. This claim is made at a moment when workers all over Britain are 'speaking' massively: in demonstrations, strikes, in the 'extraordinarily articulate and disciplined' movement of Chartism,[19] and vividly and copiously in a wealth of radical publications that are hugely various in their content. And Gaskell is representing all of this, however sketchily and condescendingly, in *Mary Barton*.

She is, we might say, a conflicted capitalist. Sometimes the growl comes out in a language, as I have discussed above, that is more moving, more true to Gaskell's idea of the poetic properties of English than anything she can give us in her own, standardised language. She gives to John Barton a coherent understanding of the labour theory of value, even if it is a version of it with which she would disagree, and she gives it to us in all the lustre of Manchester English:

> You'll say (at least many a one does), they'n getten capital an'we'n getten none, I say, our labour's our capital, and we ought to draw interest on that. They get interest on their capital somehow a' this time, while ourn is lying idle, else how could they live as they do? Besides, there's many on'em has had nought to begin wi'; there's Carsons, and Duncombes, and Mengies, and many another, as comed into Manchester with clothes to their back, and that were all, and now they're worth their tens of thousands, a'getten out of our labour. [. . .] They'n screwed us down to th' lowest peg, in order to make their great big fortunes, and build their great big houses, and we, why we're just clemming, many and many of us. (104)

This language is not difficult to read, but it is different, obviously, from that of the narrator. Its 'ourns' are mournful, the repetition of 'many and many' is melodic and balefully copious, and the abbreviated articles and prepositions suggest a way of talking that cannot luxuriate over consonants that can be understood without being sounded.

Barton makes this speech to his friend George Wilson, who has no argument to refute it except that he believes that 'th' masters suffer too' in bad times (105). The answer, the solution, lies with the reader – the middle-class reader – who is enjoined by the text to both alleviate (with alms and sympathy rather than better wages) the suffering of the poor and to display his or her own suffering during hard times. Still, Gaskell gives Barton a moment of strong and eloquent articulation, even if the thrust of the novel is that Barton misunderstands the fact that capitalists do actually risk and sometimes lose everything. Gaskell gives us a strong illustration of a political movement: she opens the novel to dissensus, to the coexistence of two worlds, even if she will not pursue 'a possible world in which the argument [the Chartist argument in this case] could count as an argument [. . .] a paradoxical world that puts together two separate worlds'.[20] The two worlds remain, jostling one another, asking us to make sense of them or to accept that multiple worlds, like multiple nations, can simply coexist if we can hold them in imagination.

The novel cannot resolve these two worlds into one because it is British, reformist and ultimately aristocratic and not French, realistic and democratic. In the democratic novel as it is developed by Honoré de Balzac and Gustave Flaubert, Rancière argues, every object, situation, person is equal: action has been overtaken by things; events by everyday life. Art is style; its content is negligible. A curiosity shop can be a poem, as it is in Balzac's *La peau de chagrin*, Rancière notes:

> In this shop, objects of all ages and from all civilizations are jumbled together. But, so, too, art objects and religious and luxury objects are jumbled together with objects from ordinary life: stuffed crocodiles, monkeys or boas seem to smile at church windows or to want to bite various busts. A Sèvres vase rubs shoulders with an Egyptian sphinx, Madame Du Barry gazes at an Indian pipe, and a pneumatic tube pokes the emperor Augustus in the eye. This shop where everything is jumbled together composes, says Balzac, an endless poem. The poem is double: it is the poem of the great equality of things noble and vile, ancient and modern, decorative and utilitarian. But it is also, conversely, the deployment of objects that are all also and at the same time fossils of an age, hieroglyphics of a civilization.[21]

Sèvres vases, sphinxes and pneumatic tubes are all part of the known bourgeois world: readers can interpret these objects without commentary from the narrator.

In *Mary Barton*, the object world is exotic and requires too much explanation to become the kind of archaeological evidence that it provides in Balzac. John Barton's silk scarf is an investment that must be explained as such: it is an item bought in good times that can be pawned in bad in order to feed a starving neighbour; a geranium on a window sill is not a random houseplant but a deep signifier of a labouring-class domesticity of which middle-class readers may be entirely unaware. The objects in this landscape are subjects that must be given a discourse by the narrator. They are not ready, in literary or historical terms, for objectification. Gaskell's unnamed narrator is a first-person narrator who is not officially a character[22] and in fact gives every impression of being the author – the same 'I' of the preface seems to be the 'I' who narrates. The effect of this is that the novel takes place in a kind of twilight zone of authorial creation/observation. But the narrator, because she is officially intradiegetic, can engage only gingerly in one of the most important formal devices of the novel: free indirect discourse. Jem Wilson's thoughts, for example, are articulated in free indirect discourse for two brief sentences and then revert to indirect discourse: 'Mary loved another! Oh! How should he bear it?' (220).

The subjectivity of the poor, perhaps, does not need this narration: the language of mill and millinery workers can be adequately represented by the friend of the poor who thinks for them and who can adequately represent them from the 'outside'. But perhaps they simply do not read enough to have the kinds of thoughts that narrators engaging in free indirect discourse so often like to quote – the flotsam and jetsam of bad novels in the case of Emma Bovary and Catherine Morland; Casaubon's bad philology; Dombey's bad business. Gaskell surrounds her characters with literary allusions, but they belong to the narrator: they are not the stuff of a character's thoughts. Occasionally a biblical quotation or a line from Robert Burns emerges as the thought of a character, but in general the recycled verbiage that makes up free indirect discourse is not part of the subjective world of the characters. Moreover, *Mary Barton*'s narrator is not removed from the action. The narrator of *Madame Bovary* is nothing like Madame Bovary and has no sympathy with her. Emma Bovary is '[t]he sentimental person [who] requires the ideal pleasures of literature and art to be concrete pleasures'.[23] The narrator is an objective artist. Emma Bovary must die so that the narrator can live, having rid himself of the build-up of her kitsch, which would destroy his soul if he could not actively disavow it by killing her off. Gaskell's narrator seems to be the very 'I' of the preface; that is, she seems to be Elizabeth Gaskell herself. Not only is she not removed from the action, but she seems to be recording action and creating a novel by turns. But like Flaubert's narrator, Gaskell, our author and narrator, also kills a character. John Barton must die because he requires that his political actions result in concrete political changes. With the failure of the People's Charter, he becomes a trade unionist.[24] He only becomes open to the narrator's solution, which is to accept and be comforted by the milk of the master's kindness, on his deathbed – and in fact he dies in John Carson's (the mill owner's) forgiving arms, his trade unionism extinguished at every level.

Gaskell's novel reduces politics to feeling; it removes the labouring-class characters from the public sphere in which they are seeking to represent themselves and returns them to, or attempts to return them to – in what will, hopefully, be the 'sequel' to the novel – private, affective relationships with each other and with their employers. The ultimate solution of *Mary Barton*, Gaskell's Unitarian liberal solution, is charity, which is why her novel is ultimately aristocratic.[25] *Mary Barton* is a melodrama and not a realist novel, and it is profoundly not the democratic novel described by Rancière in his analysis of Balzac and Flaubert, writers who are not prescribing reforms but working out styles of realistic representation.

And this rescues Mary Barton's characters as subjects, in one of the strangest of literary historical turns: it is in this deeply un-'psychological' novel that characters get to have subjectivities; they wish to represent themselves, and the author ultimately, unwittingly, colludes with her characters in that wish. Emma Bovary's 'interior self' is made up of the litter of the romances she reads, and the narrator's ventriloquising of this language shames her – for her excessive purchases, for her ideas of romance, for her tacky suicide. Free indirect discourse of this kind humiliates characters and gives readers a kind of frisson and a kind of fright, because the thoughts any of us might think and not speak are very often thoughts that are less original, acute, smart, ironic and knowing than those of a narrator who can invent, narrate, ironise and refine them. In fact, many of us may go around with only very partially modified 'lines' from various grubby sources floating around in our silent narratives of ourselves – lines we are glad there is no narrator around to cast in the kind of squirm-inducing display that free indirect discourse can create. Indeed, perhaps free indirect discourse is not so much a representation of subjectivity as a representation of the intertextuality of representations of subjectivity, including those we make to ourselves about ourselves. Not so much telepathy, omniscience or an ultimate instance of the police, free indirect discourse is a kind of satire of the way in which we all recycle language – and is itself another kind of recycling. It is a poem written over a valentine turned into the wadding for a gun that might kill someone. Or cause an author to have to kill someone.

Free indirect discourse makes characters poor so that narrators can remain rich: narrators are, after all, in control of the means of production of this kind of subjectivity effect, and the character cannot be greater than its narrator. In the case of fiction, the idea of the writer/narrator as capitalist seems pretty fair, since the labour of the character is, after all, accomplished by the author/narrator. But at the moment of free indirect discourse, the narrator splits away from that creation; an act of disavowal allows a narrator to remove herself from her own creation, giving us the characters we think of as people (even though they are made up of textual bits and pieces that the narrator nets into sentences), the ones with whom we identify, however mistakenly, however correctly.

Free indirect discourse may be cruel but, at least with respect to readers, it is democratic: it assumes an interiority that can only be narrated by a superhuman being, and it assumes that interiority is very often (in and out of fiction) a literary technique. Readers get to share the power of the narrator; they are equal, for the duration of reading, to their head of state, the ruler of the novel's world. But it is not democratic where characters are concerned, for characters are impoverished by free indirect discourse. Subjectivity is, in that mode of narration, a literary effect, sometimes literally, as when characters' thoughts are, like Emma's, bits and pieces of bad romances. Characters who are spared this invasion – like those in *Mary Barton* – remain intact as possible subjects. Their interiority is unknown, but it is not non-existent. Gaskell's characters are poor in spirit, poor in material goods, poor in intellectual accomplishment, but they are wealthier than the average fictional character that will succeed them in that they can potentially represent themselves. Gaskell leaves a margin of freedom in the first-person narrator that prevents free indirect discourse, and the same can be said of the linguistic rupture of the text. The language of her characters is too radically different from that of the narrator to allow the voices of characters and narrator to mingle in the nearly seamless way that free indirect discourse requires. Her characters' thoughts and feelings can be translated by a sympathetic narrator, but they are not represented from the inside. This gap, which is maintained in the epigraphs, main text and footnotes, is a space of freedom for the characters, who cannot, finally, be spoken for in their entirety as subjects and who therefore have yet to be represented fully in novelistic terms. In leaving open that possibility in the future, Gaskell leaves it to the labouring-class characters themselves. This may be why she removes her characters to suburban Toronto at the novel's end: the ramifications of that self-representation will be safely distant.

Coda

We might expect that essentially white-collar characters in a late twentieth-century metafiction would fare better in terms of representation than do the poor of an industrial novel by a liberal Victorian. History returns as farce in Gilbert Sorrentino's 1979 novel *Mulligan Stew*, in which we find a satire of the plight of a writer who 'loses touch' with his characters because they literally walk off the job, hoping to be employed by better writers. Martin Halpin, a character in a novel in progress called *Red Guinea* (which is being written inside *Mulligan Stew*), by the washed-up, would-be postmodernist Antony Lamont, is outraged to have been 'plucked out of the wry, the amused footnote in which I have resided, faceless, for all these years in the work of that gentlemanly Irishman, Mr. Joyce. [. . .] "An old gardener" so I've been these thirty-odd years, an old gardener who has never gardened, never even seen [. . .] a garden, and happy not to have seen one, by God!'[26] Halpin and his co-character Ned Beaumont, who was previously employed by Dashiell Hammett in *The Glass Key*, want to leave the Lamont novel, but they are anxious. Halpin asks, 'If we should desert this novel, will we ever find employment again? [. . .] [W]ill the desertion be construed as proof of our unreliability?

Authors can be strange' (89). These novelistic workers are horrified by the novel in which they find themselves: the words they have to say, the sex they have to perform, the fact that the cabin in the woods seems to have been stolen from another writer (because it is such a cliché) – a suspicion that is confirmed when mail arrives for a character in another novel. Quitting the novel, like the political activity in *Mary Barton*, is obviously risky. Like the advocates of the six points of the People's Charter, the characters in *Mulligan Stew* want better representation. But in this twentieth-century novel, the striking characters do not plan to represent themselves. They have no selves to represent: their only existence lies in what they have done on the page; Halpin is terrified of an upcoming restaurant scene because he has never eaten before. These characters are post-psychological; they cannot be narrated from within: they are closer to typographic than human characters. They wish to be represented, but not as themselves. They want good situations, good roles, and comfortable places on the page.

Chartism was treated by the terrified middle class like a revolutionary movement precisely because of its demand that the labouring class be allowed to represent itself. It was entirely liberal in its demands and yet entirely revolutionary, because the wrong group of people were demanding that their ability to think beyond their immediate ken and outside their own rank be given the recognition of parliamentary participation, both as voters and as members. The demand for greater (larger, fuller, more accurate) representation is denied in *Mary Barton* on two fronts, that of the novel and that of the state. As Chartists well knew, and as Catherine Gallagher has argued in terms of the 'industrial reformation' of the novel, these forms of representation are deeply involved in the nineteenth century and regularly analogised to one another, perhaps most famously in Eliot's novel of the first Reform Act, *Middlemarch*.

In *Mulligan Stew*, the desire for better representation (in the 1970s it is a question of lifestyle) begins to be addressed when Beaumont leaves the cabin, finds a colony of unemployed characters awaiting new authors (authorities), and finally convinces Halpin to join him. They have no agency, either their own or the employment kind through which white-collar workers in the 1970s might have sought new work. Although omniscient narration has theoretically declined by the late twentieth century – both in literary history and in this novel – these characters do not seem to have the option of becoming first-person narrators. Why not write memoirs about their lives as characters? Even in 1979, 'personalities' were engaged in such projects. In this novel, and in the literary project – modern and postmodern – of which it is a part, the representation of such a self is impossible. Omniscience returns with a particular vengeance when the post-psychological novel insists on its own status, and that of 'everyone' in it, as paper and ink. It may be that all novels are finally omnisciently narrated – whether they are focalised, written in the first person, postmodern and dispersed, or otherwise lacking an apparent central authority. The narrator always 'knows' more than she tells, and the novelist, of course, knows even more than that. And our pleasure in narration requires this gappiness. 'Curiosity, suspense and surprise', Meir Sternberg points out, 'are all driven by wanting to know more, by knowing that we do not know enough.'[27] We are poor in knowledge as readers. What we always know is that there is all this stuff we do not know. We sign up for the gappiness and then enjoy it; it is a gappiness we already know in the face of other kinds of omniscience to which we also give our consent – that of the US government, for example, recently revealed by Edward Snowden in all its splendour, to our largely silent amazement and acceptance. The pleasure of the text is also the pleasure of consenting to not knowing, to knowing that we do not know and having that be a condition of our being in the world. We do not identify with characters because they are like people but because we are like characters, relying on forms of omniscience – governments, gravity, laws of the market, expert advice and so on – to keep narrating various aspects of reality for us. Omniscience hangs around as an omnipresent narrative and epistemological form. Disembodied but not disempowered, dismembered but not defunctioned. You can walk out, but you cannot walk away. The democracy of literature is always outside of it, I would argue, in acts of interpretation that link its modes of knowing and being to our own lived experience. '[I]nterpretations are themselves real changes', Rancière writes, 'when they transform the forms of visibility a common world may take and, with them, the capacities that ordinary bodies may exercise in that world over a new landscape of the common.'[28] They must also transform the forms of invisibility that govern our passivity, our acquiescence to all 'narration' that is extradiegetic. Narration should be part of the common world; it should be not only visible but also and always audible, legible, comprehensible and accessible. Since technology, law and power will keep changing the meaning of all of the words just listed, the work of noticing narration requires a major humanitarian effort by the poor and our philosophers, by the poor and our novelists.

Notes

1. C. M. Jackson-Houlston, *Ballads, Songs, and Snatches: The Appropriation of Folk Song and Popular Culture in British Nineteenth-Century Realist Prose* (Aldershot: Ashgate, 1999), 108.
2. Elizabeth Cleghorn Gaskell, *Mary Barton: A Tale of Manchester Life* (Peterborough: Broadview, 2000), 124. All page references in this chapter are to this edition.
3. Martin Hewitt, 'Radicalism and the Working Class: The Case of Samuel Bamford', *Historical Journal*, 34:4 (1991), 873 (873–92).
4. See Jacques Rancière, 'The Putting to Death of Emma Bovary', in *The Politics of Literature*, trans. Julie Rose (Cambridge: Polity, 2011), 49–71, and *The Philosopher and His Poor*, trans. Andrew Parker (Durham, NC: Duke University Press, 2004).
5. Quoted in Rancière, *The Philosopher and His Poor*, 137.
6. Gregory Vargo, 'The World the Chartists Made: An Underground History of the Early Victorian Novel', 2010, MS, n.p.
7. Mike Sanders, *The Poetry of Chartism: Aesthetics, Politics, History* (Cambridge: Cambridge University Press, 2012), 8. See also Martha Vicinus, *The Industrial Muse: A Study of Nineteenth-Century British Working Class Literature* (London: Croom Helm, 1974); David Vincent, *Bread, Knowledge and Freedom: A Study of Nineteenth-Century Working Class Autobiography* (London and New York: Methuen, 1981); and Jonathan Rose, *The Intellectual Life of the Nineteenth-Century Working Class* (New Haven, CT: Yale University Press, 2003).
8. Ian Haywood (ed.), *The Literature of Struggle: An Anthology of Chartist Fiction* (Aldershot: Scolar, 1995), ix.
9. Quoted in Catherine Gallagher, *The Industrial Reformation of English Fiction: Social Discourse and Narrative Form, 1832–1867* (Chicago: University of Chicago Press, 1988), 224.
10. Haywood, *The Revolution in Popular Literature: Print, Politics, and the People, 1790–1860* (Cambridge: Cambridge University Press, 2004), 141.
11. Vargo, 'The World the Chartists Made'.

12. Hallam Tennyson, *Alfred Lord Tennyson: A Memoir* (London: Macmillan, 1897), 386.
13. Gordon Bigelow, *Fiction, Famine, and the Rise of Economics in Victorian Britain and Ireland* (Cambridge: Cambridge University Press, 2003), 148.
14. Hewitt, 'Radicalism and the Working Class', 877.
15. Rancière, *The Politics of Literature*, 12.
16. Priyanka A. Jacob, 'The Art of the Hoard: Secrets, Keepsakes, and Lingering Things in the Victorian Novel', PhD dissertation, Princeton University, forthcoming.
17. Andrew Parker, introduction to Rancière, *The Philosopher and His Poor*, ix.
18. Rancière, *The Politics of Literature*, 4.
19. Dorothy Thompson points out that British workers 'responded to hunger by forming a nationwide movement around a political programme instead of by more traditional means of protest like food rioting, arson, begging, poaching, or praying'. See her *Early Chartists* (Columbia: University of South Carolina Press, 1971), 12.
20. Rancière, *Dissensus: On Politics and Aesthetics*, trans. Steven Corcoran (London: Continuum, 2010), 39.
21. Rancière, *The Politics of Literature*, 15.
22. That is to say, a first-person narrator like Pip or Jane Eyre can ventriloquise their younger selves, but Gaskell's narrator offers no self, younger or current, to thus narrate.
23. Rancière, *The Politics of Literature*, 51.
24. Patrick Brantlinger argues that '[w]hereas Mrs. Gaskell presents Barton's Chartism sympathetically', she identifies his trade unionism with his turn to violence. See his 'The Case against Trade Unions in Early Victorian Fiction', *Victorian Studies*, 13:1 (1969), 37 (37–52).
25. See Lauren M. E. Goodlad, '"Making the Working Man Like Me": Charity, Pastorship, and Middle-Class Identity in Nineteenth-Century Britain; Thomas Chalmers and Dr. James Phillips Kay', *Victorian Studies*, 43:4 (2001), 591–617.
26. Gilbert Sorrentino, *Mulligan Stew: A Novel* (Normal, IL: Dalkey Archive, 1996), 25.
27. Meir Sternberg, 'Omniscience in Narrative Construction: Old Challenges and New', *Poetics Today*, 28:4 (2007), 730 (683–794).
28. Rancière, *The Politics of Literature*, 30.

7

'Broiled in Hell-fire': Melville, Rancière and the Heresy of Literarity
Grace Hellyer

In an early chapter of *Moby-Dick*, the narrator circles around the question of what it might mean to render the mode of dignity and grandeur proper to the democratic subject:

> this august dignity I treat of, is not the dignity of kings and robes, but that abounding dignity which has no robed investiture. Thou shalt see it shining in the arm that wields a pick or drives a spike; that democratic dignity which, on all hands, radiates without end from God; Himself! The great God absolute! The center and circumference of all democracy! His omnipresence, our divine equality![1]

The narrator draws a distinction here between 'man, in the ideal' and men, who 'may seem detestable as joint stock companies and nations'[2]. This distinction, he suggests, will give a paradoxical quality to his writing, causing him to ascribe 'high qualities' to 'low' subjects such as 'meanest mariners, and renegades, and castaways':[3]

> if I shall touch that workman's arm with some ethereal light; if I shall spread a rainbow over his disastrous set of sun; then against all mortal critics bear me out in it, thou just Spirit of Equality, which has spread one royal mantle of humanity over all my kind! Bear me out in it, thou great democratic God![4]

Starting from the presupposition that *Moby-Dick* constitutes an attempt to write as if the Declaration of Independence made a difference, this chapter will explore the question of what such an attempt might entail.[5] In a letter to Nathaniel Hawthorne from the period of the novel's composition, Melville hints at a heresy at the heart of the novel, describing it as 'broiled' in 'hell-fire', and as having a secret motto: 'Ego non baptiso te in nomine – but make out the rest yourself.'[6] The heresy turns out to be Ahab's Promethean attack on nature – the words are placed in his mouth as he baptises his newly forged harpoon in the blood of several of the 'pagan' members of his crew – but I want to look past this moment of high drama at a different mode of heresy, one that also shapes the text, disrupting and warping the categories that structure its representation of the doomed crew of the *Pequod*.

In *The Names of History*, Rancière sets himself the task of expanding on a new poetics of knowledge proper to the democratic age and the aesthetic regime of the arts. He explores the ways in which historical discourse responded to the challenge posed by the age of revolutions, and places a certain conception of literature at the heart of this response, contending that history must borrow from literature in order to generate a mode of historical discourse that does not foreclose on the inherently 'heretical' nature of its subject matter.[7] The situation that demands the modification of historical discourse is the removal of the figure of the king as the proper subject of history and the contingency this opens up with relation to the naming of subjects and events. In order to claim its place as a science and as a form suited to the age of democracy, he argues, historical discourse had to abolish narratives organised around the primacy of proper names and events. This new contingency of naming opened up a space of vertigo, a void – 'a terrain where the very meaning of a subject or an event is shaken'.[8]

Rancière compares the social science approach of the Annales historians to this shift to one he associates with the work of Jules Michelet and names 'romantic republican'.[9] Rather than working as an external voice narrating the meaning of historical events, Michelet's rhetorical gesture was to exact a kind of speech from the mute visibility of things and groups, replacing the figure of the king with personified abstractions like 'the people' and 'the nation'. This depends on the idea of a kind of unconscious life beneath visible reality and opens up the work of the historian as a 'romantic territorialisation of meaning'.[10] However, Rancière tells us, this territorialisation still works to contain and neutralise the inherently heretical nature of the new subjects of history because it presupposes that '[a]ll speech production can be represented as the exact expression of what gives it a place, of its own legitimacy'.[11]

Another way of putting this is that Michelet's representation of subjects and speech acts as precise expressions of place means that there can be 'no possible heresy'.[12] Heresy, in Rancière's account, is brought into being as an excess of words that emerges with the democratic movements of the seventeenth century. These are words that cannot be attributed to the traditional subjects of history but nonetheless demand recognition; the words of subjects that speak out of turn disrupting the givenness of the Platonic logic that assigns subjects and voices to their place:

> heresy is not a particular object of the history of mentalities. It poses, rather, the question of the very possibility of such a history. The history of mentalities is possible insofar as heresy is back in its place, assigned to its time and place. For heresy is the very essence of what the paperwork of the poor and the revolution of the children of the Book manifest. It is the excess of speech, the violence that comes through the book, about the book. If heresy tears apart the social body for questions of words, it is because it is first of all the very disturbance of the speaker: the disturbance of life seized by writing, of the life that is separated from itself, that turns against itself because of writing. Heresy is the life of meaning, inasmuch as it resists all play of nature and of its symbolization.[13]

This concept of 'heresy', for Rancière, must become the given of modern historical discourse. It represents the greatest challenge to any attempt to represent the new subjects of history – the masses, the workers, the poor – because it limits the possibility of their definitive representation. It guarantees that the object of history cannot fully coincide with either the discourse used to describe it or the place that it comes from. The various strategies that Rancière takes up in *The Names of History*, including the scientific specificity of the Annales school and Michelet's romantic republicanism, are ways of dealing with the problem of this heresy that 'seizes the new history in the face of its impossible beginning: the democratic disorder of speech born from the void and from abolished royal legitimacy'.[14] They are shown to be false solutions because they attempt to eradicate the problem of heresy rather than incorporating it into their mode of representation as a limit or impasse. Only a 'poetics of knowledge', which is to say a mode of historical discourse that borrows from the new literature of the aesthetic regime, is able to generate a mode of discourse adequate to the representation of its new subject – a mode of representation that does not foreclose on its inherently heretical nature.

The idea of heresy first appears in one of the articles that Rancière wrote between 1975 and 1981 for the journal *Les Revoltes logiques*. In 'Heretical Knowledge and the Emancipation of the Poor' he explores 'the relations that developed [...] on the boundary between popular and scholarly space' in French workers' culture between 1830 and 1850. In encounters between 'semi-schooled proletarians and semi-proletarian scholars', he argues, 'the idea of emancipation took shape between two poles: that of a theory of language and a science of life.'[15] Here, heresy denotes the forced entry of the plebeian into reason. If the plebeian is the one who is excluded from 'the speech that makes history' then the inaugural scene of political subjectification is one in which the plebeian recognises their capacity to claim and enact that speech.[16] For many nineteenth-century workers, Rancière argues, this involved 'the transformation of their material universe into a universe of intellectual determinations'.[17]

> The person who emancipates himself is the one for whom anything can be made into writing, and any writing at all into a textbook. Recognition in oneself of the 'sign of intelligence' was correlative with the intellectual redepiction of the surrounding universe.[18]

The scientific projects of the poor in the early to mid nineteenth century constituted an appropriation of the culture of enlightenment that involved taking the everyday objects of life and turning them into objects of knowledge. This entailed the transformation of the world into writing – the establishment of 'translatability between the world of everyday material experience and the world of science'.[19] The establishment of this symbolic relationship of analogy, Rancière shows, was the way in which those supposed to be excluded from thought, whose business was not to think and who had no natural entry into the world of natural reason, forced their way in.

It is this tearing away from the mode of being proper to one's station that constitutes heresy, understood as a power of separation: 'a voice separated from the body, a body separated from the place'.[20] It is a dissensual activity, denoting 'a difference between sense and sense: a difference within the same, a sameness of the opposite'.[21] Rancière deduces the existence of politics, not from some essence of the community, but from the fact that 'the common is divided'.[22] There is politics, Rancière tells us, 'because speaking is not the same as speaking, because there is not even an agreement on what a sense means'.[23] Thus a political disagreement could take place in a speech situation where the underlying dispute is not actually related to what the two parties are arguing, but rather the prior assumptions structuring the speech situation – whether one of the parties is capable of speaking like a proper citizen, or merely of making the noisy vocalisations of the suffering and complaining animal. This disagreement comes into play as historians – even as they tried to found their discourse on the Copernican Revolution that replaced the living, speaking body of the king with the figure of the masses – baulked at including the speech and writing of the masses into their representation of them. Rancière links the historian's mistrust of 'the paperwork of the poor' with the work of Thomas Hobbes, who saw the body politic as ailing from the effects of seditious words and phrases. Hobbes saw himself as witnessing a kind of revolution of the children of the Book in which 'the principle of political legitimacy [was] defeated, fragmented in the multiplication of speech and speakers who come to enact [. . .] the fantastical legitimacy of a people that has arisen between the lines of ancient history and of biblical writing'.[24] This fantastical legitimacy, enacted by anyone who cared to take up the excess of words, to tear names and figures from their context and apply them where they have no place to, was for Hobbes the symptom of a disorder of knowledge that threatened the legitimacy of politics. For Rancière, however, this speaking out of turn is related both to the new force of literary that he associates with the aesthetic regime and to the ambiguous body of the revolutionary event.

Although he is critical of Michelet's approach to the problem of heresy, Rancière returns to it in a later work on the politics of literature, naming it as exemplary of a romantic republican politics of literature:

> When Michelet describes the festivities in celebration of Federation in the towns and villages of France, he enthusiastically evokes the written testimonies of local orators. But he doesn't quote any of these testimonies. The reason for this is clear: the rhetoric of the village republican is made up of words and images borrowed from the rhetoric of the orators of the capital, which itself borrows from the rhetoric of antiquity learnt in the colleges of the monarchy. For this borrowed voice, which is the voice of the militants in the Republic, Michelet substitutes

another voice, the voice of the Republic in person, as harmony between bodies and meanings. He therefore tells us what is speaking through the written works of the village orators: the voice of the earth and of harvests, or the battle of the generations. Michelet is an ardent republican. But he is a republican of the age of literature and, in the age of literature, mute things speak of the Republic better than republican orators.[25]

Here Michelet's strategy points towards the difference between the politics of social agents and the politics of literature, for it explicitly opposes the way in which republicans evoked the classical mode of active speech in order to publicly stage their equality to the mode of politics proper to literature. This is a 'new regime of signification that strips the will to signify and speech-in-action of their privileges' opposing to them 'a different equality in a different language'.[26] Here, literature leaves 'the racket of the democratic stage in order to tunnel into the depths of society; by inventing this hermeneutics of the social body, this reading of the laws of the world on the body of mundane things'.[27]

This passage from Michelet offers a useful way into *Moby-Dick*'s contradictory poetics, which do not offer a clear-cut instance of the kind of realist novel that Rancière frames as the most prominent form of the emergent aesthetic regime. Instead, it is a text poised in the act of breaking away from forms like the epic and the romance, and as such offers an interesting testing ground for Rancière's account of the democratic aesthetic. The novel offers a vision of the world presented by a consciousness that seems to order it primarily in terms of the old way of conceiving of the significance of human action. The corrosion of this formal principle of action is effected by the novel's detailed focus on the processes of manual labour, to be sure, and by its merging of the world of thought and the world of work via Ishmael's narration, but also – and more importantly, I want to suggest – by the way in which the background of this world becomes foregrounded: a world of mute yet speaking life whose avatar is the leviathan. Ishmael's failure to catalogue, count or define this world enacts the waning of the representational norms that structure his account of the grandeur and dignity of whaling.

The novel offers an astonishingly detailed account of the business of whaling, the various species of whales and their characteristics, and also the written and visual cultures dedicated to the representation of whaling and whales. As Cesare Cesarino and many other critics have pointed out, the narrator draws on a wide array of different types of writing in order to bring this world into being:

> zoological taxonomies; etymological investigations; cetacean anatomies; literary and pictorial histories of the whale; political economies of the whale along with attendant financial-statistical analysis; numberless manual-like lists; descriptions and explanations of whaling equipment, of customs and discipline, of etiquette, and even of victuals, and so on.[28]

The narrator describes the culture and economic structures surrounding the whaling industry, and also the characteristics of the diverse crew of the *Pequod*, representative of the culture of the whaling industry in general. Ishmael frames his representation of the culture of whaling as an attempt to demonstrate its historical significance and give it a grandeur and nobility that would set it apart from more banal, routine forms of work. The business of whaling, he tells us, is regarded as 'a rather unpoetical and disreputable pursuit' not 'accounted on a level with what are called the liberal professions'.[29] In order to lend the work of whaling the dignity of more reputable professions, Ishmael's approach is to present it in the mode in which great actions were rendered in what Rancière would call the representative regime.

There is a distinctly ironic note in those passages in 'The Advocate' where Ishmael responds to the charge that whaling is mere butchery by comparing it to soldiery and goes on to describe the burning of all domestic lamps lit by whale oil as 'shrines' burning in honour of whalers.[30] In this peripatetic homage he oscillates between demonstrating the 'aesthetic nobility' of whaling by citing references in biblical, classical and secular literature and citing the amount of money paid to whalers in Britain between 1750 and 1788 and the yearly profits of the American whaling industry. Perhaps his most interesting ploy is to align the whaling industry with great historical events:

> For many years past the whale-ship has been the pioneer in ferreting out the remotest and least known parts of the earth. [...] They may celebrate as they will the heroes of exploring expeditions, your Cooks, and your Krusensterns; but I say that scores of anonymous Captains

> have sailed out of Nantucket that were as great, and greater than your Cook and your Krusenstern. For in their succorless empty-handedness, they, in the heathenish sharked waters, and by the beaches of unrecorded, javelin islands, battled with virgin wonders and terrors that Cook with all his marines and muskets would not have dared. All that is made such a flourish of in the old South Sea voyages, those things were but the life-time commonplaces of our heroic Nantucketers.[31]

Here Ishmael invokes a classical logic of plot, of the tracing of the causes and effect surrounding great actions, telling us that the business of whaling has set off 'sequential issues' of historical import as a result of the courage and enterprising natures of captains forced to travel off the charts in search of whales. He explicitly aligns the history of whaling with the history of the actions of great men; his 'anonymous captains' who voyage in search of profit, he tells us, are greater than those great explorers whose actions are thought to be the proper subjects of history because they did not have the benefit of armies. This conferring of heroic dignity and historical significance on the business of whaling is congruent with Ishmael's account of his intention to represent democratic dignity by paradoxically assigning high qualities to low subjects. However, the irony that haunts Ishmael's grandiose rhetoric signals that this is a false solution to the problem that the text sets up; that inscribing the whaling industry in a heroic framework is not an adequate means of respecting the democratic dignity of its workers. This is because it sustains the hierarchy that it invokes rather than dissolving it; it widens the circle of the subjects that can be proper subjects of literature while sustaining an implicit division between proper and improper subjects.

For Rancière, the aesthetic break takes place when a particular logic is overthrown – a logic that subordinates the interpretation of life to the logic of actions. *Moby-Dick* is very clearly galvanised by this old formal register that arranged the text around the logic of the actions of the salient individual, with the style of its narration evoking the classical register of speech-as-action that Rancière puts at the centre of the representative regime. According to Ishmael, whaling is great because it is a 'great action' of economic and imperial expansion associated with the discovery of continents and the development of industrial processes. However, it is striking that the democratic dignity that Ishmael is concerned with representing when he frames whaling as a historically significant practice composed of a series of heroic actions performed by great, albeit working, men cannot quite extend to cooks and carpenters.

When it is concerned with the representation of the crew of the *Pequod*, the text often sustains a distinction, either implicitly or explicitly, between the precepts and affects of anonymous life and the logic of actions that underpins the representation of certain salient individuals. This is particularly apparent with the representation of Ahab, the demonically heroic individual whose heretical quest structures the narrative. The text is seized, overtaken by its fascination with Ahab, who functions formally as a return of the hierarchical modes of literary production characteristic of Rancière's representative regime. The stakes of this seizure become especially apparent in the sections that seem explicitly to invoke the dramatic form. Here, Ahab's Shakespearean rhetoric and the biblical resonance that inflects the speech of the Nantucketers give the dialogue a distinctly early-modern resonance. After Ahab's great quest is disclosed to the crew and he obtains their allegiance, there follows a series of dramatic monologues that break with the first-person narration that has carried through the text up until this point, by first Ahab and then Starbuck, then Stubb. These monologues are followed by 'Midnight, Forecastle' in which the dialogue of the carousing sailors is represented in the form of a play script.

This formal intrusion of the dramatic script finds a faint echo later in the text in a section describing the ship's carpenter and his interaction with Ahab. This section reveals the paradox that haunts Ishmael's attempt to realise the principles of equality in his writing. Ishmael's construction of the culture of the whaling industry operates on one level as what Rancière calls a 'history of mentalities' in that it often represents individuals as an extension of their function. Although he himself writes as one who is capable of engaging in manual labour and contemplation at one and the same time, he often tends to ascribe only a kind of manual cunning to his fellow workers. In 'The Carpenter' Ishmael offers his subject as a practical instance of the problem of the representation and conception of democracy:

> Seat thyself Sultanically among the moons of Saturn, and take high abstracted man alone; and he seems a point of wonder, a grandeur and a woe. But from the same point, take mankind in mass, and for the most part, they seem a mob of unnecessary duplicates, both contemporary and hereditary.[32]

The carpenter, 'far from furnishing an example of the high, humane abstraction',[33] is characterised by an 'impersonal stolidity' that shades off 'into the surrounding infinite of things'.[34] He appears to Ishmael to have a paradoxical mode of life between human animation 'pauselessly active in uncounted modes' and the deathlike indifference of the world of natural objects: 'the general stolidity discernible in the whole visible world [which] [...] ignores you, though you dig foundations for cathedrals.'[35] This culminates in an account of the carpenter as lacking in anything that Ishmael recognises as intelligence, as a creature totally identical with his function as a labourer:

> You might almost say, that this strange uncompromisedness in him involved a sort of unintelligence; for in his numerous trades, he did not seem to work so much by reason or by instinct, or simply because he had been tutored to it, or by any intermixture of all these, even or uneven; but merely by a kind of deaf and dumb, spontaneous literal process. He was a pure manipulator; his brain, if he had ever had one, must have early oozed along into the muscles of his fingers. He was like one of those unreasoning but still highly useful, *multum in parvo*, Sheffield contrivances, assuming the exterior – though a little swelled – of a common pocket knife; but containing, not only blades of various sizes, but also screw-drivers, cork-screws, tweezers, awls, pens, rulers, nail-filers, countersinkers.[36]

Here the carpenter's mode of being is represented as identical with the pure immanence of sensation. His immersion in the 'spontaneous literal processes' of work is such that there is absolutely no separation of his mental and physical life; his brain has 'oozed' into the muscles of his fingers. Ishmael goes so far as to announce that although the carpenter does not have 'a common soul' he has 'a subtle something that somehow anomalously did its duty'; an 'unaccountable, cunning life-principle [...] that kept him a great part of the time soliloquizing; but only like an unreasoning wheel'.[37] Unlike Ishmael's thoughts, which detach themselves from his work and engage in the active interpretation of his world, the thoughts of the carpenter hum along mechanically like a wheel. He is represented as imprisoned in a circle of utility that contains his entire being and of which his thoughts and actions are a perfect expression. The being of the carpenter, then, is presented as totally commensurate with his function – he operates as a staging of the total coincidence of sense and sense wherein there can be no possible heresy.

The closely following exchange between Ahab and the carpenter offers a kind of meta-political representation of a non-dissensual speech situation in the sense that it is structured by Ishmael's prior determination of the concrete inequality of the speakers:

> 'Then tell me; art thou not an arrant, all-grasping, intermeddling, monopolising, heathenish old scamp, to be one day making legs, and the next day coffins to clap them in, and yet again life-buoys out of those same coffins? Thou art as unprincipled as the gods, and as much of a jack-of-all-trades.'
>
> 'But I do not mean anything, sir. I do as I do.'
>
> 'The gods again. Hark ye, dost thou not ever sing working about a coffin? The Titans, they say, hummed snatches when chipping out the craters for volcanoes; and the grave-digger in the play sings, spade in hand. Dost thou never?'
>
> 'Sing, sir? Do I sing? Oh, I'm indifferent enough, sir, for that; but the reason why the grave-digger made music must have been because there was none in his spade, sir. But the caulking mallet is full of it. Hark to it.'[38]

Here the evocation of the grave-digger reinforces the Shakespearean register of the scene, invoking the formal separation of the low character from the high and implicitly framing the speech encounter as a departure from the freedom of the novelistic form. Here, Ahab's moody and adroitly humorous discourse demonstrates his rhetorical mastery and the depth of his tragic consciousness, with the carpenter's responses operating in a fundamentally different register – like the automatic tics of a machine. A similar shift away from the novelistic register and towards a form more suggestive of a comic, dramatic monologue also characterises the interaction of Stubb with the ship's cook when he requests a whale steak from the body that he has been instrumental in acquiring. Here, the representation of the carpenter, like that of the cook in the earlier scene, is a performance of non-participation: the demonstration of the temperamental incapacity of individuals engaged in prosaic forms of labour to participate in the meaningful speech and action of the more heroic individuals engaged in the dangerous business of hunting and killing whales. It is striking, however, that even as Ishmael encloses the carpenter within the circle of mute life trapped in the circle of production and utility, his own contemplative activity exists on the margin of the division between the prosaic world and the world of art, calling into question the grounds of his own distinction. On the one hand, his workers' history operates so as to set up a history of mentalities that tends to reduce the workers to functions of their station or occupation, as we have seen in the account of the carpenter, creating a separation between the activity of thought and a mode of existence excluded from that activity, reduced to a mere expression of function. On the other hand, his writing turns the world of work into a thing of words, words that could be taken up by anyone, acting as a demonstration of the entrance of the worker into the world of thought and reason.

In a letter to Hawthorne, written during the period when he composed *Moby-Dick*, Melville turns over the question of his commitment to democratic equality:

> I am told, my fellow-man, that there is an aristocracy of the brain. Some men have boldly advocated and asserted it. [. . .] And I can well perceive, I think, how a man of superior mind can, by its intense cultivation, bring himself, as it were, into a certain spontaneous aristocracy of feeling, – exceedingly nice and fastidious, – similar to that which, in an English Howard, conveys a torpedo-fish thrill at the slightest contact with a social plebian.[39]

Ishmael's account of the carpenter seems touched by just this 'torpedo-fish thrill' of revulsion at the thought of the distance between himself and the carpenter. He establishes a division, with himself and Ahab as members of a 'spontaneous aristocracy of feeling' from which the carpenter is excluded. If democratic equality with his crew often seems to be imperceptible to Ishmael, however, I want to suggest that it becomes perceptible through the paradoxical appearance of the whale; specifically, its staging in his writings as a being that undoes many of the hierarchical distinctions that structure his account of the carpenter.

Like the French revolutionaries, Ishmael attempts to take up the power of speech in action of classical antiquity and use it to animate the world of work with democratic dignity. This kind of poetics, however, cannot take hold of the object that he takes up at the centre of his narration. His representation of the mode of being of sperm whales refuses to fit into the categories presupposed by the literature of the representative regime; it interrupts the connection between a certain idea of speech and the Aristotelian idea of the superiority of action over life, opening up a new and distinct sensorium. Ishmael's presentation of the whale displays a fascination with a mode of existence that collapses the logic that distinguishes the worker from the thinker, active speech from mere voice, carpenters and cooks from captains. The chapters in which Ishmael offers a practical anatomical account of the sperm whale, designed to render its mode of being intelligible, circle around the problem of formulating a new poetics of knowledge, searching for perceptible traces of a paradoxical thought that coincides with non-thought, for a way of perceiving the world that disrupts its self-evidence. It is as if Ishmael can only discover an escape from the paradox imposed by his understanding of democracy as an ideal haunted by practical evidence of inequality by leaving a world structured by his sense of what constitutes meaningful human speech and action.

Ishmael begins with a meditation on the gaze of the whale, noting that the distance between its eyes suggests a divided field of vision composed of two distinct pictures from either side of the head. He compares this with the human gaze, speculating that the brain of the whale, unlike that of a human, may be capable of 'attentively examining two distinct prospects' and also distinct objects of thought at the same time.[40] This two-ness in the mind of the whale and its perception of the world signals the way in which Ishmael's account of the leviathan will rupture the self-evident ideas that structure his perception. The eccentric sensory capacities of the whale create a gap, a dissonance in the world of sense, a division between sense and sense that drives a wedge into Ishmael's narration, dislodging his conception of the meaning of human speech and action. It is interesting that the contemplative subtlety and facility that Ishmael ascribes to the whale is directly linked to an impairing of its capacity for action, with its divided vision creating 'a helpless perplexity of volition' when the whale is under attack.[41]

In 'The Prairie', the narrator examines the 'phrenology' of the whale, noting in particular the combination of the impression of featurelessness created by the absence of the nose, and the impression of 'genius' imparted by its massive 'brow':

> But how? Genius in the Sperm Whale? Has the Sperm Whale ever written a book, spoken a speech? No, his great genius is declared in his doing nothing particular to prove it.[42]

The paradox, for Ishmael, is the idea of a genius whose particular nature resides in the absence of any concrete manifestations of genius, such as action, expression or speech. Lacking such a framework on which to hang his sense of the significance of the being of the whale, Ishmael despairs of being able to read and interpret it even as he positions it as an object that invites interpretation – 'how may unlettered Ishmael hope to read the awful Chaldee of the Sperm Whale's brow? I but put that brow before you. Read it if you can.'[43] There is no way for the whale to manifest the potentiality that Ishmael reads slumbering in the vast curvature of its front, and it is this paradox of significance and inaction that carries through the subsequent anatomical sections. In the following chapter, 'The Nut', Ishmael notes that the brain of the whale is positioned so far behind its 'forehead' that his prior phrenological reading was based on 'an entire delusion'.[44] Trying to read the impress of mental activity in the forehead is impossible so he turns to the brain itself, noting its smallness relative to the size of the animal, and speculating that the spine itself, resembling small interlinked skulls, may actually be part of its substance. This subversion of the dichotomy of mind and body again offers a kind of challenge to the hierarchical distinctions that structure his sense of human life, meaning and action.

Ishmael's account of the tail of the leviathan again foregrounds the creature's capacity to combine opposing characteristics. Here Ishmael focuses on the tail's ability to simultaneously convey the impression of power and playfulness – 'where infantileness of ease undulates through a Titanism of power'.[45] He describes coming across the whale playing 'kitten-like' on the surface of the ocean, and marvels that 'still you see his power in his play'.[46] There is also a paradox at work in the mode of expressiveness proper to the tail. The narrator tells us, 'At times there are gestures in it, which, though they would well grace the hand of man, remain wholly inexplicable.'[47] So although the tail has expressive power, it is not the kind of power possessed and wilfully deployed by the skilled orator whose gestures support active and directed speech. This is a bodily expressivity that cannot clearly or explicitly be linked to conscious volition. Instead, the communicative power of the tail is associated with a 'mystic force [. . .] akin to Free-Mason signs and symbols' through which the whale is able to 'intelligently [converse] with the world'.[48] Indeed, the entire body of the whale is said to be animated by paradoxical impressions that the narrator despairs of ever fully comprehending:

> Dissect him how I may, then, I but go skin deep; I know him not, and never will. But if I know not even the tail of this whale, how understand his head? much more, how comprehend his face, when face he has none? Thou shalt see my back parts, my tail, he seems to say, but my face shall not be seen. But I cannot completely make out his back parts; and hint what he will about his face, I say again he has no face.[49]

Ishmael's account of the sperm whale seems driven by an obscure desire for proximity to or knowledge of a paradoxical agency that seems to enter into an implicit opposition to Ahab's expressive forcefulness and ability to bend others towards the ends that he wills. This power without face whose volition and purpose remain impossible mysteries and around which his life as a whaler is organised is at the centre of the narrative. The enigmatic expressive power of the whale, whether it is in the face or the tail, eludes Ishmael's interpretative capacities and opens up a gap in the old paradigm 'that linked the appearance of beauty to the realization of a science of proportion and expression'.[50] The truth of the whale resides in an indeterminacy that invites interpretation by a science of proportion and expression even as it makes a final interpretation impossible. Its narration creates a subtle dispute with the logic of action and plot that structures the narrative – the logic that opposes Ahab and Stubb's heroic agency to the anonymous life of carpenters and cooks. It renders Ishmael's accounting of intelligences and functions litigious by operating as a dissensual supplement, disturbing his account of the activities and functions proper to the various members of the crew within the hierarchical sensible distributions that structure life on board the *Pequod*.

The tales surrounding the famous Moby-Dick operate in a curious tension with Ishmael's account of the genus of the sperm whale because the notorious white whale fits more easily into the classical logic of plot. This is largely because Ahab's perverse interpretation of Moby-Dick, in line with the mythology that surrounds its actions and its history, deliberately forces it into the old paradigm of meaning in action. Ahab dismisses Starbuck's claim that the whale is merely animal and that it is absurd, even blasphemous, to assign it a part in his human conflict, making it into a mask behind which lurk all the inscrutable malignancies that thwart human will and action. According to the narrative shared by the crew of the *Town-Ho*, the white whale intervenes actively and with seemingly directed intention in the tense struggle between master and crew member, dragging Radney, the brutally oppressive mate, to his death before the heroic and embittered Steelkilt can kill him, thus condemning himself to death. The sperm whale that Ishmael anatomises, however, is not comprehensible through the conventional framework used to describe human action. Its mode of being is irreducible to the logic of plot that hangs meaning on intention, action and the logic of causes and effects. In Ishmael's study of the whale, his attention turns away from the logic of actions that informs his representation of the struggle between Ahab and Moby-Dick and towards the interpretation of mute life. Here he circles around the impossible fact that the 'genius' and the significance of the whale lie in its doing nothing, discovering that its activities are readable only in a paradigm that suspends action, that puts its fascination to one side in favour of the interpretation of mute life.

Likewise, the fragmented and heterogeneous discourses adequate to the sperm whale's articulation create a rupture with 'the old organic paradigm that dominated the way discourse and the work were thought'.[51] Although Ishmael's discourse is organised around the articulation of a unified organism, it does not conform to the Platonic ideal of a discourse 'that takes up the image of a living being, given all the elements that make up an organism, and only those'.[52] His narration fragments world literature, indifferently mixing the sacred and the profane, the high and the low, the scientific and the fictional. His heretical discursive productions are inaugurated by the figure of the sub-sub-librarian, the archivist who mixes texts indifferently, refraining from articulating anything about the subject of the extracts or offering an account of how they are connected. The sub-sub presents a proliferation of texts that circle around their subject without offering a direct presentation of it, placing biblical references alongside historical ones, texts that use the whale as a figure of speech alongside those that actually take the whale as their subject, texts that describe uses for the products obtained by processing the body of the whale alongside those that offer an empirical account of the living whale in its natural environment. This principle of disorganisation is the necessary presupposition of writing that takes on board the problem of naming subjects and states in a modern world in which the distinction between sacred and profane literature no longer holds and there are only texts that can be taken up or discarded in the labour of narration. The sub-sub-librarian is the curator of a multiplicity of texts detached from any transcendent organising principle, and his disorderly archive is the immanent plane of undifferentiated material out of which *Moby-Dick* is spun. It inaugurates a principle of indifference as a kind of presupposition of the text.

Against the impersonality of the sea, the poetic construction of the floating factory/community of the *Pequod* is a performance of the dissensual powers of literary. Ultimately the most signal aspect of this endeavour is the metaphoric elaboration of the sperm whale. This mysterious being, curiously presented as a textual as much as an actual object, invokes a mode of representation that is irreducible to the logic of mentalities that often seems to underpin Ishmael's elaboration of the hierarchically ordered modes of being that make up the world of the whaling industry. Ishmael's rigorous mapping of the uncertainties that haunt his representation of the sperm whale disclose more than anything else the democratic excess of words that disrupts any final designation of subjects and places. Thus, the presentation of democratic dignity is displaced from the representation of the crew and the world of work and located in the body of the whale, a mysterious object poised between sacred mystery and a raw product to be harvested and transformed into commodities. In tearing the body of the whale away from its routine appropriation by capital, Ishmael casts light on the way that he and his fellow crew members are also appropriated.

Moby-Dick's style is characterised by a kind of rhythmic oscillation between dramatic accounts of great events, scholarly speculative digressions, prosaic accounts of the processes of manual labour, and the moments of reverie that punctuate the life of work. Thus, the passage from Ishmael's anatomical and philosophical meditations on the sperm whale to gruelling, detailed accounts of the industrial processing of its body is bridged by a dramatic account of the hunting of a whale, Pip's abandonment at sea, and the famous opening section of 'A Squeeze of the Hand'. Pip is a young, black crew member who loses his senses after being cut adrift during a whale hunt and retrieved only after the whale has been secured. In this instance, Stubb refuses to turn back the boats from their pursuit after Pip loses his nerve and jumps from the boat into the water, having previously warned him: 'We can't afford to lose whales by the likes of you; a whale would sell for thirty times what you would, Pip, in Alabama.'[53] This brutal equation of the market value of Pip's living body and the dead body of the whale highlights the peculiarity of Ishmael's cetological and anatomical writings, namely that Ishmael insists on engaging with the body of the whale in terms that are not dictated by market value. It is through this assay of the whale that he seems to ascertain a different way of conceiving of the value of human life, and the way in which a kind of being in common can be constituted. He reads a strangely embodied democracy in the body of the whale as something opposed on the one hand to Ahab's imperial values, and on the other to the commercial values of the whaling trade. His account of processing the spermaceti harvested from the body of the whale is framed as the expression of a universal impulse towards unity, a kind of displacement of a utopian notion of being in common onto the body of the whale:

> as I snuffed up that uncontaminated aroma, – literally and truly, like the smell of spring violets; I declare to you, that for the time I lived as in a musky meadow; I forgot all about our horrible oath; in that inexpressible sperm [. . .] and I found myself unwittingly squeezing my co-laborers' hands in it, mistaking their hands for the gentle globules. [. . .] Oh! my dear fellow beings, why should we longer cherish any social acerbities, or know the slightest ill-humor or envy! Come; let us squeeze hands all round; nay, let us all squeeze ourselves into each other; let us squeeze ourselves universally into the very milk and sperm of kindness.[54]

Even as the very whale whose value has been measured against Pip's is processed into the raw product that will become a commodity, Ishmael makes the material substance – spermaceti – into the sensible embodiment of a community in palpable possession of its own idea. The framing of this phantasmatic representation of being in common, created in a manner that is explicitly framed against the grain of the oath that has previously bound them together, by a ruthless economic logic that calculates the values of individuals against that of whale blubber, constitutes the construction of a dispute within the text. Thus, the whale operates as a kind of machine of thought that pulls at the threads that hold Ishmael's narrative in place, a modification of the thinkable that resounds through the text.

Notes

1. Herman Melville, *Moby-Dick* (London: Penguin Classics, 1998 [1851]), 126.
2. Ibid.
3. Ibid.
4. Ibid., 127.
5. In a letter to Nathaniel Hawthorne, written during the period of *Moby-Dick*'s composition, Herman Melville compares his situation as a writer to that of Shakespeare and suggests that he is capable of a more 'full' and 'frank' articulation because 'the Declaration of Independence makes a difference'. Melville [1819–91], *Correspondence: The Writings of Herman Melville: The Northwestern-Newberry Edition*, ed. Lynn Horth (Evanston, IL: Northwestern University Press, 1993), 122.
6. Ibid., 196.
7. This is one of Rancière's earliest accounts of that concept of 'literarity' that plays such an important role in his account of aesthetic modernity. Here literature is conceived as constituting its own kind of truth procedure, and this as the reason that historical discourse is required to draw on it in order to generate a mode of representation adequate to its new subject.
8. Jacques Rancière, *The Names of History: On the Poetics of Knowledge* (Minneapolis: University of Minnesota Press, 1994), 2–3.
9. Ibid., 98. The Annales school sought to release history from 'the indeterminacy of the words and phrases of stories', thus transforming into real cognition what was still only the 'novel of human life'. They saw themselves as writing in the light of a Copernican Revolution that replaced the king with the masses, so they set themselves the task of extracting data from the masses and presenting events in a purely objective and scientific mode. Rancière argues that this in effect constitutes the destruction of history and its replacement by the social sciences; that the empiricism of the Annales school makes it impossible to account for the uniqueness of events and subjects; that it suppresses their singularity by presenting them as mere functions of scientific abstractions – periods of time, geographical locations and forces (Rancière, *The Names of History*, 5).
10. Ibid., 58.
11. Ibid., 67.
12. Ibid.

13. Ibid., 67–8.
14. Ibid., 90.
15. Rancière, *Staging the People: The Proletarian and His Double*, trans. David Fernbach (London: Verso, 2011), 37.
16. Ibid.
17. Ibid., 38.
18. Ibid., 39.
19. Ibid., 40.
20. Ibid., 68.
21. Ibid., 1.
22. Ibid. Rancière explains this in terms of the disagreement. He describes a fundamental instance of this disagreement preceding Aristotle's claim that man is a political animal because he is a speaking animal, showing that beneath this apparent anthropological grounding of politics there is a prior distinction between the merely animal capacity of voice, which only expresses pleasure or displeasure, and speech, denoting the proper capacity of speaking and discussing. This presupposition, this a priori that could structure a speech situation without being the subject spoken about, is a privileged instance of the object of a properly political dispute or disagreement.
23. Rancière, 'The Thinking of Dissensus: Politics and Aesthetics', in Paul Bowman and Richard Stamp (eds), *Reading Rancière* (London: Continuum, 2011), 2.
24. Rancière, *The Names of History*, 20.
25. Rancière, *The Politics of Literature*, trans. Julie Rose (Cambridge: Polity, 2011), 20–1.
26. Ibid., 20.
27. Ibid., 21.
28. Cesare Cesarino, *Modernity at Sea: Melville, Marx, Conrad in Crisis* (Minneapolis: University of Minnesota Press, 2002), 76.
29. Melville, *Moby-Dick*, 118.
30. Ibid., 119.
31. Ibid., 119–20.
32. Ibid., 508.
33. Ibid.
34. Ibid., 509.
35. Ibid.
36. Ibid., 510.
37. Ibid.
38. Ibid., 573–4.
39. Melville, *Correspondence*, 190.

40. Melville, *Moby-Dick*, 361.
41. Ibid.
42. Ibid., 380.
43. Ibid.
44. Ibid., 381.
45. Ibid., 411.
46. Ibid., 412.
47. Ibid., 414.
48. Ibid.
49. Ibid.
50. Rancière, *Aisthesis: Scenes from the Aesthetic Regime of Art*, trans. Zakir Paul (London: Verso, 2013), 4.
51. Ibid., 8.
52. Ibid.
53. Melville, *Moby-Dick*, 454.
54. Ibid., 455.

8

Why Maggie Tulliver Had To Be Killed
Emily Steinlight

'To kill people or to marry them is to beg the question,' writes William Dean Howells in a study of literary heroines, 'but into some corner the novelist is commonly driven who deals with a problem. [. . .] How life would have solved the problem of Maggie Tulliver I am not quite prepared to say; but I have my revolt against George Eliot's solution.'[1] Howells's protest against the ending of *The Mill on the Floss* is understandable, and pretty widely shared. The flash flood that drowns the protagonist seems to impose on the plot a certain logic of cruel necessity, leaving readers to lament Eliot's judgement that such a character as Maggie cannot be allowed to survive. John Ruskin's complaint was different: 'There is not a single person in the book of the smallest importance to anybody in the world but themselves,' he fumed, 'or whose qualities deserved so much as a line of printer's type in their description.'[2] Where Howells takes issue with the extraordinary circumstances of Maggie's death, Ruskin objects to the gross ordinariness of her life, unconvinced she should exist in the first place. On the face of it, these critiques seem opposed: Howells valorises Maggie as a unique individual who deserves a better fate, while Ruskin writes her off as part of a demographic set of worthless figures (somewhat ironically, since his criticism of *Bleak House* in the same essay is that Dickens registers the deaths of his characters with the statistical indifference of an actuary). Yet the two in fact share a premise: that something called 'life' is tasked with solving narrative problems, and that a novel can be assessed by the power it exerts to make characters live or die in narrative time.

With that premise in mind, this chapter asks a simple question: why does Eliot's novel kill its protagonist? I borrow this question from an essay by Jacques Rancière, which famously asks the same of *Madame Bovary*.[3] Yet it yields a different answer in Eliot's case than in Gustave Flaubert's, and not solely because Maggie perishes in a stroke of divine violence rather than by slow and agonising suicide. Whereas Emma Bovary, in Rancière's reading, dies for her refusal to separate literature and life, Maggie's fate is not sealed by a transgression against art. If she shares with Emma that sense of the oppressiveness of everyday existence, an unnameable discontent with home and a longing for aesthetic or erotic experience that has no specific object, she is divested of any idealising impulse to beautify life, any novelistic fantasy of living otherwise. Eliot's heroine indeed renounces novel-reading because she knows too well that art will only ever be a partial pleasure. Walter Scott's novels may enthral her imagination, as they do Emma's, but they cannot sate Maggie or compensate her for what she lacks: 'some explanation of this hard, real life', of her family's sudden destitution, 'the unhappy-looking father seated at the dull breakfast-table; the childish bewildered mother; the little sordid tasks that filled the hours'.[4] Literature, she reasons, can only intensify her restlessness, leaving her prey to the 'seductive guidance of illimitable wants' and longing for more than her circumstances will allow (348, 338). There is thus no need to sentence her to death, like Flaubert's heroine, for 'the crime of having abused the equivalence of art and life'.[5] And if this equivalence is a threat to the specificity of art that Flaubert has brought upon himself, by Rancière's account, through a pervasive free indirect discourse that makes literary language indistinguishable from the everyday and depersonalises narration, Eliot faces no such threat at the level of form.[6] Though rigorous and polemical in its attention to the everyday, *The Mill on the Floss* never fully slides into free indirect discourse, instead maintaining a distinct and personal (if unidentified) narrative voice, a transcendent intelligence that floats above the dull patter of the village life it frames. So if Maggie's death, too, arises out of a dilemma of realist form, as I suggest it does, that dilemma hinges on a different linkage between art and life – one that swerves from the logic of individual punishment that the putting to death of a character might imply.

In seeking to be, as Eliot puts it, 'the nearest thing to life', realism binds art to life in a double sense. The novel stakes its form on life not only in the biographical sense of lived experience but also in the totalised biological sense captured by vital statistics. And these two registers, though never fully separable, never quite line up in realist fiction. Life, in its biological sense, necessarily extends beyond the personal and names a markedly different narrative object from character and from plot. Perhaps, then, Eliot's novel elaborates a different problem in cutting short the life of its protagonist. Such literary deaths expose fiction to the seemingly alien question of which lives are worth preserving. They point toward a peculiar recognition of disposability that at once shapes and unsettles realist form. Insofar as the novel makes itself accountable for the disposability of its own materials, the lives and deaths of characters might be grasped in part as narrative determinations made at the level of population.

There is no shortage of explanations, of course, for what befalls Maggie: that she dies the death of the fallen woman she became in reputation if not in deed, sunk by a wayward desire that carries her away from domestic duty; that she is doomed, conversely, by a fatal allegiance to home and a quasi-incestuous attachment to the domineering brother who dies locked in an eternal embrace with her; that she is sacrificed on the altar of historical necessity. There are cases to be made for all these readings. But what if the reason for the novel's catastrophic climax is actually no reason at all, and we are left with the apparently simpler and far less hermeneutically satisfying answer that Maggie's death occurred by chance? This is liable to sound obvious, on the one hand, or just plain wrong on the other: obvious, since the story ends with natural disaster; wrong, since plot entails purpose, and since this novel's denouement invites allegorical readings that make it anything but random. Still, Eliot's narration insists on unpredictability – and that insistence, rather than a mere pretence to keep readers guessing and to preserve the illusion of open possibility, marks a particular approach to causation.

In asking whether the novel can live with chance, and how chance intersects with narrative determinations about life, I want to consider the politics of realist fiction in the terms offered by Rancière's account of the modern literary regime. His work makes chance elemental to fiction, above all in claiming that literature articulates a single ambivalent truth: that 'anything can happen to anyone'.[7] For Rancière, this means that anyone may be a literary subject, but it also means that the novel owes no particular dignity to its subjects. In what follows, I will ask what this truth – this indeterminacy with regard to subject and plot – would entail for Eliot's novel and for many of the key terms of narrative theory. What becomes of character, elemental as it is to fiction, if the novel's handling of life hinges on chance? What might then follow about realism's historical project as it mediates between the biographical and the biological? Here, the stakes are particularly high in the case of the *Bildungsroman*, with its presumed ambition to align the biographical plot of individual development with a historical process of social incorporation.[8] And what are the pressures on chance itself when it is called into service? I want to stress that what it has to contend with is not just determinism, its assumed opposite; it also confronts the probabilistic systems that made chance governable and, at times, appealed to it as a means of disavowing agency for the state's own casualties. Then, too, in fiction, it comes under the different pressures of narrative form itself.

Demos or population?

I turn first to Rancière, whose work illuminates a surprising set of answers to these questions. His account of the literary, while not expressly concerned with any single generic category, enables a substantial reconsideration of the politics of realist form. Rancière, to be sure, voices no commitment to the specificity of realism. The novel is the 'genre without genre',[9] and his insistence on defining literature simply as the art of writing, without any qualifications or rules of correspondence between style and subject, entails a certain indifference to generic and formal distinctions. Yet his readings of nineteenth-century novels implicitly revise what it means to call those novels realist: most obviously, in suggesting that literature does not deal in representation. Rejecting the mimetic view of fiction as a reflection of social totality and of the recognised spatio-temporal ordering of everyday experience,[10] Rancière defines literature as a redistribution of the sensible: a disordering of space, time and attention. *Madame Bovary*, rather than a cynical tale of *embourgeoisement* and commodity fetishism, becomes in Rancière's reading 'the literary equivalent of working-class emancipation' even in attesting that someone as socially inconsequential as Emma Bovary, a half-educated farmer's daughter, demands aesthetic pleasures to which she is not entitled.[11] This approach to realism contrasts sharply with the claims of Fredric Jameson, who has long held the novel complicit in normalising and stabilising the bourgeois social order, affirming its measures of time, space, and economic equivalence, and acclimatising readers to the rhythms of capitalist work.[12] Jameson's recent *Antinomies of Realism* upholds this view of the realist novel's formal investment in a new status quo it helped rationalise: realism, he argues, 'requires a conviction as to the massive weight and persistence of the present as such, and an aesthetic need to avoid recognition of deep structural social change [. . .] and contradictory tendencies within the social order'.[13] For Rancière, by contrast, fiction does not affirm but fractures the representational order of the social world.

This is the shared terrain of aesthetics and politics. Politics, for Rancière, does not name a form of ordering or administration but, on the contrary, a disorder that prevents the political community from ever reaching a final or sufficient form. Literature, he suggests, makes this politicity palpable even in the descriptive excess and disproportioning of words to bodies that Georg Lukács (notably, in his critique of naturalism and modernism) took as signs of alienation and political capitulation. Its subjects, like the subjects of politics, are neither unique individuals nor social parts seeking to be represented as such but an anonymous, multiple and indeterminate *demos* exceeding the established count of those presumed to constitute the social body.

At the level of character, Rancière's account of the distribution of the sensible bears comparing with Alex Woloch's formalist study of minor characters and of the uneven distribution of character space. *The One vs. the Many* stipulates that while anyone might happen to be the protagonist of a nineteenth-century novel, 'only one character is'.[14] For Woloch, chance selection is not wholly emancipatory and certainly not levelling; yet the incursion of minor characters into the space occupied by the central figure foregrounds the relative arbitrariness of the novel's focalisation and of the resulting distribution of attention. For Rancière, by contrast, the hierarchy of subjects is so thoroughly undone by literature's new distribution of the sensible that all such divisions of narrative space and focus are perpetually compromised not only by other human figures but also by the mute voices of things that take on unexpected powers of speech.

Such an approach to the novel's human material goes some way toward explaining one of the prevailing critical objections to nineteenth-century fiction: too much! Ruskin's response to Eliot's novel bears this out, and it points to the political stakes of a certain excess he found there. While his complaint appears to be with the lowness or ordinariness of its chosen subjects, which Eliot's narration periodically steps in to defend, this complaint masks a recognition of a more radical challenge that Rancière would call aesthetic indifference: fiction no longer admits any distinction between what is ordinary and what is extraordinary. Realism's interest in mass life met the routine charge that novelists were peopling their fictional worlds with superfluous characters, wasted lives, subjects unworthy of narration; in fact, Woloch's claim that realist novels are 'structurally destabilized not by too many details [. . .] but by *too many people*' gets pretty directly stated in nineteenth-century criticism.[15] Such excess is to be expected in the Dickensian or Balzacian city novel, while the provincial setting of *The Mill on the Floss* seems a world apart from the frenetic buzz of *Bleak House* or *Père Goriot*. But Ruskin felt an unsettling oversaturation of bodies, voices and sensations even in St. Ogg's, dismissing Eliot's small rural population of characters, major and minor, as the human 'sweepings out of a Pentonville omnibus'. His objections to the feverish and depraved character of modern literature in general correlate, in his analysis, with demographic density. Ruskin attributes fiction's fascination with 'physical corruption' and 'moral disease' to human aggregation: it is the outcome, he suggests, 'of the hot fermentation and unwholesome secrecy of the population crowded into large cities', all persons becoming 'infectious' to each other by their proximity.[16] His response to Eliot's slow-paced, backdated novel of provincial life, which he does not hesitate to class with the 'railway novel', extends this diagnosis beyond the literal setting of the city. This strongly suggests that literary excess is never simply demographic – and Rancière's argument that fiction never simply reflects a countable social whole is well taken.

Even so, the uncounted surplus that constitutes the subjects of politics and of literature alike cannot be fully detached from a new governing logic that demands that life be quantified in the first place (not just in the form of a census of individual units but also in impersonal statistical projections). If the surplus, the part of those who have no part, presents itself as a threat to the social order, we can also understand it as a product of that order. In the most bluntly historical sense, it arises as the redundant population that facilitated capitalist production. And it corresponds with a science of government that necessarily assumes more people than it is concerned to handle. Indeed, such demographic excess had been theorised as the very basis for the inequality that Thomas Malthus saw as intrinsic to excessive human reproduction. This bears emphasising, even if one wishes to agree with Rancière that the count of the uncounted offers an immanent response to the very forms of order that produce it. Realist fiction, insofar as it claims the populace as its object, never simply mirrors these forms of order. Yet an approach to population that treats certain bodies as fungible or ill-adapted for survival nonetheless hangs over the nineteenth-century novel's decisions regarding the distribution of life. In the case of *The Mill on the Floss*, it seems to offer one explanation for an ending that has been criticised on one side because it seems arbitrary and on the other because it seems deterministic.[17]

Chance's necessity

The politics of realism, however, depend not only on the aleatory character of the subjects it claims and the language it adopts but also on its temporal organisation. For Rancière, the novel's aesthetic indifference extends beyond the selection of figures and the laws of style to the assumed primacy of the event. *Madame Bovary*, in his reading, refuses the Aristotelian privileging of a poetics of action over passive description – a hierarchy made militant in Lukács's 'Narrate or Describe?'. Indeed, Rancière locates, in the novel, an internal resistance to narrative time and sequence; 'the abolition of the representative hierarchy in fiction', he argues, 'does not simply consist in introducing common people and the prose of the everyday into the realm of high art [. . .] It entails something more radical which is the destruction of the representational form of the event and of the connection of events as an "arrangement of actions".'[18] It would seem, indeed, that plot is the enemy of what Rancière calls 'life', which is not a series of identifiable deeds and inherently consequential events but an impersonal flow of sensations, Deleuzian haecceities, aesthetic micro-events.[19] For life to claim its place in form, both the ordering of plot and the distinction between what does and does not fall into plot's apparent causal sequence must become subject to a kind of radical chance, an essential indeterminacy, on which realism paradoxically depends.

Chance is elemental to realism. This much was clear to Lukács, for whom history itself grinds to a stop once narrative ceases to allow for the unforeseen. But in order for the chance event to ramify, he argues, narration must transform it into something quite different: necessity. Turning back to the question of why Eliot's novel abruptly cuts short its slow historical *Bildung* and drowns its protagonist, then, requires some attention to what it would mean to call this ending a chance event. Eliot's plot, of course, is not merely actuarial – nor are realist fiction's events reducible to 'crass accident', which Lukács would distinguish from true chance (112). To call a flood accidental seems incoherent anyway, as if geological and ecological processes were usually steered by some intention that fell asleep at the wheel. The opposite is true of narrative. If we define plot, with Peter Brooks, as 'an embracing concept for the design and intention of narrative, a structure for those meanings that are developed through temporal succession',[20] then the events that form its sequence (say, the sudden death of a character) can obviously never be inadvertent even where they must appear so.

And Eliot prepares the way for her denouement so carefully that it is not as sudden as it looks. The event of the flood is heavily foreshadowed in repeated references to past inundations, and the Tulliver siblings' death by water is both predicted literally in Mrs Tulliver's constant fear of her children drowning and hinted at figuratively in the novel's metaphoric vocabulary. We see Maggie picturing the river Floss in childhood whenever she reads, in *The Pilgrim's Progress*, of 'the river over which there was no bridge' (45); though the line is not glossed, readers will recall this image as John Bunyan's metaphor for death. We see it, too, in Maggie's childhood fascination with the image of an accused 'witch' being drowned; together with the narrator's and characters' repeated descriptions of Maggie's own witch-like qualities, this illustration from Daniel Defoe's *Political History of the Devil* seems chillingly prescient. One can locate countless other signs pointing toward the same future, cataclysmic though it is. For Jameson, it is 'no accident' that Eliot repeatedly consigns characters to a watery grave, and the ending of *The Mill on the Floss* proves that realism, try as it might, cannot do away with those providential notions of destiny that Eliot's narrators perpetually disavow. Why this death is Maggie's destiny, Jameson does not stop to explain.

Rancière's contribution to the current volume, which explicitly engages theories of realist fiction, loosens the seemingly obvious connection between sequence and causation. His focus here is on narrative time, which Lukács and Auerbach, in different ways, have understood as key to the formal relation between fiction and historical process. His gambit is to locate a surprising discovery in *Mimesis*. Seizing on Auerbach's odd choice to illustrate the 'sense of reality' created in fiction via a 'random occurrence' in *To the Lighthouse* that is unconnected to any 'planned continuity of action', he suggests that 'fiction reaches its highest historical achievement when it loses what seemed to constitute it, namely the causal connection between the events.'[21] This claim sounds untenable if one takes plot to be a requirement of narrative. Virtually all forms of novel theory and narrative analysis, from formalist and structuralist criticism to Lukácsian and Jamesonian dialectics, rely on the interpretable character of a sequence of events. Brooks, indeed, identifies temporality as the novel's most irreducible meaning-making device – so much so, he suggests, that fiction's preterite tense gets read as the present because we take for granted that there is a future we are waiting to reach, and it is thus 'best to speak of the *anticipation of retrospection* as our chief tool in making sense of narrative'.[22] But such sense-making requires a peculiar leap of logic. Because of the chronological structure of narrative, Brooks acknowledges, 'prior events, causes, are only so retrospectively, in a reading back from the end'.[23] In effect, this makes the Humean inductive fallacy the standard mode of narrative interpretation: turning ordinality into causation by reading backwards. Rancière has good reason, then, to track a resistance to causal sequence, and even to the primacy of the event, in the novel's very form.

So the appeal to chance in Eliot's novel is paradoxically necessary for the very reason it is formally impossible: it aims to counter the tendency of plot to temporalise events into a sequence of causes leading to a known conclusion. If chance kills Maggie, it is what keeps realism alive; without it, argues Lukács, 'all narration is dead and abstract. No writer can portray life if he eliminates the fortuitous.'[24] But chance is tough to plot in the past tense. It requires the narrative to proceed as if it were unfinished at the time of reading, and the narrator to stand apart from authorial agency over the plot. Eliot upholds the contingency of circumstance, rejecting Novalis's 'questionable aphorism' that character is destiny; Maggie's 'history', she contends, 'is hardly to be predicted even from the completest knowledge of characteristics'

(418). Even in eschewing prediction, though, the narrator points, cagily yet proleptically, toward a future known to the novel and yet not knowable in advance: 'Maggie's destiny [. . .] is at present hidden, and we must wait for it to reveal itself like the course of an unmapped river: we only know that the river is full and rapid, and that for all rivers there is the same final home' (418). This simile prepares for its own collapse into metonymy, since the future rests on the non-arbitrariness of the two terms linked by figurative language: Maggie's destiny is not *like* a river, it *is* the river. The future already exists and is merely hidden; and how could it be otherwise, especially in a historical novel? But if we take the force of that collapsed simile between story and river, then what is 'hidden', what we do not yet know, is just what we already know: destiny names the channel of chance causes rolling toward death, that 'same final home' toward which all life flows.

Eliot's metonym, then, routes us toward a familiar alignment of narrative with the death drive. Brooks would understand this as a universal condition of narrative, a formal expression of the 'time-boundedness' of existence; 'plot', he submits, 'is the internal logic of the discourse of mortality.'[25] But the novel's impulse to narrate untimely death has more particular meaning in a century that made life a scientific object ('the set of functions that resist death') and aimed to govern it as an economic and political quantum. Those techniques for making live and letting die that Foucault calls biopower change the stakes of the life story. If the death drive itself knows no history, its narrative work takes on historical weight in a text where biological existence is so fraught.

Realism's 'gross sum'

There is, as I have suggested, a distinct ideological context in which chance becomes a means of operationalising life and death. Here, we might recall Ruskin's complaint that realist novels are overpopulated and that our attention is wasted on such lives as Eliot animates. This complaint owes much to a premise that at first seems quite foreign to literary criticism: the Malthusian theory of a quantitatively excessive human species. This theory shaped much of the era's thinking about the systemic function of chance events in causing both life and death on a mass scale. We see its traces when *The Mill on the Floss* registers the peculiar sense of an excess of human material.

Even in St. Ogg's, life seems to require justification against the charge of superfluity. This is clear in the first chapter of Book Fourth, which beats Ruskin to the punch in affirming his contempt for a cast of characters unworthy of a line of type. Eliot's narrator reflects here on the triviality of the novel's population and on what Marx would call the 'idiocy of rural life' by first taking the reader elsewhere, evoking a touristic view of 'ruined villages' along the banks of the Rhône, long since swallowed by the river's sudden rise (282). This dreary scene – 'dismal remnants of commonplace houses, which in their best days were but the sign of a sordid life' – offers a parallel for the oppressive provincialism of the novel's own setting and populace, which cosmopolitan readers will object is 'surely the most prosaic form of human life' (283). If Eliot's ventriloquising of objections enables her defence of the novel's anti-idealist programme, it does so by re-evaluating rather than falsifying the terms of the objection. 'Prosaic form' has an ironic edge, since the Hegelian 'prose of the world' is the stuff of realist form. And form is the very thing that promises to fashion a single life or set of lives into biographical narrative, thus giving them value. But that promise is disarmingly broken by the repetition of the words 'life', 'lives' and the verb 'to live', which appear no fewer than fourteen times in the three paragraphs opening this famous chapter, their usage switching between the cultural modes of life and biological generalisation. Thoughts of those skeletal structures destroyed by floods, the narrator remarks, 'oppress me with the feeling that human life – very much of it – is a narrow, ugly, grovelling existence, which even calamity does not elevate' (283).

If Eliot's extended narrative interjection answers a demand to justify life, it does so precisely by not justifying it. The aesthetic response to this other scene, rather than redeeming the 'sordid life' of the Tullivers and Dodsons, becomes a biological perspective on the species: a mass of mere existence obliterated by meaningless catastrophes, rarely rising to the level of history. The narrator admits to 'a cruel conviction' that 'the lives these ruins are traces of were part of a gross sum of obscure vitality, that will be swept into the same oblivion with the generations of ants and beavers' (283). While Eliot's 'The Natural History of German Life' rejected the Gradgrindian notion 'that the relations of men to their neighbours may be settled by algebraic equations', she is not so far from treating population in those terms here, where human existence awaits its value without the aid of mathematics.[26]

A particular sense of life's socio-economic status and its potential calculability lies at the back of these reflections, captured unnervingly in the narrator's consciousness of a 'gross sum of obscure vitality'. This phrase voices the statistical premise of the *Essay on Population*, which insisted on a perpetual imbalance between human numbers and their allotted resources, with permanent inequality as its result. Lest we imagine such misanthropy is unique to this text, the Malthusian formula is only the plainest articulation of the normal governing logic of political economy, for which life becomes waste material, 'ugly' and 'grovelling', once it cannot be instrumentalised. Even remote history, as is clear in that passage from Eliot's novel, looks different through the grid of human life's economic functionalisation. This is the framework in which Eliot's scenes of destruction take on their narrative logic. If the flood that swallows Maggie and Tom is a sequel to this scene of mass death, it is also hinged on the spectre of excessive life that these ruins metonymise but fail to dignify.

There is, of course, a way of accounting for such seemingly random catastrophes as the flash flood that cuts short the life story. What looks like the essential unpredictability of nature becomes, via Malthus, part of a regulatory system intrinsic to the natural order. The *Essay on Population* made seemingly random events – bad harvests, epidemics and so forth – into semi-predictable patterns that operate to keep human numbers from exceeding their allotted resources. This is a prime example of what Ian Hacking calls the taming of chance: the making of statistical laws of probability that undercut determinism while also resisting the merely random. That view allowed Malthus to see the most disastrous forms of chance, paradoxically, as having a telos: checks built into the natural order, which of course follows the laws of political economy.

Is this appeal to nature's self-regulatory techniques, then, the logic of necessity that drives the novel? I would argue otherwise. In fact, it is just this mode of reasoning – co-opting chance as destiny – that the plot invalidates. Eliot shows just what interests profit by making unforeseen circumstance into an excuse for wilful inaction: Stephen Guest, the son of a wealthy industrialist, uses it to his advantage as he and Maggie (whose cousin Lucy he is engaged to marry) row a great distance down the river when unexpectedly left alone together. Putting down the oars as they drift down the Floss, Stephen exclaims, 'See Maggie, how everything has come without our seeking [. . .] See how the tide is carrying us out' (485). His cessation of action calls attention to itself, qualifying his words; while the current may bear them along without any effort, he has been actively rowing according to his own wishes, taking advantage of Maggie's characteristic 'fits of absence'. Stephen's reading of the river's flow lets him off the hook by placing agency outside him in the realm of natural phenomena with their own vectors and velocities. He takes it as proof that some combination of natural law and chance (the pull of the current, the compulsive force of sexual instinct, and propitious circumstances) has won out over his and Maggie's social obligations, and that this outcome justifies itself.

Eliot has a name for such reasoning, though it is not stated here: this is egoism in its purest form. Anticipating Bulstrode in *Middlemarch*, who can convince himself that the universe is providentially arranged to fulfil his most self-serving wishes, Stephen reads circumstances as conspiring to yield the result he wants, proving his elopement with Maggie is 'the only right thing' and that 'everything has concurred to point it out to us' (485). This sense of his own centrality to events – his sense of *protagonism*, we might as well say – is symptomatic of those egocentric pattern-making tendencies at the heart of narrative itself. Audrey Jaffe has attested to this in a talk on Hardy: 'In realist narrative, [the] ability to find in a series of random events a pattern out of which a character's life story emerges signals the subject's primacy: the realist subject, his majesty the ego, is [. . .] the one for whom all random events have meaning.'[27] Stephen, taking himself as the subject favoured by chance, and giving his own life biographical form, seems to mistake his significance not just to the cosmos but also to this plot – latecomer and 'Guest' that he is. (Indeed, his belated entry into the story on which his presence has such outsized effects masterfully aligns his formal role to his social impact.) But in placing himself alongside Maggie at the centre of those events in the novel's plot that most pointedly invite interpretation, he is merely following our own standard reading practice: constellating meaning around an individual subject. Maggie rejects Stephen's justification, and rejects desire, though her choice does not save her.[28] On the one hand, it is difficult not to recall that picture of the woman being drowned to test whether she is a witch: damned if you do, damned if you don't. On the other hand, Maggie's subsequent death reminds us that no individual is the chosen subject of chance turned into destiny. And it does so by showing that the position of protagonist – however symbolically central – can be the most hazardous in the novel.

Here, Rancière's claim that 'anything can happen to anyone' takes on peculiar resonance.[29] This claim binds together, even in disconnecting, the problem of character and that of plot. It is not just that the novel's subjects and their ways of speaking and being must be unbound from any automatic correlation to an assigned social place; the abolition of representational hierarchy also requires the perceived logic of events to come apart. Eliot's plots indeed untether the course of a life from destiny in the strict sense. Narrative may insist on some essential relation between the proairetic and the hermeneutic, but that relation never quite does away with contingency. It is not that things couldn't be otherwise; it's just that they weren't. Such rationality is not quite emancipating; indeed, it creeps toward a certain nihilism that seems uncharacteristic of Eliot. Perhaps, the story suggests, we have simply failed to learn what Rancière calls the devil's lesson: that life is without rhyme or reason.

This is not to suggest that Eliot surrenders all agency to the seemingly random force of nature, giving up on history and giving way to narrative laissez-faire. The Floss itself channels the contingency of natural and social causes. History can alter the course of a river, as we see, and a river, in turn, can swallow 'the grand historic life of humanity' (283) as well as its lesser forms. Maggie's and Tom's deaths occur at the junction of two causes: natural disaster (the flood itself) and the collision of bodies against a distinctly social object (the floating fragments of industrial machinery used to retrofit the mill to the new demands of steam power – those blunt historical facts that crash against and capsize the siblings' little boat). History is, indeed, what hurts. It disproves Mr Tulliver's favourite tautology that 'water is water' and 'a river's a river' – the sole argument of his suit against the neighbour who diverts this power source from Dorlcote Mill. Water is not just water; it is also a commodity, and the Floss is a conduit to national and imperial commerce whose flux uproots the mill and the home. Tulliver's formula fails to grasp the practical challenge he faces: the capitalist valuation process, which makes the commodity a middle term between money and more money, ensures that x never simply equals x. If we blame Maggie's death on machinery, then, the novel's heroine becomes a casualty of the developmental forces of modernity (personified in Stephen, the arriviste whose erotic magnetism, like his fortune, is industrially produced).[30] But as the flood-marks on the town's local structures reveal, what we are seeing is not just some external social force eroding, as the pastor Dr Kenn says elegiacally, all 'obligation which has its roots in the past'. The sleepy archaism of St. Ogg's is deceptive, as Eliot hints early on: 'the present time was like the level plain where men lose their belief in volcanoes and earthquakes, thinking [. . .] the giant forces that used to shake the earth have been laid to sleep.' The past appears as a physical record of cataclysmic events, and the comfort of tradition mobilises destructive forces of its own.

If we see the scientific subtext of this appeal to geological consciousness – the loss of belief in volcanoes and earthquakes as a gauge of false security – we should also see its political stakes. These figures of natural disaster write the novel's historical span into the debates between uniformitarianism and catastrophism that were largely concluded by the time of the novel's publication. The reminder of those sudden, catastrophic events through which Georges Cuvier had argued life forms went extinct unsettles the more gradualist and progressive story of change that had come to displace it. In placing social history in the timespan of geological change, Eliot is not just making scientific knowledge into a historical and political metaphor. The vocabularies of geology and of politics are so intertwined from the start that Cuvier called volcanic eruptions 'revolutions' – and his theory of sudden change affirms a vision of history in which continuity can be ruptured by radical transformation. Eliot makes geological tremors palpable in persons as well as environments: even during Maggie's devotional phase, we are told, some 'volcanic upheavals of imprisoned passions' are perceptible just beneath the surface of her outward tranquillity (306), and conversations between characters rise to emotional 'flood-marks which are never reached again' (349). Even on the small temporal scale of Maggie's own development, organic processes are similarly unsettling; the naturalising idiom of germination and growth gets transmuted into a sign of rupture and discontinuity: 'a girl', we're told, may 'hold forces within her as the living plant-seed does, which will make a way for themselves, often in a shattering, violent manner' (247).

With this in mind, it is not so clear that Eliot's fiction, as Jameson argues in *Antinomies of Realism*, follows a single 'ideological intent [. . .] to affirm historical continuity (as against the radical breaks of modernity)', or that realism in general, as he once argued, is 'threatened by any suggestion that the world is not natural, but historical, and subject to radical change'.[31] Nature and history are not either/or propositions. And the slow, meliorist version of history we later see in *Middlemarch*, in which everything moves imperceptibly toward organic integration and 'the growing good of the world', looks far less stable in *The Mill on the Floss*. Contra its narrator's own claim to trace, in the dilatory time of development, 'the onward tendency of human things', this is a novel in which change happens violently (284). Instead of naturalising its social world as a stable mimetic object, Eliot's novel fractures any organic continuity in the succession of events.

For Jameson, the 'great flood that sweeps away the protagonists of *The Mill on the Floss*' is symptomatic of realism's need to kill its darlings, and ultimately to kill realism itself. The entire narrative project of realism lies on the dialectical fault line between 'destiny' and 'the eternal present', its plot holding open an imagined space between 'the irrevocable time of the event' and the demand for 'an open, undecided future'.[32] That dialectic is indeed essential to the novel form. But *The Mill on the Floss* might demand a different reading. Its temporality decouples realism from the ideological ends we usually see it as serving: plotting life in developmental time, integrating characters into a continuous organic community, and, in the *Bildungsroman*, mapping a fantasy form of national history onto the individual's coming of age. What is unsettling about this novel is not the ordinariness of its characters; it is that the plot gives up its fidelity to character. Life cannot solve the problem of Maggie Tulliver except by adding her to 'that gross sum of obscure vitality'. Attached as this text is to its protagonist, it simply cannot allow that attachment to dictate the logic of events. The novel's narrativity, its sequencing of events into plot, is on the one hand formally necessary and, on the other, undone by the demands of realism itself, which refuses to grant any individual the privilege of being the subject through whom time becomes meaning.

Notes

1. William Dean Howells, *Heroines of Fiction*, vol. 2 (New York: Harper, 1903), 53.

2. John Ruskin, 'Fiction, Fair and Foul', part 5, in *The Works of John Ruskin*, vol. 34, ed. E. T. Cook and Alexander Wedderburn (London: Allen, 1908), 377 (370–94).
3. Jacques Rancière, 'Why Emma Bovary Had To Be Killed', *Critical Inquiry*, 34 (2008), 233–48.
4. George Eliot, *The Mill on the Floss* (London: Penguin, 2003), 298. All page references in this chapter are to this edition.
5. Rancière, 'The Putting to Death of Emma Bovary: Literature, Democracy and Medicine', in *The Politics of Literature*, trans. Julie Rose (Cambridge: Polity, 2011), 59 (49–71).
6. For a contrasting view, see Auerbach, who suggests that Flaubert's mode of writing is not truly free indirect discourse because the narration – rather than merging seamlessly with the thoughts of the character – frequently expresses Emma's thoughts in terms that are beyond her powers of reflection or articulation. Where Rancière sees an essentially de-hierarchising process and a depersonalisation of narration in this novel's form, Auerbach sees a consistent divide between the acuity of Flaubert's narrative perspective and the 'stupidity' of the character and her world. Erich Auerbach, 'On the Serious Imitation of the Everyday', in Gustave Flaubert, *Madame Bovary*, Norton Critical Edition, ed. Margaret Cohen (New York: Norton, 2005), 430 (423–49).
7. Rancière, *The Politics of Literature*, 156.
8. See especially Franco Moretti, *The Way of the World: The Bildungsroman in European Culture* (London: Verso, 2000), 15–73.
9. See Rancière, *The Flesh of Words: The Politics of Writing*, trans. Charlotte Mandell (Stanford: Stanford University Press, 2004), 83. Cf. Jameson's claim that the novel, owing to its heterogeneity, 'is the end of genre'; Fredric Jameson, *The Political Unconscious: Narrative as a Socially Symbolic Act* (Ithaca: Cornell University Press, 1981), 151. For Jameson, unlike Rancière, this internal multiplicity has an ideological character; it is the outcome of the novel's effort to process the residue of other (sometimes obsolete) narrative forms, to mediate and 'harmonize heterogeneous narrative paradigms which have their own specific and contradictory ideological meaning' (144). This 'formal sedimentation', argues Jameson, is the novel's way of safely containing, reconciling, and thus effectively neutralising the political possibilities of all existing forms (140). Rancière approaches this sedimentation with less essential suspicion.
10. See especially Auerbach, 'On the Serious Imitation of the Everyday', and Georg Lukács, 'Narrate or Describe?', in *Writer and Critic,*

and Other Essays, ed. and trans. Arthur D. Kahn (New York: Grosset, 1970), 110–48. In rejecting a mimetic account of realism, Rancière perhaps implicitly returns to Tzvetan Todorov's formalist understanding of fiction as constructing rather than imitating a real world; see especially *Genres in Discourse*, trans. Catherine Porter (Cambridge: Cambridge University Press, 1990), 39.
11. Contrast, for example, Lukács's tart dismissal of *Madame Bovary*'s failed realism: 'Flaubert confused life with the everyday existence of the ordinary bourgeois.' Lukács, 'Narrate or Describe?', 125.
12. Jameson, *The Political Unconscious*, 152.
13. Jameson, *Antinomies of Realism* (London: Verso, 2013), 145.
14. Alex Woloch, *The One vs. the Many: Minor Characters and the Space of the Protagonist in the Novel* (Princeton: Princeton University Press, 2003), 31.
15. Rancière cites Armand de Pontmartin's attack on Edmond About and Flaubert as an example of this reaction, which he diagnoses as a response to the aesthetic interruption of social hierarchy: 'A tide of beings and things, a tide of superfluous bodies, floods the novel,' writes Rancière; and critics who objected to it were not wrong to feel its political charge: 'This tide, for Pontmartin and his ilk [. . .] is called democracy.' *The Politics of Literature*, 39.
16. Ruskin, 'Fiction, Fair and Foul', 156.
17. See, for example, U. C. Knoepflmacher, *George Eliot's Early Novels: The Limits of Realism* (Berkeley: University of California Press, 1968), 237–9; cf. Jameson, *Antinomies of Realism*, 154–62. Knoepflmacher complains, even while acknowledging multiple explanations for Maggie's death, that the sudden deluge nonetheless seems 'capricious and unjust' (238). To his reasoning, 'freedom and accident [. . .] are irrevocably at odds' in this novel (239). Jameson, by contrast, finds Eliot's denouement fatalistic rather than accidental, so that even natural disasters look less like organic processes than melodramatic stagecraft in the service of an overdetermined meaning.
18. Rancière, 'Fictions of Time', in this volume, 34.
19. See Rancière, 'Why Emma Bovary Had To Be Killed', 241; 'The Putting to Death of Emma Bovary', 61.
20. Peter Brooks, *Reading for the Plot: Design and Intention in Narrative* (Cambridge, MA: Harvard University Press, 1992), 10.
21. Rancière, 'Fictions of Time', this volume, 28.
22. Brooks, *Reading for the Plot*, 23.
23. Ibid., 29.

24. Lukács, 'Narrate or Describe?', 112.
25. Brooks, *Reading for the Plot*, 22.
26. See Eliot, 'The Natural History of German Life', in *George Eliot: Selected Critical Writings*, ed. Rosemary Ashton (Oxford: Oxford University Press, 1992), 260–95.
27. Audrey Jaffe, 'Half and Half in Casterbridge', American Comparative Literature Association, University of Washington, Sheraton Hotel, Seattle, 27 March 2015, 7.
28. Here, my reading differs from Sara Ahmed's, which intriguingly aligns Maggie's 'wilfulness' with the broader problem of character in Eliot's novel; Ahmed suggests that the protagonist's characterisation as 'wilful' (by her family and by readers) becomes an instance of the injustice of attribution. As against this strain of ascribed wilfulness, however, the novel notably places Maggie in a situation with Stephen in which her lack of conscious will exposes her to social danger, and it further shows that her subsequent assertion of will (toward renunciation rather than the pursuit of pleasure) makes no difference to the end she meets. See Ahmed, 'Willful Parts: Problem Characters or the Problem of Character', *New Literary History*, 42 (2011), 231–53.
29. Rancière, *The Politics of Literature*, 156.
30. Such an explanation, however, does not account for the death of her brother, who has dutifully followed the adaptive demands of industrialisation and of the *Bildungsroman*, slowing working to master the vocational skills that allow him to succeed within a newly industrialised money economy.
31. Jameson, *Antinomies of Realism*, 120; *The Political Unconscious*, 193.
32. Jameson, *Antinomies of Realism*, 161, 18.

9

The Meaning in the Detail: Literature and the Detritus of the Nineteenth Century in Jacques Rancière and Walter Benjamin

Alison Ross

Notwithstanding the critical remarks Jacques Rancière occasionally makes about Walter Benjamin,[1] a number of commentators have pointed to parallels between the two thinkers. In general, these parallels focus on their evidently shared sceptical attitude to the approaches of the social sciences (Rancière) or historicism (Benjamin) to history. Kristin Ross, for instance, argues that Benjamin and Rancière share the motivation 'to blast [...] "a unique experience of the past" out of the "continuum of history" for the purpose of wresting meaning from the past for the present'.[2] Similarly, Hayden White writes that in his book *The Names of History* 'Rancière takes up arms on behalf of Walter Benjamin's idea that the story of the victors must be balanced, even supplanted, by the story of the vanquished, the abject and the downcast of history.'[3]

It is true that each thinker pursues an approach to 'the past' which aims to rescue the possibilities of past revolutionary energies. The premise of the approach is that historicist practices of truth strip the past of its actuality in the present. For Benjamin, the counter term to the closure of history in 'the past' is theology, whereas for Rancière it is the literary, itself understood as the disavowed part of the practice of historical writing. In each case the supposedly insignificant refuse of the nineteenth century is called upon to support the position. Benjamin credits the nineteenth century's refuse with epistemological significance for history. Rancière, on the other hand, draws attention to the logic that governs the way such refuse can claim a noticeable position. He argues that the focus on refuse is one facet of the general interest in hitherto unimportant social, natural and institutional details in nineteenth-century literature. According to him, this literary 'aesthetic revolution' underpins and precedes the 'social revolution'.[4] The distinction between these positions is telling.

The first position leads to a messianic theory of history, which contemplates the idea that each moment of the past be restored to significance. Ultimately, it is this thesis of 'fulfilled' or 'redeemed' time that constitutes Benjamin's distinctive conception of revolution. In 'On the Concept of History' Benjamin writes:

> The chronicler who narrates events without distinguishing between major and minor ones acts in accord with the following truth: nothing that has ever happened should be regarded as lost to history. Of course only a redeemed mankind is granted the fullness of its past – which is to say, only for a redeemed mankind has its past become citable in all its moments. Each moment it has lived becomes a citation *à l'ordre du jour*. And that day is Judgment Day.[5]

The second focuses instead on the literary pedigree of the realisation of the possibility that what had seemed obscure or obsolete might shift into the foreground. Since it puts forward an explanation for the significance of the refuse to which Benjamin grants epistemological probity, Rancière's position should be able to account for Benjamin's strategy. However, the positions are ultimately irreconcilable: Benjamin's position on the nineteenth century is based in his commitment to a quasi-Hegelian idea of historical truth, which does not belong to the same conceptual universe as Rancière's emphasis on the historical contingency of what at any given moment commands attention.

The irreconcilability has its source in their respective conceptions of language. In his early 1916 essay on language Benjamin attacks the theory of conventional meaning as 'bourgeois', defending instead the Adamic conception of naming language as an eminently cognitive relation to the essence of things. The relation between language and knowledge is guaranteed by 'the creative word of God'.[6] In contrast, the core of Rancière's position stems from his insistence on the merely conventional basis of language use. The conventional basis of the meanings assigned to words, which is ultimately tested in their capacity for effective communication, fuels his contention that any regime of perception is susceptible to fundamental alteration. The position is explicitly critical of the way claims to 'knowledge' endorse established regimes of perception. The various critical remarks Rancière makes of Benjamin may all be located in this general framework: he holds Benjamin's treatment of the commodity form to be a treatment of the literary commodity housed in the shops depicted in Balzac's novels[7] and he contends elsewhere that the meaning Benjamin ascribes to the nineteenth-century commodity form is reducible to the 'arbitrary position of the interpreter'.[8] Together, these remarks amount to the following position: Benjamin's claims regarding the refuse of history are not, as he believes, epistemologically grounded, but instead consist in an interpretation of the idea of the commodity that is communicated in nineteenth-century French literature. The critical intervention against the aesthetic, semblance properties of the commodity form that Benjamin makes is bound by the modern literary conception of truth and its practices of determining the inclusion of objects that warrant literary treatment. It might be objected that the criticisms Rancière makes about the literary horizon of Benjamin's position on the commodity do not stick. After all, the argument that the strategy of attending to the detail of old commodities was first deployed in a literary context does not amount to perpetual literary ownership of the strategy.[9] Despite Rancière's dissatisfaction with Benjamin's position, I will argue here that their shared fascination with the presumed meaningfulness of various types of detritus from the nineteenth century is worth scrutiny, especially since in each thinker these forms may carry, as part of the claim regarding their collective significance, motivational capacity. The respective position each takes on this nest of issues can be framed in relation to their incompatible assumptions regarding the relevance of modern literature for emancipatory practices.

This chapter has three main parts: first, I set out the problem of the literary communication of meaning through a comparative analysis of these writers' inclusive epistemologies of aesthetic form; next, I consider the different implications that each attaches to the presumed meaningfulness of the detritus of the nineteenth century; and finally, I examine the specific mechanisms that grant to refuse and detritus the status of a collective truth-telling position. The general point I wish to highlight is the discrepant implications of their respective treatment of the assumption that discarded refuse from the past can communicate complicated meanings. There are technical questions to consider here: among them, how are seemingly random instances of refuse and detritus from the nineteenth century able to cross the threshold from their status as merely incidental elements of the past into sites able to communicate vital meanings in the present? If there is no a priori feature that warrants this communicability, what is the principle of selection under which refuse is able to convey meaning? Examining such questions can help to elucidate whether, as many commentators have asserted in passing, there are important points of affinity between these two thinkers' approaches to history. Or do their different perspectives on the significance of literary innovations in the nineteenth century undermine the premise of such comparisons?

The literary communication of detail

Historical studies of modern literature point to the unrestrained principle of potential relevance that comes to the fore in nineteenth-century literature. Against earlier aesthetic practices in which style was aligned to topic, modern literature witnesses an explosion in what topics may be treated and how they may be written about. The earlier strict hierarchy in which depictions of noble action required poetic treatment and ordinary life was treated in the low genre of comedy loses its hold. With the erosion of the conventions underpinning the hierarchy of *belles lettres*, serious literary attention may be conferred on anything at all. The detail of the shift in aesthetic convention that occurs with the modern European novel has been systematically treated in various places.[10] Rancière, who considers this shift to be an 'aesthetic revolution', does not offer another such treatment. Rather, in his conception of the 'aesthetic regime of the arts' he endorses what he considers to be the egalitarian implications of the shift. He also argues that the writers who did so much to prompt and install the shift in how and on what aesthetic value is conferred often attempt to block the evidence of the contingency of social order that their writing had done so much to uncover. Rancière's focus falls on modern literature because he is interested in the literary articulation of political ideals like democracy and equality that emerge in the era of modern revolutions. For instance, he argues that Gustave Flaubert's principle that 'style is an absolute way of looking at things' enables him to treat the mediocre affairs of a farm girl in *Madame Bovary*. However, he also argues that this famous character's literary suicide would more accurately be seen as an act in which the author 'kills' her. Flaubert had Emma Bovary put to death for her arrogant presumption that despite being a mere farm girl, she could claim to exercise her aesthetic taste and that the territory of such taste was not 'fine art' but the design of the mundane features of her life and surroundings, such as ensuring that matching vases adorn the mantelpiece. Rancière comments:

> literature means to her a nice blotting pad and an artistic writing case. Art in her life means nice curtains on her windows, paper sconces for the candles, trinkets for her watch, a pair of blue vases on the mantelpiece, an ivory work box with a silver gilt thimble, and so on.
>
> Such is the disease that the pure artist wants to display as the contrary of his art. We can give it its name: the aestheticization of everyday life. The expression does not yet exist at that time for sure. But the concern does. [. . .] Flaubert already deals with what Adorno will spell out as the problem of kitsch. Kitsch does not mean bad art, outmoded art. It is true that the kind of art which is available to the poor people is in general the one that the aesthetes have already rejected. But the problem lies deeper. Kitsch in fact means art incorporated into anybody's life, art become part of the scenery and the furnishings of everyday life. In that respect, *Madame Bovary* is the first antikitsch manifesto.[11]

Although he argues that Flaubert's anti-egalitarian orientation is discernible in his narrative choices, the general premise of Rancière's position on the 'aesthetic revolution' of nineteenth-century literature is that the political commitments of authors are irrelevant for assessing the politics of the literature attached to their name. In 'The Politics of Literature' he recounts the different political evaluations of Flaubert's work. Despite Flaubert's famous indifference towards politics, the immediate reception of his work held it to be dangerously democratic. This judgement is contrasted with the criticism of a raft of twentieth-century critics like Sartre that its ethos is elitist. For Rancière, none of these characterisations adequately captures the democratic political field, which the style deployed in Flaubert's corpus opens up, or the premise of equality that shapes his selection of topics and themes. Crucially, the political field that his choice of topic and style puts in play renders Flaubert's indifference to politics otiose and exceeds therefore the hold of authorial 'intention'. Hence Rancière insists that the politics of literature has nothing to do with the politics of writers.[12] Indeed, how could it when Flaubert's corpus is the basis of such mutually incompatible positions regarding the politics it supposedly expresses? The politics of literature is not about the expression of an author's political views. It is about the way words partition the sensible, the way that the democratic use of words makes visible new ways of experiencing the heterogeneous field of sensibility. This field is unmarked in the sense that nothing claims attention or stands out against other elements that would be in the background. It becomes marked once aspects of it are selected for literary description. As such, Rancière's focus falls on the new distribution of the sensible that is opened up in nineteenth-century literature. This new distribution has a direct impact on the semantic integrity of the category of literature.

To stay with the example of Flaubert, Rancière argues that the depiction of micro-sensations in his writing aligns him to the democratic 'aesthetic revolution'. Spinoza had attempted the dissolution of the world into atoms. Flaubert gives idiosyncratic Spinozist voice to the micro-world of feeling around his characters. In doing so he shows that one consequence of the dissolution of the hierarchy of *belles lettres* is the tenuous nature of the category of 'literature'. The entry of prosaic worlds and words into 'literature' undermines the clarity of the distinction between the autonomous field of literary production and the merely prosaic world. With the emergence of topics like 'dust' as appropriate for capture in literary style the literary field is altered and the constitutive features of its definition undergo a fundamental challenge. As we will see, the challenge also affects the constitution of other disciplinary practices; it brings, for instance, literary technique to the heart of the practice of history. The point that interests me here is that this alteration of the literary field is signalled, in large part, by the advent of the realisation that if anything at all is susceptible to literary representation, anything at all can be made into a vehicle for meaningful experience. This 'literary' point is also one of the drivers of the shift in nineteenth-century historical writing to the interest in capturing the historical significance of prosaic features of life, like Jules Michelet's poetic descriptions of the mud in the French villages. In the case of Flaubert, the mechanism able to confer significance on the detritus of life is 'style' but its method seems to be the indirect communication of meaning. Hence Rancière claims that Flaubert's description of micro-sensations is used to depict how characters fall in love:

> When Emma falls for Rodolphe, she perceives little gleams of gold about his pupils, smells a perfume of lemon and vanilla, and looks at

the long plume of dust raised by the stagecoach. And when she first falls for Leon, 'weeds streamed out in the limpid water like green wigs tossed away. Now and then some fine-legged insects alighted on the tip of a reed or crawled over a water-lily leaf. The sunshine darted its rays through the little blue bubbles on the wavelets that kept forming and breaking.' This is what happens: 'little blue bubbles' on wavelets in the sunshine, or swirls of dust raised by the wind. This is what the characters feel and what makes them happy: a pure flood of sensations.[13]

In this description of Flaubert, Rancière's focus is on the way that, in their literary treatment, ephemera become meaningful. In this particular case, the literary description of ephemera gives indirect expression to the feeling of love experienced by the characters. In their capacity to communicate literary meaning in this manner such ephemera also contribute to a new, general schema of meaning that has the potential to unravel the fabric of social convention. In this regard, Flaubert's description of the microsensations of his characters' feelings uses a democratic sensibility regarding what is relevant for the literary communication of meaning. His choices foreground what, from the perspective of *belles lettres*, would have been considered unimportant material and topics. Despite Flaubert's intended indifference to politics, his attention to the nascent realm of disordered sensation is what, on Rancière's account, uncovers the truth of contingency that underpins the various forms of social order. The literary depiction of this realm of sensation as meaningful is eloquent testimony for the thesis regarding the contingency of social order. For Rancière, modern literature puts in play new common worlds moulded from this nascent realm of sensation, as well as freeing up the capacities of the bodies that inhabit them.

This cluster of themes receives a pointedly different treatment in Benjamin's writing on literature. In his famous essay 'The Storyteller: Reflections on the Works of Nikolai Leskov', as well as his various discussions of Marcel Proust and Charles Baudelaire, Benjamin is interested in the way modern literary genres, such as the novel, relate to the depleted conditions of access to collective meaning, or tradition. The emphasis in Benjamin's position across these pieces varies. In the essay on the storyteller the diagnosis of the modern novel as a type of writing produced in isolation and devoured in solitude is shaped by the nostalgic evocation of a pre-modern past. The novel is the only form of prose literature completely cut off from the oral tradition. The 'birthplace of the novel is the individual in his isolation', and it addresses another isolated individual, the reader.[14] According to Benjamin, the storyteller imparted practical wisdom, which was absorbed in a state of distraction as his listeners pursued other activities, such as weaving, in the background. A similar set of concerns also frame his various discussions of Proust. In the 1929 essay 'The Image of Proust', the novelist is praised for the way he contends with the difficulty modern deracinated life presents for experience (*Erfahrung*), understood as tradition. The significance of Proust's extraordinary autobiographical novel *In Search of Lost Time* can be located here: on the one hand, Proust's writing attempts to evoke the conditions for the 'recollection' of his childhood; on the other, his novel synthetically constructs the conditions necessary for experience, which is manifest in the picture he provides for the reader of an epoch in which those conditions are unravelling. Ultimately, however, it is telling that Proust describes an experience of personal, rather than collective, memory. I will return to this point below. Although the approach and prominent themes in Benjamin's late discussions of literature are not at all compatible with Rancière's diagnostic analysis of modern literature as part of the modern framework of social revolution, there are points of affinity between Rancière's approach to the changing specifications of literary meaning and the structure of Benjamin's epistemology across his corpus. Furthermore, the concern with the conditions for the communication of shared meaning is a feature of Benjamin's epistemology and his writing on literature, although each of these contexts gives the topic distinct inflections.

In his late work on history, Benjamin defends a quasi-Hegelian conception of historical truth. Historical moments are able to bear truth and specific historical moments can be said to embody absolute truths. Hence in his *Arcades Project* Benjamin argues that the nineteenth century bears the truth of human history per se. His approach to history is anchored in the contrast between the merely 'arbitrary' selection of material that traditional historians comment on and discuss, and the idea that his collection of the detritus of the nineteenth century offers an 'essential' experience of truth.[15] The contrast is not merely rhetorical since it is supported by an array of concepts, amongst them the idea that there is a 'historical index' that points uniquely from the refuse of the nineteenth century to its 'redemption' or historical 'legibility' or 'readability' in the twentieth. What I would like to focus on here is that Benjamin extends the field of potential significance of things so that it includes the disused commodities, outmoded fashions and other 'refuse' of the nineteenth century, but that this generous principle of inclusion cleaves to the stated epistemological motivation of arriving at knowledge of the century. Unlike Rancière's analytic account of the principles of inclusion operative in nineteenth-century literature, which presupposes the relativity of the protocols governing what counts as art in the different regimes of the arts and highlights the specificity of the modern notion of significance as ubiquitous, in Benjamin's understanding truth is found specifically in extremity. The rubbish and detritus of the century do not figure in the history of the nineteenth century as new tests of style. They figure as the way to understand the truth of history and they do so against what his work calls 'semblance'. The universality of the claim is worth considering. In the famous preface to his *Trauerspiel* book he argues that '[t]he naked and manifest existence of the factual' is unable to reveal anything. Rather, the 'totality of its history' is the schema of revelation for an idea's truth.

> On the one hand [the origin] needs to be recognized as a process of restoration and re-establishment, but, on the other hand, and precisely because of this, as something imperfect and incomplete. There takes place in every original phenomenon a determination of the form in which an idea will constantly confront the historical world, until it is revealed fulfilled, in the totality of its history. Origin is not, therefore, discovered by the examination of actual findings, but it is related to their history and their subsequent development.[16]

In the *Arcades* the problem of 'fathoming an origin' is pursued in 'the origin of the forms and mutations of the Paris arcades from their beginning to their decline'.[17] Decay and ruin counter the false attractions of the semblance form; they become the sites of vital historical meaning and rightfully claim attention. In Benjamin's view what they show is 'truth', and he defines truth as an intention-less state.[18]

Unlike Rancière, who credits the nineteenth-century novel with loosening the organised paths of perception that order social reality in advance and claims that it does so by its elucidation in words of the speech of otherwise mute things, Benjamin is interested in the vitiated wishes of the past carried in the old commodities. He cites in support of his position the surrealist's view that vital 'political meanings' are communicated in 'outmoded' commodity forms, like fashion, or former icons of bourgeois life, like the grand piano.[19] Truth is thus intention-less because it is a feature of the materialist construction of historical detail, rather than a partial perspective on it. The experience of historical truth must bypass the limited perspective of an interpreter in order to have its collective purchase and claim. In this respect, the idea of historical truth that is deployed specifically aims to exceed the significance accorded to the retrieval of merely personal memory that is identified in Benjamin's discussion of Proust.

The ways historical detritus accrues significance

Rancière's contrast between the significance of will and action in what he calls the 'representative regime of the arts' and the dissolution of these in the 'aesthetic regime' is a relevant point of comparison here. According to the terms of the contrast, the will and action of heroic individuals belonged to the realm of the poetical, and prosaic life had its own sphere. It was noble action that was appropriate for poetic representation. When ordinary things enter the space of aesthetic significance with the aesthetic regime of the arts, so too does the problem of the technique to be used in poetic depictions of what is without will, narrative arc, or voice. Hence the perspective of Immanuel Kant's aesthetics on intention, which views its presence as a limiting factor on aesthetic judgement, is not relevant here. Kant had argued that the singular experience of nature's beauties had more significance than works of art because the former were not constrained by the mark of human intention and the distracting effort to trace its path in the exercise of aesthetic judgement.[20] Rancière is not opposing, as Kant did, the distorting effects of intentional human products on one side with pure beauty on the other; but tracking the implications of the presence of merely ordinary things within the aesthetic space that had been formerly reserved for noble topics. The position disregards the distinction between nature's phenomena and the products of history. In this framework, what is important is that these ordinary things are mute and without a noble narrative arc. Because these things are mute, they require literary evocation, but precisely because they are mute such evocation is never final. The traditional aesthetic question of intention has no stalling effect on the capacity of mute things to stimulate writing, or on the consequences of this capacity. Non-intentional phenomena such as dust swirling in the breeze, or sunlight falling on reeds in the river, as well as things that bear the traces of intention, like the decaying products of the old commodity forms, acquire their aesthetic significance through the same channel of indiscriminate democratic attention to anything, and with the same indeterminate effects.

Literary evocation stimulates new evocations of such things, and neither is the energy devoted to this perpetual attempt to capture mute surroundings restricted to the literary field. The mud in the French villages that Jules Michelet describes in his republican history is an object of literary-historical depiction. The sewers of Paris in Victor Hugo's novels and the shops in Balzac are also forms of 'mute speech', which conjure up the democratic sensibility of the nineteenth century.[21] Rancière wants to credit this revolution with opening up the possibility that worlds presumed to be passive, to be without the noble agents whose narrative arcs alone warrant poetic depiction, would come to alter the established settings of social communication. The route he takes to this point is historical since many of his studies use archival work to show that people presumed to be without intellectual competence thought and wrote, and claimed therefore the prerogatives of the leisured class despite not being free, as the members of this class were, from manual occupation.[22] Further, it is the way the past is written that gives rise to new constellations. This is the 'literary' core of 'history'.[23] What is striking in the comparison with Benjamin is that despite the epistemological questions at the heart of Rancière's study of the different regimes of the arts, his study of the aesthetic regime forecloses the question of how these things attract vital meaning in virtue of its default assumption that the meaning they bear, or the way they can wander into the foreground as an object of literary attention, is contingent. The emphasis is on the possibility of such rearrangement of 'foreground' and 'background' components. In this respect, although the indiscriminate entry of ordinary objects and people into literature promises a rough parallel to Benjamin's conception of truth as 'intention-less', it is not just without the epistemological aspiration of Benjamin's idea that truth resides in extremity, in the idea it defends of the contingency of social order, it also explicitly undermines the presumption that things bear articulable knowledge of history. The way he frames historical contingencies as potentially politically significant is precisely what motivates Rancière's position on intention. In other words, his political agenda mandates the redundancy of aesthetic intentions. The limiting foreground these intentions select have no purchase on the diverse potential of the meaning they assemble unawares, as Flaubert's example shows.

Viewed from this perspective, the disagreement between these authors regarding the salience of modern literature for the experience of collective meaning is at the nub of their respective approaches to history. Benjamin's contrast between rescuing the past through historical knowledge and Proustian, personal memory implies that literature is an insufficient vehicle for stimulating revolutionary motivation in the present. More pertinently, Benjamin complains about the limited horizons of the modern novel in the individual contexts of its production and reception; whereas Rancière endorses the communicative possibilities of literary interpretation as these exceed the peculiar intentions of the authorial voice. Literary interpretation is not, on this view, able to be entirely distinguished from 'real change', and it is able to exceed the authorial limitations or 'partiality' of its construction. Against the epistemological stipulations Benjamin places on the effective use of the past, recounting a story in an indirect, literary voice is Rancière's mode of practising motivating, historical recollection in the present.

Literature and the motivating perception of collective meanings from the past

In the first published English version of 'The Politics of Literature', Rancière claims that the scene in which Benjamin's *Arcades* is set is not the Paris arcades, but the shops of Balzac's novels.[24] It is the commodities in these 'literary' shops that drive Benjamin's use of the theory of the commodity fetish. Rancière argues in an earlier essay on Benjamin that the meaning attached to the commodities boils down to the arbitrary view of their interpreter.[25] In the revised version of 'The Politics of Literature', the specific claim about the shops in the Balzac novels as the scene for the *Arcades* is dropped.[26] However, he retains the general argument that interpreting a scene in a way that gives it new meaning is the literary mark of the modern. It is not things themselves, but the potential meaning they carry that is important. As we saw above, there is an ontological presupposition here: namely, that the field of heterogeneous sensibility is marked out with contingent meanings that do not in any way exhaust its possibilities. The reinterpretation of mute things in Michelet's poetic history or Hugo's novels is the background for the potential political significance of the 'aesthetic revolution'. However, the political outcomes of the nineteenth-century aesthetic revolution are tenuous. They are void when the revolution descends into an endless hermeneutics of mute 'things'. The potential emancipatory yield of 'mute speech' is the democratic ethos it installs such that what is in the background, or presumed to be passive and unremarkable, can speak and thereby show the contingency of the arrangement under which it was presumed to be inconsequential and thus silent. The assertion that Benjamin's take on the nineteenth century draws on a literary technique is not just a claim for the priority that literature has in providing the infrastructure of possibilities for the different critical 'theories' of modern politics. Nor is it a reductive claim about the literary components of historical writing. Its aim is more fundamental: it disputes the logic of the claim that literary 'interpretations' are politically ineffectual. The claim is relevant for assessing Rancière's style of writing. Rancière asserts, against the Marxist dictum that the point is not to interpret but to 'change the world', that 'interpretations are themselves real changes'.[27] The very cogency of the opposition between a 'real change' and a mere 'interpretation' is a hermeneutic 'plot' that was, he argues, uniquely articulated in modern literature. This plot has an afterlife in fields that deny the pertinence of the literary to social order. The point is made throughout Rancière's corpus.

Hence in *Disagreement* he looks at the retelling of the Aventine Hill secession. He emphasises not 'the original' act of secession, but the importance of Simon Ballanche's nineteenth-century retelling of the story. The modern reinterpretation of the slave rebellion intervenes in the revolutions of the early nineteenth century.[28] The literary space of word use – that is, their capacity to redefine meaning – has a practical dimension for the perception of order in social life. In this respect, when Rancière criticises Benjamin for imparting an arbitrary meaning to the old commodities, this need not be taken as a comprehensive rejection of the position. In fact, the effect of the criticism is to highlight that Benjamin is retelling a scene and not, as he presents it, providing us with knowledge of a past century's intention-less truth. This retelling can be evaluated, in Rancière's view, according to its capacity 'to transform the forms of visibility a common world may take, and with them, the capacities that ordinary bodies may exercise in that world over a new landscape of the common'.[29] His real criticism of Benjamin, therefore, is that his specific retelling locks the past in the past; his account of redemption is stultifying because it focuses on the potentially endless hermeneutic study of the things from the arcades, not the people who made them.[30] In this context the evocative activity of mute speech becomes what he calls 'metapolitics'; it becomes an endless speech that annuls the communicative acts pertinent for political shifts in perception. We might also say that the position ascribed to Benjamin is one that expunges the 'literary' dimension from 'history'. What is clear in this criticism is the conditional form of Rancière's endorsement of the tactic of imbuing the mute with speech in the aesthetic regime.[31]

On the other hand, it is reasonable to ask how the perception of new meanings comes about on Rancière's model of the retelling of the past. Once again the contrast between Rancière and Benjamin is instructive. Each has a distinct approach to the question of how the perception of 'collective truth' shapes motivation. And the position of literature in their respective accounts is once again a key marker for these differences.

Despite the general thrust of Benjamin's comments on historical truth, his conceptualisation of the collective truth of history is entirely dependent on the contingent way individuals arrive at meaningful comprehension of complex, counterfactual ideas. The perception of the idea that old commodities express the vitiated wishes of the nineteenth century for an emancipated life cannot, however, one assumes, be easily achieved for a mass of revolutionary agents leafing through the dossiers of the *Arcades*. The contingencies involved in the reception of the telling of past events and people are, in contrast, openly acknowledged in Rancière's literary-philosophical style. In *The Ignorant Schoolmaster*, for instance, he writes against the 'madmen [...] who want to be right'. And he counters that equality is not 'decreed' nor 'passively received', but takes place in an 'act, verified, at each step by those marchers who, in their constant attention to themselves and in their endless revolving around the truth, find the right sentences to make themselves understood by others'.[32] The truth 'revolved around' is collective insofar as it can be expressed intelligibly.

But since this truth breaks apart the false consensus that assumes 'equality' can be decreed, Rancière understands truth to stem from, and involve the communication to others of, an individual's experience of truth. Hence, 'equality in act' rather than 'decree' involves work on the self. Crucially the 'truth' involved here is existential: it is understood as the repudiation of the posture of mastery. For Rancière, it is how collective meaning is perceived, communicated and worked on at the level of the individual that counts.

This individual dimension would seem to be missing from Benjamin's *Arcades Project* given that his aspiration is to establish the legibility of the truth of the nineteenth century in the vital historical meaning carried by its detritus. Nonetheless, the project of historical legibility requires a recipient sensitive enough to decode the complex meaning this refuse conveys and to effectively communicate this to others. And Benjamin does attempt to accommodate the problem, even if his *Arcades Project* does not easily resolve it. Benjamin's starting point, after all, is that Marxist theory is too anaemic to convey motivation and what is needed is a way of making the meaning of history 'graphically perceptible', that is, experienceable for individuals.[33] The truth of history becomes meaningful *only* when it is experienced as such by an individual. In this respect, Benjamin's *Arcades Project* endorses the terms of his 'Storyteller' essay's contrast between the degraded communication involved in the relay of information in news reporting and the practical wisdom imparted by the storyteller. The positivist historians of the nineteenth century merely convey the past as 'information', Benjamin claims; the *Arcades*, in contrast, aims to instil knowledge of history able to claim collective veracity. Such veracity is loosely akin to the 'practical wisdom' the storyteller once shared with his listeners. The difficulty, as I mentioned above, is how this wisdom is arrived at.

To be sure, then, the word 'collective' is not reducible to the 'communicability' of meaning. Neither Benjamin nor Rancière considers mere communicability to be a sufficient threshold for collective significance to accrue its requisite value. For Benjamin information may communicate 'news' (the 'Storyteller' essay) or 'historical events' (*The Arcades Project*) but not in a way that compellingly addresses the experience of its recipient.[34] Hence the need for a materialist approach able to make history graphically perceptible is integral to the *Project*, even if its exact mechanisms remain vague. Similarly, the corollary of Rancière's view that politics consists in the alteration of the way sensibility, understood as the perceptible meaning of the common, is distributed is that such alteration is not merely a subjectively perceptible feature of a situation but that it occurs in a politically meaningful way only when its successful communication alters the distribution of roles in a social space.

It is here, I think, that the significance of Rancière's emphasis on literature can help to sharpen our appreciation of what is distinctive in his approach to the nineteenth century. Like Benjamin, Rancière's archival practice of history locates a deficit in historical writing when it provides explanations of events that circumvent the experience of participants in historical processes. Unlike Benjamin, whose approach to collective memory prioritises what is shared in tradition, Rancière works from the inverse proposition: his account is interested in what would make new meanings collectively understood, that is to say, what would make them effective. The absence of any filters in his treatment of what may be significant and how it may be significant is thus not merely a tactic that allows him to grasp the dynamics of the so-called aesthetic regime of the arts; it is also an expression of his openness to where political ruptures might occur. When the use of words in ways that challenge the prevailing distribution of the sensible reaches the threshold of 'politics', they do so because they communicate in a politically relevant way. But, like in Benjamin, there is a critical conception of the limits of intention that supports this position. What is significant for our purposes is that Rancière stages this conception in the literary style of his writing, and refutes therefore the association in Benjamin's discussions of Proust and the novel the idea of the limitation of modern literature to personal memory and isolated individual production and reception. Rancière refers in his discussion of the poetic historian Jules Michelet to the anonymous murmurings of history[35] and castigates historians who try to exclude the literary dimensions of their vocation; he also uses the free indirect style, which blurs the identification of a narrative voice in respect to the topic or views it represents.[36] When he resists the idea that the politics of literature can in any sense be reducible to the politics or intentions of the author, this is his way of protecting the possibilities of meaning that arise uniquely in nineteenth-century literature when background figures and objects move into the foreground as topics for poetic depiction. As we have seen, the suspension of the relevance of authorial 'intention' in Rancière's approach to the analysis of the aesthetic regime leaves us with a potentially infinite surge of material with no given principle of organisation. His position on the aesthetic regime thus contrasts with the role and purpose of detritus in Benjamin's theory of history. In Benjamin's case, the criticism of intention also holds for individual experience. He writes about the role that moods like distraction and boredom play in the acquisition of experience.[37] Experience (*Erfahrung*) arises from these non-intentional moods, and truth and knowledge are not the yield of intention but features of the historical process of decay. The evocation of meaning through subjective conditions like mood and style shows that each thinker prizes the relevance of the existentially gripping experience of meaning for motivation. This is the common feature of their approach to the past. Its most significant corollary is the way it entails a critical perspective on 'theories' of politics; they are inevitably futile exercises when they fail to address individuals' existential experience of meaning. It is because Rancière's approach depends on an avowedly literary style, however, that in his case even this critical point has a 'literary' basis. Rancière's writing does not outline a 'theory' of art, or literature, or politics; it is a literary exercise forged from and attempting to share with other intelligent beings an emphatic experience of meaning. This meaning is the repudiation of the posture of mastery, which he considers to be one legacy of the modern literary revolution in meaning. His upbraiding of Flaubert on the grounds that his intentions are irrelevant to the meaning of Emma Bovary's life has its basis in this perspective.

I have argued here that Benjamin and Rancière have irreconcilable perspectives on the significance of literary innovations in the nineteenth century. Their different assessments of the implications and meaning of nineteenth-century literary innovations are stark: Benjamin's epistemological approach to history is foreign to the ontological assumption that drives Rancière's interest in the literary attention lavished on hitherto ignored details of social life. It is Benjamin's insistence on historical knowledge that ultimately excludes the pertinence of literature from his project of stimulating revolutionary motivation through the recovered detritus of the century. In contrast, the avowedly literary perspective of Rancière's approach to history meets up with his analysis of the significance of nineteenth-century literature. The variability in topic and style of the latter is adopted as a case study and a strategy for how to subject the authority-bearing posture of 'theory' to scrutiny. Benjamin and Rancière each think that an epistemological proof of the past suffering of others is not sufficient to fuel motivation in the present. Individuals need to experience such meaning in order to act. Rancière thinks literary technique is some kind of answer to this problem. And this is because, in his view, when the past is given an epochal stature, we lose our capacity to focus on the potentially revelatory details of the here and now. In this sense the merely personal horizon of Proustian memory is not necessarily indicative, as Benjamin had thought, of the limitations of the modern novel form in the age of individualism, but a sign of its significance.

Notes

1. See Jacques Rancière, 'The Archaeomodern Turn', in M. P. Steinberg (ed.), *Walter Benjamin and the Demands of History* (Ithaca: Cornell University Press, 1996), 24–41.
2. Kristin Ross, introduction to Jacques Rancière, *The Ignorant Schoolmaster: Five Lessons in Intellectual Emancipation*, trans. Kristin Ross (Stanford: Stanford University Press, 1991), xxi (vii–xxiii). She goes on to ask about the writing practices that could 'allow an episode from the past to become an episode in the present' (xxi), and argues that storytelling, or recounting, is, in Rancière's writing, a practice of equality that fulfils his motivation to reset the present through an episode from the past (xxii). She also mentions the aversion to authority in his mode of writing voice, which is poetic and elusive. To contextualise this comparison, it should be noted that in Benjamin it is not any episode of the past that could become an episode in the present, but the nineteenth century that becomes uniquely legible in the twentieth; what he calls the 'historical index' (the nineteenth century) points forward to its redemption (in the twentieth). Further, he explicitly pits his practice of 'historical citation', in which the decay of history reveals the image as the ineradicable primal phenomenon of history, against 'storytelling', which is the privilege of the victors and which consigns past suffering to oblivion. See Walter Benjamin, *The Arcades Project*, trans. Howard Eiland and Kevin McLaughlin (Cambridge, MA: Belknap Press, 1999), 476 (N11, 4). Similar obstacles present themselves for the accuracy of the comparison on the question of the voice. Benjamin avoids the use of

the personal pronoun and writes as if he is describing how things are. Like other suggestions of an affinity in the literature, the parallel is suggestive, but does require qualification. Other places where the suggested connection between Rancière and Benjamin is made include Kevin Newmark, 'A Poetics of Sharing: Political Economy in a Prose Poem by Baudelaire', *Symposium: The Canadian Journal of Continental Philosophy*, 15:2 (2011), 57–81.

3. As mentioned in the previous note, White's use of 'story' to describe the restoration of the vanquished would require qualification as a position that could be ascribed to Benjamin. Hayden White, 'Foreword: Rancière's Revisionism', in Jacques Rancière, *The Names of History: On the Poetics of Historical Knowledge*, trans. Hassan Melehy (Minneapolis: University of Minnesota Press, 1994), vii–xix.

4. Rancière, *Aisthesis: Scenes from the Aesthetic Regime of Art*, trans. Zakir Paul (London and New York: Verso, 2013).

5. Walter Benjamin, 'On the Concept of History', in *Selected Writings, Vol. 4: 1938–1940*, ed. Howard Eiland and Michael W. Jennings, trans. Edmund Jephcott et al. (Cambridge, MA, and London: Belknap Press, 2003), 394 (389–401).

6. Benjamin, 'On Language as Such and on the Language of Man', trans. Edmund Jephcott, in *Selected Writings, Vol. 1: 1913–1926*, ed. Marcus Bullock and Michael W. Jennings (Cambridge, MA, and London: Belknap Press, 1996), 68 (62–75).

7. Rancière, 'The Politics of Literature', *Sub-Stance*, issue 103, 33:1, 20–1 (10–24).

8. Rancière, 'The Archaeomodern Turn', 37.

9. Rancière does not rest with the criticism of performative self-contradiction, however. He adds the objection that Benjamin entombs past revolutionary energies in the purism of the silent commodity form. The claim that the meaning attached to the commodity form is arbitrary is thus intended as a riposte both to Benjamin's epistemology and to the tone of pathos for what is lost that characterises his 'rescuing critique'. See Rancière, 'The Archaeomodern Turn', 38.

10. Erich Auerbach's *Mimesis: The Representation of Reality in Western Literature*, trans. Willard R. Trask (Princeton: Princeton University Press, 1953) is perhaps the most comprehensive account. Rancière disputes the pivotal role that Auerbach's account gives to scripture as the transition point from Homer to modern European literature, but he concurs with many other features of the account. See Rancière, *The Politics of Aesthetics*, trans. Gabriel Rockhill (London: Continuum, 2004), 59–69, and *The Flesh of Words: The*

Politics of Writing (Stanford: Stanford University Press, 2004), 74–7; see also Auerbach, *Mimesis*, 14–23. We could also mention here G. W. F. Hegel's prescient complaints about literary uses of irony in his *Aesthetics: Lectures on Fine Art*, vol. 1, trans. T. M. Knox (Oxford: Clarendon Press, 1998), 79–81. Hegel also deploys the terminology of the indifference about what is represented and how it is done that is used in Rancière's descriptions of the aesthetic regime of the arts. I have examined the relation between Rancière's 'aesthetic regime of the arts' and Hegel's analysis of the dissolution of romanticism in Alison Ross, 'Equality in the Romantic Art Form: The Hegelian Background to Jacques Rancière's Aesthetic Revolution', in J-P. Deranty and A. Ross (eds), *Jacques Rancière and the Contemporary Scene: The Philosophy of Radical Equality* (London and New York: Continuum, 2012), 87–99.
11. Rancière, 'Why Emma Bovary Had To Be Killed', *Critical Inquiry*, 34 (2008), 239–40 (233–48).
12. Rancière, 'The Politics of Literature', 10.
13. Rancière, 'Why Emma Bovary Had To Be Killed', 242.
14. Benjamin, 'The Storyteller: Reflections on the Works of Nikolai Leskov', in *Selected Writings, Vol. 3: 1935–1938*, ed. Howard Eiland and Michael W. Jennings, trans. Edmund Jephcott, Howard Eiland et al. (Cambridge, MA, and London: Belknap Press, 2002), 146 (143–67).
15. Benjamin, *The Arcades Project*, 475 (N10a, 1).
16. Benjamin, *The Origin of German Tragic Drama*, trans. John Osborne (London and New York: Verso, 2009), 45–6.
17. Benjamin, *The Arcades Project*, 462 (N2a, 4).
18. Benjamin, *The Origin of German Tragic Drama*, 36.
19. Benjamin, 'Surrealism: The Last Snapshot of the European Intelligentsia', in *Selected Writings, Vol. 2: 1927–1934*, ed. Michael W. Jennings, Howard Eiland and Gary Smith, trans. Rodney Livingstone et al. (Cambridge, MA, and London: Belknap Press, 1999), 207–22. Although Benjamin challenges the relevance of literature for political insights when he claims that the surrealists produce 'watchwords and slogans' but not 'literature' (208), important features of the perspective of his *Arcades Project* were nonetheless forged in his early essay on Goethe's novel *Elective Affinities*. In that superb example of literary criticism he makes it clear that he is pursuing the external perspective of truth in order to avoid the 'chaos' of captivation by material, sensuous form. This entails taking the vantage point of the novella in Goethe's novel against the mythic

perspective of the novel. See Benjamin, 'Goethe's *Elective Affinities*', in *Selected Writings, Vol. 1: 1913–1926*, 329 (297–361). A similar dependence on literary models characterises the evolution of his view on historical truth. As noted above, the theory of truth and the claims regarding the knowledge of history in his late work are adapted from his early preface to his study of the German mourning plays, *The Origin of German Tragic Drama*.

20. Immanuel Kant, *Critique of Judgment*, trans. W. S. Pluhar (Indianapolis: Hackett, 1987), §42, 166–7.
21. Rancière, *Mute Speech: Literature, Critical Theory, and Politics*, trans. James Swenson (New York: Columbia University Press, 2011), esp. 52–73.
22. Rancière, *The Nights of Labor: The Workers' Dream in Nineteenth-Century France*, trans. J. Drury (Philadelphia: Temple University Press, 1989). See also the 'literary' colour he gives to the title of this work when he comments that it contains a reference to the French translation of Shakespeare's *Twelfth Night* as *La Nuit des Rois*; Rancière, 'Work, Identity, Subject', in Deranty and Ross, *Jacques Rancière and the Contemporary Scene*, 206 (205–17).
23. Rancière, *The Names of History*, esp. 2 and 103.
24. Rancière, 'The Politics of Literature', 10–24.
25. Rancière, 'The Archaeomodern Turn', 24–41.
26. Rancière, 'The Politics of Literature', in *The Politics of Literature*, trans. Julie Rose (Cambridge: Polity Press, 2011), 3–31.
27. Ibid., 30.
28. He calls Ballanche's retelling 'retrospective prophecy' (51). Jacques Rancière, *Disagreement: Politics and Philosophy*, trans. Julie Rose (Minneapolis: University of Minnesota Press, 1998), 24–6, 50–1.
29. Rancière, 'The Politics of Literature', in *The Politics of Literature*, 30.
30. Rancière, 'The Archaeomodern Turn', 24–41.
31. Hayden White's 'Foreword: Rancière's Revisionism' misses just this point when he parses the anonymous murmurings of the people in Jules Michelet as if this were the object of Rancière's veneration (xvi). Rancière's attitude to this revolution is not just conditional, it is explicitly ambivalent – on the one hand, the anonymous are the ones who will speak, but on the other, their very presentation as vehicles of 'anonymous murmurings' of history which the historian brings to speech is the problem (Michelet, Rancière complains, does not cite the archives in which these people do speak). The point is made in a different context in Rancière's criticism of Benjamin's

alleged substitution of the analysis of commodities for labourers in 'The Archaeomodern Turn'. The displacement here is a silencing, no less than Michelet's oppressive poetics that speaks for others in the mode of the conditional; Rancière, *The Names of History*, 54.
32. Rancière, *The Ignorant Schoolmaster*, 72.
33. Benjamin, *The Arcades Project*, 460 (N1a, 6).
34. The references to the communication of information in the 'Storyteller' essay and the ideal of presenting 'history as it really was' in his *Arcades Project* can be found respectively in *Selected Writings, Vol. 3*, 147, and the *Arcades*, 463 (N3, 4).
35. Rancière, *The Names of History*, 56–7.
36. For instance in Rancière's *The Ignorant Schoolmaster* it is not clear whether and when it is Jacotot who speaks and when it is Rancière, or whether the narrative voice aims at an impersonal tone properly distinguished from either the author or the subject of his analysis. The lack of clarity is deliberate since the text is both a study of a practice of revolutionary emancipation (Jacotot) and an intervention in contemporary debates in France regarding educational reform (Rancière). This context is set out in Kristin Ross's introduction.
37. See on 'distraction' Benjamin, 'The Artwork in the Age of its Mechanical Reproducibility (third version)', in *Selected Writings, Vol. 4*, 264, and on 'boredom' 'The Storyteller', in *Selected Writings, Vol. 3*, 149.

III Contemporaneities

10

Ineluctable Modality of the Sensible: Poverty and Form in *Ulysses*

Julian Murphet

'His true Penelope was Flaubert'

Gustave Flaubert, Jacques Rancière's exemplary hero of the aesthetic regime, is also – despite Rancière's ongoing effort to use that example to dismantle the very thesis of literary modernity – one of the totemic figures in the critical establishment of modernism. Ezra Pound famously put it that modern poets have more to learn from the prose of Flaubert than from any other writer: 'I believe no man can now write really good verse unless he knows Stendhal and Flaubert. [...] To put it more strongly, he will learn more about the art of charging words from Flaubert from all the floribund sixteenth-century dramatists.'[1] Pound made telling claims for the art of James Joyce in similar terms: 'English prose catches up with Flaubert,' he said of Joyce's *Dubliners* (1914); and still more significantly he hailed *Ulysses* (1922) as 'the first [book] which, inheriting from Flaubert, continues the development of Flaubertian art from the point where he left it in his last unfinished book', *Bouvard et Pécuchet*.[2] Still further, Pound averred that 'Joyce has taken up the art of writing where Flaubert left it [...]; he has brought it to a degree of greater efficiency, of greater compactness; he has swallowed the *Tentation de St Antoine* whole, it serves as comparison for a single episode in *Ulysses*. *Ulysses* has more form than any novel of Flaubert's.'[3] This double insistence, on the superiority of form in *Ulysses* relative to Flaubert's work, and on its consummate extension of the last, unfinished Flaubertian experiment in *Bouvard et Pécuchet*, certainly requires some comment, since it flies in the face of a certain persistent orthodoxy regarding Joyce's masterpiece: that its central claim to critical recognition rests upon what Eliot identified as its discovery of the 'mythic method' – 'manipulating a continuous parallelism between contemporaneity and antiquity [. . .] a way of controlling, of ordering, of giving a shape and a significance to the immense panorama of futility and anarchy which is contemporary history'[4] – that Rancière himself has seen fit to echo in his only published reflection on Joyce.[5] If, however, in concert with a growing chorus of recent critical attention, *Ulysses* is perceived less as a testament to 'myth' and more along the lines of Pound's approbation, we may begin to make out some of the ways in which this 'modern epic' both exemplifies the aesthetic regime of the arts, and subjects its very conditions of possibility to a process of radical formal interrogation.[6] We may even see why Joyce was the most faithful of Flaubert's readers, precisely in his willingness to mutate the DNA of his prose.[7]

To be sure, Rancière emphatically declares that the condition of 'literature' is also the condition of its extinction, its uneasy proximity to 'the noise of non-sense' with which it is uncannily coextensive.[8] And, on his reading, this constitutive contradiction is precisely Flaubert's legacy. His essay on Borges strives to resist any too precipitous agreement with the Argentinian's 'modernist' claims that *Bouvard et Pécuchet* 'explodes the genre of the realist novel that [Flaubert] himself created'.[9] For Rancière, of course, there is no question of any 'explosion', no notable 'break', only an intensification of the inaugural contradiction in which *Madame Bovary* had itself been conceived. Common to both texts is 'the Flaubertian sentence that dissolves the conjunctions of the narrative, even as it produces them, reducing them to the indifferent dance of atoms of dust'.[10] The semi-autonomous sentence form is what eats away at its own genetic narrativity, by developing an autotelic interest in pure style as an index of literary truth: 'because style is the very rhythm of things dissolving, yielding to their lack of reason, their baselessness'.[11] On the one hand, there are still actions, ordered according to the immemorial stipulations of dramatic propriety canonised by Aristotle; on the other, there is 'the visionary power that imperceptibly lifts [them] up, sentence after sentence, in order to make us perceive [. . .] the music of unbound affections and perceptions, mixed together in the great indifferent flux of the Infinite'.[12] In his final work, Flaubert prefers to allegorise the entire dilemma in the eponymous figures themselves, who are forced by the immense stupidity of all they survey to retreat from any heroism of absolute style into broken *Bartleby* types by the end of the book – which only amplifies the excruciating irony of the literary situation Flaubert has arranged for himself. As Rancière puts it elsewhere,

> They return to their desks and there resign themselves to copying forever after what can then only ever be a collection of stereotypes. That is good medicine for curing the democratic disease of writing. But this good medicine is also the self-elimination of literature. Flaubert must himself copy what he makes his characters copy. He has to cancel the labour through which the prose of literature distinguished itself from the commonplaces of the prose of the world. Literary purity can't undo the tie that binds it to the democracy of writing without eliminating itself. Its own process of differentiation leads it to the point where its difference becomes indeterminable.[13]

In these terms, the 'positive contradiction' that underpins the aesthetic regime (from Hugo through to Zola) is already at a point of maximum dialectical tension, already facing a kind of interminable stasis of self-cancellation, in Flaubert's last work, beyond which it seems logically impossible for the process to evolve.

In what sense, then, might Joyce's *Ulysses* have marked not merely a continuation of this perilous experiment – bringing 'absolute style' to an asymptotic proximity with its opposite, the stupid prattle of the 'prose of the world' – but in Pound's sense a radical challenge to Flaubert's 'elimination' of literature from within the contradictions of literariness? In what follows, I play with the idea that by combining the three paradigmatic 'focalisers' of Flaubertian narrative – the ironic *Bildungsheld* (Stephen Dedalus as Frédéric Moreau), the naïve adulterous 'reader of novels' (Molly Bloom and Gerty MacDowell as Emma Bovary), and the benevolent philistine who channels circumambient *idées réçues* (Leopold Bloom as Bouvard or Pécuchet) – and by threading between and among them ample evidence of a nebulous literary power plucked from the *Tentation* (the 'indifferent dance of atoms'), Joyce does more than rejuvenate some exhausted procedures. He arranges for a strategic displacement of the primary platform of Flaubertian aesthetics, namely *style*, by a higher-order principle, or *form* itself. When Pound suggests that '*Ulysses* has more form than any novel of Flaubert's', what is at stake in the claim is a dramatic reconfiguration of the central problem of the aesthetic regime. For, as I will argue, with Joyce it is no longer a question of finding a literary style 'adequate' to 'the indifferent murmur of a-significant life'; it is, instead, a question of declaring all such styles bankrupt and consequently forgetting about 'the sheer intensity of things without rhyme or reason'[14] and attending, as it were, to *the indifferent murmur of a-significant styles*. What will now have emerged as the unavoidable aesthetic issue is precisely *what to do with all the dead styles* – an issue whose innermost counsel of despair is that none of them was ultimately any better than the others, but whose more hopeful incitation was, of course, to recombine them via the alchemy of form. Form translates in this context as the transfiguration of exhausted styles through unanticipated conjunctions in novel arrangements, none of which pretends to depict anything beyond its own disfiguration. Which is why it is so disconcerting to find Pound chastising Joyce, as the drafts of the chapters of *Ulysses* arrived on his desk: 'Also even the assing girouette of a postfuturo Gertrudo Steino proteopublic dont demand a new style per chapter.'[15] If the public did not demand it, then, as Pound himself well knew, 'the age' certainly did: a plastic 'prose kinema' made up of the *disjecta membra* of a collapsing literary order of things.[16]

What Joyce does to Flaubert – namely, redouble the 'positive contradiction' of the latter's 'theme' by passing beyond the injunctions of style to the imperative of form – is consistent with a larger argument that the aesthetic regime was subject to a certain break within its own modus operandi, a break not with the underlying lines of force or defining contradictions, but with the specific constellation of its internal apparatus. Just as 'monopoly capitalism' or imperialism differs from classical industrial capitalism without constituting a distinct mode of production in its own right, so the work of Joyce, Pound, Stein, Woolf and others might be said to mark a unique stage in the development of the aesthetic regime, a stage we may yet have every reason to persevere in naming *modernism*. For there are ways, and ways, of copying out a vast collection of stereotypes: there is the Flaubertian prophylactic membrane of style which erodes to the point of vanishing in an 'indeterminable self-elimination', and there is the Joycean proliferation and exaggeration of styles, none of which has any greater status than any other in the war against cliché, but the accumulated effect of whose concatenation is to reinvent the prophylactic altogether – as if we have been materially upgraded in our literary congress with capital, from the French letter of a worn-out sheep's intestine to the modern British Empire of versatile rubbers. 'Grammar and style!' Beckett expostulated. 'To me they seem to have become as irrelevant as a Biedermeier bathing suit or the imperturbability of a gentleman.'[17] In their place, as part of an international avant-garde, the modernists advocated an attention to form as such, as a supersession of these Victorian hangovers.

The key difference between Flaubert's generation and Joyce's thus consisted in a shift from the claim that 'there were neither beautiful nor vile subjects',[18] provided all were held compact in the matrix of a rigorous, impersonal style, to the still more outrageous claim that *there are neither perfect nor imperfect styles*. By the early 1920s, for a congeries of reasons, it must have appeared inevitable to serious literary artists that the goal of some absolute or immaculately indifferent stylistic medium – as the path beyond mere subject matter and into the sublimity of form – was a dead or dying cause. That older aesthetic faith in the perfectly honed sentence as 'an absolute way of seeing things', such that those things, in their abandoned muteness, might at last speak, had buckled under an assortment of pressures, some internal to literary history, others extrinsic. The critical paradox of any approach to 'writing degree zero' is that every achieved approximation – every Flaubertian, Hemingwayesque or Steinian sentence, for instance – becomes an imitable (and parodiable) thing in itself, no more 'absolute' than any other, even the most ornate rhetorical period of the baroque. The sixty-six years separating the publication of *Madame Bovary* from that of *Ulysses* is a period in which the disciplined faith of Flaubert is subject to wave upon wave of reaction, counter-reaction, new florid styles (Whitman's, Swinburne's, Mallarmé's, Proust's, etc.), wars against those styles, the anti-aesthetics of Dada and the avant-garde, and a veritable decomposition of 'literary' language into babble, nonsense and mere sound. Moreover, and more importantly, the course of capitalism's historical intensification in the age of monopolies and imperialism included, very much, the reification of language itself, its colonisation by advertising, propaganda and the various 'jargons' and 'speech genres' of administrative reason. 'We can', wrote Adorno, 'distinguish three stages in the developing domination of needs: advertising, information and command.'[19] This domination proceeds by way of a determinate social subjugation of language as the collective substance of 'Spirit', its progressive substitution by decoration, data and diktat. The 'blow dealt to language by the technological onslaught of images' in the age of mechanical reproducibility is shadowed by the ascent of positivism as a prevailing epistemology and a system of coded imperatives posing as 'politics'. Such are the inimicable material conditions against which any 'pure style' might have striven in the early decades of the twentieth century.[20]

Petrification and presentation

Rancière has written elegantly about the perceived problem of 'petrification' in Flaubertian literature, the orphaned, stone-like qualities of a purified language with no inbuilt relation to the things it is conjuring out of nothing.[21] But in Joyce, especially in *Ulysses*, this problem is redoubled. For the problem here is that *all the speech genres available to the writer have already become petrified*. The writer does not petrify them, he does not uncouple them from intentions and causes, from meaning and purpose; he does not need to. They are already orphaned from sense by the sheer force of an immanent petrification that sinks far deeper than artistic fiat. Hugh Kenner sums up the dilemma of *Ulysses*' writer-figure, Stephen Dedalus, thus: 'Whatever he can say seems derived from what someone has said before.'[22] The Dublin of which Dedalus, and the young Joyce he forlornly echoes, is merely the latest scribe is itself 'in fact an eighteenth-century parody', a 'fossil city' where undead language games and superannuated rhetoric walk the streets in the guise of persons, in a mordant excuse for a 'cultural heritage'.[23] Fallenness is the very condition of speech here, as much for the emptiness of everyday exchange as for the manner in which a trapped subjectivity might yet 'rattle its prison-bars' in an unexpected turn of phrase. There is no high style that hasn't long succumbed to premature fossilisation in this desert of signs. And to pretend to 'purify' any of this petrified speech would be to obscure the native genius of a form of social utterance for which these stricken words are still the fuel of a distributed, demotic intelligence. Kenner gets this right:

> That is why the clichés he listened to didn't drive Joyce to despair as those of Rouen and Paris drove Flaubert. In Dublin words, even dead words, are consciously used. Parasites and travelling salesmen drop polysyllables into place with an air. [...] So the usual criterion of style, that it disappear like glass before the reality of the subject, doesn't apply to [Joyce's] pages. The language of Dublin is the subject;

his books are about words, the complexity is there, in the way people talk [...] So Joyce embalms in cadences what Dublin embalms in music, and entraps in the amber of learned multiple puns the futile vigour which the Dubliner, gazing into his peat-coloured Guinness, must generate in language because its counterpart has slipped out of life. (11–12)

To that extent, Dublin could be grasped as a living laboratory for testing the literary situation of monopoly capitalism itself: the embalmed linguistic 'vigour' of the Irish capital serving as an allegorical Petri dish from which to speculate about the blasted roots of language under the imperatives of 'advertising, information, and command'. Here the test of literature, as of the vulgar wordplay of an average Dublin citizen, is not any messianic injunction '*donner un sense plus pure aux mots de la tribu*',[24] but what can yet be made of the surviving vestiges of a once-living language – via techniques of cannibalisation and pastiche, irony and satire, *bricolage* and collage. To write amidst the ruins of a fallen language is to write *about* those ruins, but not necessarily in accents of despair, or with any wish to burnish a lost glory. It is equally possible to rejoin Nietzsche's stoic intelligence, standing before the 'hard and rigid' edifice of petrified conceptual abstractions, and making free with it – he 'smashes this framework, jumbles it up and ironically re-assembles it, pairing the most unlike things and dividing those things which are closest to one another', creating out of his own free wit a 'masterpiece of pretence' with which to weather the storm of fatuity.[25] Such a masterpiece of pretence is *Ulysses*, a text whose formal ingenuity is precisely comparable to that of the Dublin wag adduced by Kenner: dead words, consciously used, in new combinations. The result is not an extreme rarefication of the evaporating meniscus of style, but an ever-thickening, palimpsestic patina of all the dead styles that continue to haunt the premises of fiction.

If the end is something properly called *form*, however, we need to be precise about what that might mean in a 'post-stylistic' literary space. We can begin by articulating some of the advantages that accrue to a simultaneous elaboration of all the prototypical Flaubertian 'focalisers' – *Bildungsheld*; reader of novels; petit-bourgeois philistine – as well as that other, fully depersonalised carrier of discourse that is the narrative voice of the *Tentation* (and which Joyce studies tends to classify as 'The Arranger' of *Ulysses*).

For once it has been decreed that the novel will not privilege any one of these frames of discourse, but accommodate each of them in turn as a bearer of textual authority, it follows that there can be no single style capable of stringing them together on a plane of consistency. Rather, the inaugural decision to pluralise the novelistic 'point of view' into a triptych shadowed by a burgeoning fourth order determines a proliferation of stylistic tempers and modes – from flagrant pastiche ('Nausicaa'), through sub-generically surcharged monologue ('Penelope'), ironic-pedantic monologue ('Proteus'), the absentminded possibilism of the Bloomian stream of consciousness ('Calypso' through 'Hades'), the various zones of discursive interpenetration ('Aeolus' and 'Scylla and Charybdis'), on up to the truly polyphonic symphonies of the later chapters of Part II – each of which is tethered 'in the last instance' to some derivative aspect of one or other of the four prevailing narratological climates. If such formal dependency is clearest in the three chapters of the Telemachiad, the opening movement of the Odyssey, and the closing chapter of the Nostos, nevertheless, it is clear that *Ulysses*' overall stylistic multiplicity is determined by this founding quadrangulation of its base points: the Flaubertian types of Frédéric Moreau, Mme Bovary, Bouvard and Pécuchet, and the visionary 'dance of the atoms'. The delicious ironies that had regulated the episodic narration of *Sentimental Education*; the stylistic purities of *Madame Bovary* which had allowed the 'nothing' to resound in the proliferation of provincial banality; the heavy satire of *Bouvard et Pécuchet*'s insoluble quest narrative; and the rhapsodic intensities of the *Tentation* – what had seemed arguably consistent at the level of an oeuvre must now, compressed between the covers of one book, betray intolerable inequalities of tone and mood, wild discrepancies of voice, and a large amount of noise generated by the transitions between them. 'Absolute style' buckles absolutely under such prodigious pressures, and the resulting discordance has already signalled the exhaustion of a superannuated aesthetic ideology.

With the ideal of any single, cohesive, 'pure' stylistic element shattered by a congeries of intra- and extra-aesthetic forces, the supposedly immanent connection that 'absolute style' had had with 'the democratic principle of equality' to begin with is problematised.[26] Rancière's argument about the politics of literature has nothing to do with the political opinions of authors, nor with the ideological 'commitment' of the work itself to this or that social tendency; it has even less to do with the 'negative dialectics' of the work's formal withdrawal from utility and interest. Rather, literature and democracy are said to share a differential participation in the 'principle of equality', which is simply the abolition, specific to each of them, of the authorised orders of things that had yoked words and bodies in hierarchical relations since the dawn of the social. If political democracy institutes a 'redistribution of the sensible' according to which the obscure 'parts with no part' suddenly become visible and audible on the stage of politics, literature discovers the means (at roughly the same time, though there appears to be no causal link here) to dismantle centuries' worth of legislation as to what can be said, when and how, about whom and what, thanks to the radical 'democracy of the letter' itself. Instead of a situation where every 'word has a well-determined point of origin and point of destination, and is thus inscribed in an ordered arrangement of bodies in their place and in their function',[27] we have a situation that allows for *anybody whatever* to write, and to read, the mute-loquacious letter's errant trajectory across the field of the perceptible. In that deviant and promiscuous passage, literature simultaneously enacts a 'redistribution of the sensible' of its own, violating the sanctioned system of differences that had regulated the fixed relations between genres, voices and styles, in order to 'tunnel into the depths' and there reveal three interpenetrating and conflicting regimes of equality: (1) the perfect equality of all possible subjects, and the availability of any word or genre to express them; (2) the mute speech of commodities whose formal equality as aliquot parts of value is shadowed by a loquacious, feverish fetishism; and (3) 'the molecular democracy of the states of things with no rhyme or reason'.[28] If there was any single aesthetic force coordinating this astonishing triple accession to the literary 'principle of equality', it was the absolutisation of style that allowed Flaubert and his disciples to cultivate a tonal indifference toward the swarming intensities unleashed by it. At this level, the 'individualities' discerned by literary egalitarianism penetrate far below the surface of the 'humanist' order of things, beneath the molar forms on which the 'representative regime' had based its operations; these 'are replaced by prehuman individualities, resulting from an indifferent intermingling of atoms: encounters with a blade of grass, a whirl of dust, the flash of a nail, a sunbeam', and so on.[29] The only technical mechanism capable of managing such haecceities without being perforated by their shattering frequencies was the 'absolute manner of seeing things' crystallised in the style of petrified indifference – that syntactic 'force of disindividualization' that presents things in a perpetual molecular vibration, 'as they are, in their "absoluteness"'.[30]

But this is, to say the least, a most peculiar politics. The 'disorder of representation' amounts, at this most radical edge of literarity, to the disclosure of an atomism that can have no relation to the stage of political dissensus – since no human interest could descend this deeply into the vibrating chaos of 'the great river of the infinite'.[31] The literary 'principle of equality' is set on a scale properly incommensurable with the scale of political democracy; the chasm opened up between molar bodies and molecular intensities is finally too vast to bridge. So the 'politics of literature', springing from the orphan letter's introduction of 'dissonance into the communal symphony',[32] ends up by rupturing the sound barrier of political contestation itself, and bleeds out into the indifferent babble of the universe, where literary language at last abandons its dialogical foundations in agonistic speech acts and can 'only be heard as the music of the atoms of antirepresentation that compose the novel's "story"'.[33] And it is *style* that permits such a glacial indifference to proliferate and accumulate in the interstices of novelistic discourse; *style* that withholds its tonal regard from all merely 'human' interests so that an entirely new order of things becomes both visible and sayable, and that conforms itself to these inaudible rhythms on the far side of sense in order to amplify their vibratory nullity. Without this formal prophylactic of disengagement, this sheath of depersonalisation, there can be no question of literature's attainment to its own 'principle of equality', which must now bypass the molar dimension and rush to the microscopic haecceities of 'the truth of things', registering as sheer intensities of affect and percept upon supercharged syntactical antennae.[34] And so it is *style* that, pursuing a 'politics' specific to its war against representational orthodoxy, ends up inevitably accelerating beyond the political altogether and out into the ontological as such. Style effectively dissolves its own political *raison d'être* into a quavering stake on the question of Being.

This raises significant questions about a later writer whose early ideal of 'the author' was precisely the ambivalent Flaubertian figure of an immanent *deus absconditus*: 'The artist, like the God of the creation, remains within or behind or beyond or above his handiwork, invisible, refined out of existence, indifferent, paring his fingernails.'³⁵ It was with such a scrupulous, immanent ideal of the literary (from which all mere opinion would evaporate under the heat of exactitude) that Joyce had issued his first foray in the world of published letters: *Dubliners*, if it is nothing else, is the finest approximation in English of the style of the *Trois contes* and of a now respectable 'French' style notable for its tonal reticence and modal petrification. It was in this anachronistic – but in English still quite radical – style that *Ulysses* itself had taken root, as a short story idea that then kept growing due to a metastasis of stylistic tempers and moods lodged like foreign bodies in the very fibres of that discourse. 'Stately, plump Buck Mulligan came from the stairhead, bearing a bowl of lather on which a mirror and a razor lay crossed' could well be a sentence taken from the earlier collection; but as the opening period of *Ulysses*, it establishes only an ironic, false continuity with a stylistic element here in the process of being abandoned. And the reasons for this abandonment have arguably to do with what we have said to be the 'post-political' dynamic of its literarity; with the extent to which the very stance of 'indifference' ultimately obliges the text to sink through the domain of political dissensus and percolate down into the a-signifying ontological horizon of molecularity – like some kind of syntactic 'incredible shrinking man', subsumed into meaningless immanence. For Joyce himself, during the years 1900 to 1904, had become not a Whiteheadian ontologist, but a socialist, a fact emblazoned in his earliest draft of *A Portrait of the Artist*, written in 1904 and taking the curious form of a narrative manifesto. 'Man and woman,' the text boldly concludes, 'out of you comes the nation that is to come, the lightning [*sic*] of your masses in travail; the competitive order is employed against itself, the aristocracies are supplanted; and amid the general paralysis of an insane society, the confederate will issues in action.'³⁶ That *Ulysses* is set in 1904, featuring an avatar of this same literary 'self-portrait', recently returned from the stirring political influence of socialist-nationalists in Paris, and is itself an attempt to reconcile (under duress) the implications of such a political 'distribution of the sensible' with the residual claims of the paramountcy of 'the rhythms of phrase and period, the symbols of word and allusion',³⁷ means that we are obliged to see it as a laboratory experiment in which these latter claims finally give way under the stresses of a 'general paralysis of an insane society'. In short, *Ulysses* is the prodigious literary arraignment of *style as such* for having failed to make any political difference whatever; it is the performative deconstruction of style's 'absolution' amid the complex tensions of a historical reawakening and reimagining of the political after 1917. And it performs this Herculean task not by 'eliminating' literary difference from within the movement of its own asymptotic accord with the 'prose of the world', but precisely by advancing the most radical hypothesis about form as such: that literature does not represent the world, it presents representations of the world, and in so doing trains the subject to read for the lapses and inconsistencies, the lacunae in literary space, that betray the political fault lines and contradictions latent in what is sayable in the first place. Form begins from the shambolic ruins of all petrified literary means. Like the jumbled pieces of a dozen incomplete jigsaw puzzles, it assembles them into monstrous new shapes; these shapes, through which whatever 'lurks behind [. . .] – be it something or nothing – begins to seep', are the only means by which the Real can be presented.[38] Form deposes 'pure style' in order to show the complicity of style with the police; it is what the polis is left to make out of the rubble of literary signs.

Poverty and form

> Ineluctable modality of the visible: at least that if no more, thought through my eyes. Signatures of all things I am here to read, seaspawn and seawrack, the nearing tide, that rusty boot. Snotgreen, bluesilver, rust: coloured signs.[39]

This mannered approximation of the aesthetic ideology of Flaubert, with its approbation of a 'dance of atoms' as the ultimate horizon of literarity, is helplessly ironised by the fact that the myopic Stephen Dedalus has left his corrective spectacles back at Martello Tower, and so 'sees' nothing but a miasma of indistinct shapes and colours. There is, perhaps, nothing to see on Sandymount Strand but the phantasmagoric projection of a narcissistic delusion, issuing in an onanistic 'waste of shame', and decked out in all the tricks of the 'aesthetic regime's' decadent phase: swooning onomatopoeia, Swinburnian euphony, Dowsonesque morbidity, and a distorted after-echo of the prose of the *Tentation* itself: 'His mouth moulded issuing breath, unspeeched: ooeeehah: roar of cataractic planets, globed, blazing, roaring wayawayawayawayawayaway' (60). All of which builds ironically to a poetic utterance, an aesthetic composition, whose belated appearance (in the chapter set in the house of winds) gives the game away:

> On swift sail flaming
> From storm and south
> He comes, pale vampire,
> Mouth to my mouth. (168)

The specious tropology and style of the decadent 1890s in this quatrain expose the degree to which not an 'ineluctable modality of the visible' but an exhausted distribution of the sayable is Stephen Dedalus's abiding problem. In trying 'to maintain "the sublime" / In the old sense', he is 'Wrong from the start –',[40] since there is nothing here to trouble a stable, iterative horizon of sense. True, that horizon is the achievement of the aesthetic regime itself: a late Romantic poetics flourishing in the bourgeois ruins of an aristocratic order of things. But the problem is that a determinate logic of petrification now blights the aesthetic regime from within; style succumbs to reification, and so lapses into 'representativeness'. Stephen can only write what the aesthetic regime permits him to see and say, and the result is worthless both aesthetically and politically.

It is worthless politically because of what it prevents him from seeing: in this case, the midwives and cocklepickers who share not only the beach with him but above all his poverty, which, it turns out, all of these exercises in 'aesthetic' literary stylistics have been engineered precisely not to contemplate, and not to politicise. To be sure, he finds a ready discourse for them – he is anything but slow when it comes to drumming up an idiom suited to his sense of the occasion – but that discourse is not a way of *thinking* poverty; it is a way of masking it. Stephen's entire monologue is a strategy for burying his head in the alluvial deposits of an 'aesthetic regime' that only makes a place for the poor by 'aestheticising' them; it is a strategy of denial, as we learn poignantly when he encounters his sister Dilly selling his books in 'Wandering Rocks', scant pages after she has begged a penny off their widowed father: 'She is drowning. Agenbite. Save her. Agenbite. All against us. She will drown me with her, eyes and hair. Lank coils of seaweed hair around me, my heart, my soul. Salt green death' (313). A profoundly atypical, monosyllabic prose of clipped confessions of the worst inevitably gives way to the resurgence of the decadent literary 'aesthetics' of 'Proteus', with its green salt lugubriosities.

Think, too, of how the milk-woman fares under Stephen's 'ineluctable' distribution of the sensible in the first chapter. Here is his effort to 'picture' her in prose:

> He watched her pour into the measure and thence into the jug rich white milk, not hers. Old shrunken paps. She poured again a measureful and a tilly. Old and secret she had entered from a morning world, maybe a messenger. She praised the goodness of the milk, pouring it out. Crouching by a patient cow at daybreak in the lush field, a witch on her toadstool, her wrinkled fingers quick at the squirting dugs. They lowed about her whom they knew, dewsilky cattle. Silk of the kine and poor old woman, names given her in old times. A wandering crone, lowly form of an immortal serving her conqueror and her gay betrayer, their common cuckqueen, a messenger from the secret morning. To serve or to upbraid, whether he could not tell: but scorned to beg her favour. (15)

The milk-woman is simultaneously doing symbolic time here as both the classical figure of Pallas Athena ('lowly form of an immortal [. . .] messenger from the secret morning') and a type of Irish revival romance: the feminine figure of the folk, Kathleen Ni Houlihan, of a piece with the 'dewsilky cattle' (*a shíoda na mbó*) whose milk nourishes a starving nation under a foreign yoke. In either case, it is a question of the 'symbolic principle, which refers every empirical spectacle to the metaphor of an essential form'.[41] Here again is a paradigmatic case of a prefabricated 'distribution of the sensible' foreclosing any access to the woman's 'mute speech', and the actual contours of her poverty, but not the distribution peculiar to the 'representative regime'. Let us be very clear: this is by no means a simple recrudescence of that venerable allocation of a 'vile' role to the peasant class. The kind of hostile paternalism we tend to associate with Spenser and Swift, their depictions of the Irish peasantry as villeins and cannibalistic sub-humans, is not reproduced here. Rather, what we find is an 'aesthetic' displacement of the peasant-woman's historical being into the modern-classical, and into the national-romantic.

One thing that can safely be said (and that Joyce did say) about the peasants of Ireland, circa 1904, is that they lived in poverty.[42] And poverty is, I suggest, the secret history that *Ulysses* wants to tell without telling it; a poverty so intense and harrowing that it dogs even the final moments of Bloom's long day, as he prepares for bed. To the catechist's direction to 'reduce Bloom by cross multiplication of reverses of fortune', the text responds with four successive stages of social free-fall in declining 'helotic order': poverty, mendicancy, destitution, and the 'nadir of misery: the aged impotent disfranchised ratesupported moribund lunatic pauper' (855). We are alerted via stylistic correspondence to a sinister similarity between this projected sociological declension of Bloom and an earlier rehearsal of the actually dwindling lot of Simon Dedalus: 'a small landlord, a small investor, a drinker, a good fellow, a storyteller, somebody's secretary, something in a distillery, a tax gatherer, a bankrupt and at present a praiser of his own past'[43] – to which we now must add widower and head of a household crumbling into ruin. The subsidence of the lower middle class into a lumpenproletarian abyss is the signal social fantasy gnawing restlessly at the superficial creature comforts of this great text. Think of the apparition of Bloom's old flame Josie Breen, née Powell, whom he meets on Westmoreland Street and silently reflects: 'Same blue serge dress she had two years ago, the nap bleaching. Seen its best days. Wispish hair over her ears. And that dowdy toque: three old grapes to take the harm out of it. Shabby genteel. She used to be a tasty dresser. Lines round her mouth. Only a year or so older than Molly' (200). This regrettable fall is diffracted through any number of other small vignettes, such as the late-night re-appearance of Stephen's old schoolfriend Corley, his 'breath redolent of rotten cornjuice' (708–9), homeless and out of work, 'all in', looking desperately for 'something, anything at all to do' (709); or the death of Dignam and the yawning ruin of his wife and many children; or the 'onelegged sailor' begging for alms as he growls 'The Death of Nelson' along Eccles Street earlier in the day (288–9); or indeed any of the other familiar figures – 'sandwichman, distributor of throwaways, nocturnal vagrant [. . .], blind stripling, superannuated bailiff's man' (855), etc. – whom Bloom lists as types of mendicancy.

Above all, one should not fail to recognise the absent centre of the book's most flamboyant and grotesque graveyard of styles, 'Oxen of the Sun'. Here, for roughly an hour of narrative time, Bloom and Stephen finally converge in the National Maternity Hospital, and the former sees the true depths into which the latter's acquaintances are dragging him. Behind this sentimental encounter, however, the deeper subject concerns the prolonged, three-day confinement of impoverished Mina Purefoy, giving excruciating birth to her latest infant, with a 'houseful of kids at home' already (200), and only a stingy beggar of a father to provide for them all. It is this, precisely, that the text will not represent directly; rather, by assembling a prodigious sequence of masterful stylistic pastiches in loose literary-chronological order (from the manner of the *Fratres Arvales*, through the style of Anglo-Saxon alliterative prose, Mallory's narrative voice, the pithy precision of Defoe, the witty sallies of Steele and Addison, the satiric venom of Swift, up to the voluble equipoise of Carlyle and beyond into 'a frightful jumble of pidgin English, nigger English, Cockney, Irish, Bowery slang and broken doggerel'[44]), the book constructs a thoroughly opaque and hyper-mediated *scrim of form* through which to glimpse the telltale signs of an arduous and semi-tragic parturition – the scene of a poor woman giving birth to a poor child who would be better off not being born. This quintessential scene of the social *reproduction of poverty* is one that the novel chooses not to depict, not to narrate, not to commit to any 'absolute' stylistic medium, but to be legible only as an effect of form; for it is form that laboriously mimics the scene to which no one style would be adequate.

Unlike many another book about the 'grinding poverty' (715) of the urban poor or of *la bohème*, *Ulysses* never truly dwells upon poverty's material 'plane of immanence': it does not survey the spaces of poverty for their emblematic signs or telling metonymies, 'signs that are sufficient to show misery and make it palpable for an audience,' as Rancière puts it in a different context.[45] Rather, adhering to a very different conception of 'presentation' – namely the outrageous law that *'the reader should not be told what no one present would think worth an act of attention'*[46] – *Ulysses* respects its characters', and especially Stephen's, absurd and impossible pride to the extent of never figuring the cataclysm engulfing them, other than through terse and epigrammatic figments and depths glimpsed below the tectonic shifts of an unevenly developed formal surface. It is, then, precisely by its failure to appear on the surface of representation that we begin to gauge the severity of Stephen's situation, and with it Dublin's, under the terrible pressures of 'the competitive order [. . .] employed against itself'. By segmenting its narratological focus into four incommensurable quadrants, and allowing that primordial formal fissure to generate an ever-more elaborate tracery of cracks, rifts and splinters on the surface of the prose, *Ulysses* refuses the tendency of 'absolute style' to sink without a trace from the heated agonistic confrontations necessary to rouse the 'confederate will' to action. Instead, in comic solidarity with the unwritten second volume of *Bouvard et Pécuchet*, it arraigns all literary styles before the bench of a hypothetical polis: a polis unpoliced by any 'proper' or exceptional voice, and learning to experiment constructively with the detritus of a blasted literary system. This polis recognises itself and its interests, not in any particular style, or any specific figure or genre, but in the monstrosity of a form without foundation in any law, beyond a will to depose the 'paralysis of an insane society' with an ungovernable delight in its own potential. *Ulysses* is not Bloom's book, any more than it is Stephen's or Molly's; it is conclusive proof that literary politics belongs to no subject at all, but only to the form in which all subjects and all styles are obliged to become conscious of the general conflict and 'fight it out'.[47]

Notes

1. Ezra Pound, *Literary Essays*, ed. T. S. Eliot (London: Faber and Faber, 1954), 32.
2. See Pound, 'Past History', *The English Journal*, 22 (1933), 351, and *Polite Essays* (Norfolk, CT: New Directions, 1940), 82–3.
3. Pound, *Literary Essays*, 403.
4. T. S. Eliot, 'Ulysses, Order, and Myth', in *Selected Prose of T. S. Eliot*, ed. Frank Kermode (Orlando: Harcourt, 1975), 178.
5. 'Take Joyce, and you will find a vast expanse of stereotypes without end at the same time as the ascent toward language's necessity, which would also be the necessity of myth. [... A] desire to rediscover, within "modern" triviality, the powers of myth enveloped in language.' Jacques Rancière, 'Interview for the English Edition' (with Gabriel Rockhill), in *The Politics of Aesthetics: The Distribution of the Sensible*, trans. Gabriel Rockhill (London and New York: Continuum, 2004), 59.
6. Franco Moretti, *Modern Epic: The World System from Goethe to García Márquez*, trans. Quentin Hoare (London and New York: Verso, 1996), 123–230.
7. Fredric Jameson has quipped that Joyce was Flaubert's 'favourite reader'. See Jameson, 'Aesthetics of Singularity', *New Left Review*, 92 (March/April 2015), 110.

8. Rancière, 'The Truth through the Window', in *The Politics of Literature*, trans. Julie Rose (Cambridge: Polity, 2011), 158.
9. Rancière, 'Borges and the French Disease', in *The Politics of Literature*, 137.
10. Ibid., 140.
11. Rancière, 'The Truth through the Window', 158.
12. Rancière, *Mute Speech: Literature, Critical Theory, and Politics* (New York: Columbia University Press, 2011), e-book edition, loc. 2481.
13. Rancière, 'The Politics of Literature', in *The Politics of Literature*, 27.
14. Ibid., 25.
15. Pound, letter to Joyce, 10 June 1919, *Pound/Joyce* (New York: New Directions, 1970), 157.
16. Pound, 'Hugh Selwyn Mauberley', in *Early Writings* (London: Penguin, 2005), 128.
17. Samuel Beckett, letter to Axel Kaun, 9 July 1937, in Martha Dow Feshenfeld and Lois More Overbeck (eds), *The Letters of Samuel Beckett, 1929–1940* (Cambridge: Cambridge University Press, 2009), 518.
18. Rancière, *The Politics of Literature*, 54.
19. Theodor W. Adorno, 'The Schemata of Mass Culture', in J. M. Bernstein (ed.), *The Culture Industry: Selected Essays on Mass Culture* (London: Routledge, 1991), 73.
20. Jonathan L. Beller, 'Kino-I, Kino-World: Notes on the Cinematic Mode of Production', in Nicholas Mirzoeff (ed.), *The Visual Culture Reader*, 2nd edn (London and New York: Routledge, 2002), 62.
21. Rancière, 'The Politics of Literature', 11, 21.
22. Hugh Kenner, *Ulysses*, rev. edn (Baltimore and London: Johns Hopkins University Press, 1987), 58.
23. Kenner, *Dublin's Joyce* (New York: Columbia University Press, 1987), 11.
24. Stéphane Mallarmé, 'Le tombeau d'Edgar Poe', in *Collected Poems*, ed. and trans. Henry Weinfield (Berkeley and Los Angeles: University of California Press, 1994), 71. Famously reworked by T. S. Eliot as 'To purify the dialect of the tribe', in 'Little Gidding', II, *The Complete Poems and Plays of T. S. Eliot* (London: Faber, 1969), 194.
25. Friedrich Nietzsche, 'Truth and Lie in a Non-Moral Sense', in *The Birth of Tragedy and Other Writings*, ed. Raymond Geuss and Ronald Speirs (Cambridge: Cambridge University Press, 1999), 152, 153.

26. Rancière, 'The Politics of Literature', 11.
27. Rancière, *The Flesh of Words: The Politics of Writing*, trans. Charlote Mandell (Stanford: Stanford University Press, 2004), 102.
28. Rancière, 'The Politics of Literature', 26.
29. Rancière, 'Literary Misunderstanding', in *The Politics of Literature*, 40.
30. Rancière, *Mute Speech*, loc. 2354, 2321.
31. Ibid., loc. 2369.
32. Rancière, *The Flesh of Words*, 103.
33. Rancière, *Mute Speech*, loc. 2529.
34. Rancière, 'The Politics of Literature', 14.
35. James Joyce, *A Portrait of the Artist as a Young Man*, in *A James Joyce Reader*, ed. Harry Levin (London: Penguin, 1993), 483.
36. Joyce, 'A Portrait of the Artist' (1904), in Robert Scholes and Richard M. Kain (eds), *The Workshop of Daedalus: James Joyce and the Raw Material for 'A Portrait of the Artist as a Young Man'* (Evanston, IL: Northwestern University Press, 1965), 68.
37. Ibid., 62.
38. Beckett, *Disjecta: Miscellaneous Writings and a Dramatic Fragment*, ed. Ruby Cohn (London: John Calder, 1983), 173.
39. Joyce, *Ulysses* (London: Penguin, 1992), 45.
40. Pound, 'Hugh Selwyn Mauberley', 133, 127.
41. Rancière, *Mute Speech*, loc. 2682.
42. 'A feudal peasantry [still] exists, scraping the soil but this would with a national revival or with a definite preponderance of England surely disappear.' Quoted in Richard Ellmann, *James Joyce*, rev. edn (Oxford: Oxford University Press, 1983), 237.
43. Joyce, *A Portrait of the Artist*, 512.
44. Joyce, letter of 13 March 1920, in *Letters*, vol. 1, ed. Richard Ellmann (London: Viking, 1966), 138–9.
45. Rancière, *Aisthesis: Scenes from the Aesthetic Regime of Art*, trans. Zakir Paul (London and New York: Verso, 2013), 248.
46. Kenner, *Ulysses*, 31.
47. Karl Marx, *A Contribution to the Critique of Political Economy* (Moscow: Progress Publishers, 1977), available at <https://www.marxists.org/archive/marx/works/1859/critique-pol-economy/preface.htm> (last accessed 24 September 2015).

11

The Politics of Realism in Rancière and Houellebecq
Arne De Boever

This chapter engages with Jacques Rancière's theorisation of the politics of literature and the central role that nineteenth-century French literary realism plays in it. In a first section, I assess Rancière's politics of literature from a perspective that nuances Rancière's theory of realism as democratising and equalising and considers in addition the modern novel's potential complicity with what Michel Foucault calls 'biopolitics'. This will enable me to distinguish what I call Rancière's 'performative realism' from approaches to realism that stay within the representationalist framework that he largely leaves aside. I then consider Rancière's discussion of nineteenth-century workers and workers' thought, showing how it puts his performative realism into practice. In the second half of the chapter, I mobilise this theoretical framework to make sense of contemporary French novelist Michel Houellebecq's struggle with realism and the representation of contemporary workers in his novels *Whatever* and *The Map and the Territory*. Taking my cue from Houellebecq's realism, I consider in closing what I claim to be the neglected object-oriented dimension of Rancière's politics of literature, arguing that while this dimension is essential to Rancière's discussion of literary realism, it marks a limitation of his humanising politics. At the limit of his politics but crucial to his politics of literature, then, this dimension draws out the tension between 'politics' and 'the politics of literature' that this chapter ultimately reveals.

Literature about anything, for anyone

Rancière's theorisation of the politics of literature, and of the politics of nineteenth-century French literally realism in particular, has taken many by surprise due to its stubborn refusal to assess realism within debates about its representationalism, or its aim to give an account of the world. In his work on realism, Rancière proposes that the politics of realism cannot be assessed on this count. By extension, critics of realism cannot simply claim anti-representationalism – 'realism will never be able to give an account of the world' – as a political position. For Rancière, such debates – which have generated the 'distribution of the sensible'[1] (to use one of Rancière's technical terms) that separates 'realism' from 'modernism' and 'postmodernism' – are missing the political mark. As he sees it, realism's politics consists in how it extended – redistributed – one's sense of what could and could not be written, introducing into literary representation realms of subjective experience that were previously off-limits. From such a perspective, there is no difference between, say, realist and abstract art: both challenged, in their different ways, representation's count. Similarly, when it comes to assessing the politics of realism, modernism and postmodernism, it is this challenge that must be assessed – not their representationalism or anti-representationalism.

It is largely from this perspective that Rancière can characterise the politics of literature, specifically of literary realism, as democratising and equalising. Taking Gustave Flaubert's *Madame Bovary* as an example in 'The Politics of Literature',[2] a text that rehearses many of the arguments of Rancière's earlier and challenging book *Mute Speech*,[3] Rancière points out that early commentators of Flaubert's work saw in its prose 'a fascination for detail and an indifference toward the human meaning of actions and characters that led him to give the same importance to material things and to human beings'.[4] They agreed that Flaubert's 'prose was the petrification of human action and human language'.[5] Rancière is interested, specifically, in the fact that commentators saw this as 'the symptom of democracy':[6] 'Flaubert's disregard for any difference between high and low subject matters, for any hierarchy between foreground and background, and ultimately between men and things, was the hallmark of democracy.'[7] Flaubert as well as other new writers had 'lost the sense of human action and human meaning'.[8]

Characterising the development of Flaubert's prose as the 'absolutization of style',[9] Rancière notes that such an absolutisation – which Jean-Paul Sartre would later identify as a-political and aristocratic (as opposed to democratic) – 'could only be interpreted [in Flaubert's time] as a radical egalitarian principle, upsetting the whole system of representation, the old regime of the art of writing'.[10] Thus the so-called 'aristocratic' absolutisation of style was actually the 'democratic' and radically 'egalitarian' principle of what Rancière characterises as an inhuman and petrified indifference towards the distributions of the system of literary representation. As Rancière sees it, it is for those reasons that realism is political.

One of Rancière's other and perhaps more intuitively understandable examples in this context is Victor Hugo, who in his novel *Notre-Dame de Paris* 'gives voice to the towering stones [. . .] [of] the cathedral of Notre Dame', as Gabriel Rockhill puts it in his introduction to Rancière's *Mute Speech*.[11]

> The hierarchical relationship between the intellectual and the material, between the soul and the body, is undercut as the material power of written words and stones that come to speak overthrows the cosmology of the earlier [representationalist] poetics.[12]

In this context, Rancière's association of the realist novel with 'petrification' begins to make sense. Fiction makes room for 'the primacy of language';[13] Hugo's novel is shaped by 'the principle of the equality of all represented subjects';[14] by the 'indifference of style in relation to the subject represented';[15] 'the model of writing displaces the ideal of performative speech [. . .] as act and efficacious rhetoric'.[16] In short, 'silent things take on a language of their own, meaningless objects become a system of signs.'[17] It is partly through these characteristics – present in the discussion of Flaubert as well – that Rancière arrives at the notion of 'mute speech'.

But there is more. Rancière extends this emphasis on what one could call the *whatever* of the realist novel's subject matter – an emphasis I will return to in the final part of this chapter, when I discuss the object-oriented dimension of his realism – into a reflection about the public of the realist novel as well.[18] 'Mute', Rancière further clarifies, also refers to the fact that Flaubert's prose did not have a clearly defined audience; to the fact that the realist novel was, in Rockhill's words, a 'genreless genre that freely circulates'.[19] It 'spoke to anybody, without knowing to whom it had to speak, and to whom it had not'.[20] One could thus say that it was a literature not only about *whatever*, but also for *whomever*: about anything, for anyone.[21] At its most extreme, it was a literature for those who did not read, thus effectively cancelling out (as Rancière notes[22]) its own existence, at the outer limit of the distributions that had shaped the literary public. For this reason, too, realism takes up a central place in Rancière's theorisation of the politics of literature.

One can now understand why Rancière writes at the beginning of 'The Politics of Literature' that his title does not refer to the politics of writers nor to 'the modes of representation of political events or the social structure and social struggles in their books'.[23] Literature does politics through its interruption of *what* can be represented, and *for whom*. It is in this double sense that it stands for the democratisation and equalisation of 'subjects': of the *whatevers* and *whomevers* of literary writing. It is in this double sense that it is 'mute': a stone speaking to all, even those who do not read.

From biopolitical to performative realism

Focusing on the whatever of Rancière's politics of literature, this means that with the realist novel, the scope of what is considered worthy of literary representation, of being included in literary writing, is extended to anyone and to anything – equally and democratically, as Rancière sees it. While I would agree with this assessment, and specifically with the historical dimension of it (the fact that Flaubert's contemporary commentators interpreted realism's aesthetic to be equalising and democratic), I do not think this historical dimension can mark the full limit of one's theorisation of the politics of literature, and specifically of literary realism.

In some of my own work on the contemporary novel, which engages the problem of realism's representationalism that Rancière all too quickly leaves aside, I have considered another theorisation of the politics of literary realism that I uncover in the work of some contemporary novelists engaged with realism (J. M. Coetzee, Kazuo Ishiguro, Paul Auster, Tom McCarthy and others).[24] This theory would ask one to take seriously the historical coincidence that the modern genre of the novel, which programmatically seeks to write the lives of ordinary human beings into their most intimate details (as opposed to the lives of mythical or legendary figures represented in the tales of yore), emerges at the same time that, in Michel Foucault's analysis, the transformation of Western power from sovereignty into biopolitics takes place.

In the realist novel, as Ian Watt pointed out in his study,

characters do not only have names that sound like yours or mine; they also have birthdates, even birth-times (or, for that matter, death-times: we know that Richardson's 'Clarissa died at 6:40pm on Thursday, 7 September',[25] as Watt recalls). This biographical trait is staged in the diary-writing that makes up a significant part of what is often considered to be the first English-language novel, Daniel Defoe's *Robinson Crusoe*, a novel whose full title – *The Life and Strange Surprising Adventures of Robinson Crusoe, Mariner* – reveals better its biographical drive.[26] In the modern novel, characters are so full of life 'they practically need birth certificates', as Yann Martel put it in *Life of Pi*, a contemporary rewrite of the Crusoe tale.[27]

In the famous fifth chapter of the first volume of *The History of Sexuality*, Foucault suggests there has been a shift in the history of Western power from the old, classic power of sovereignty, defined by the right to kill (a power of death), to a new, modern power of life.[28] He makes a distinction between anatomo-politics, which is focused on individual bodies and rules through disciplinary techniques, and biopolitics, which is interested in the biological life of the population (the human being as species) and governs through interventions and regulatory controls. Biopolitics tries to make (produce, foster, optimise) life rather than take it: to keep life alive to the point of near-death, if needs be. While several novel theorists had already considered the relation between the novel and anatomo-politics, specifically the disciplinary power that rules individual bodies, in my book *Narrative Care* I tried to show that some contemporary novelists through their intertextual engagement with certain classic examples of the novel-genre (the already-mentioned *Robinson Crusoe*, but also Shelley's *Frankenstein*, and others) invite one to investigate the relation between the novel – specifically, the realist novel – and biopolitics. Theorising the realist novel as a biopolitical form, then, whose programmatic attempt to write life is complicit with the shift in the history of Western power that Foucault theorises, my approach arguably looked into the underside of Rancière's claim about literary realism's democratising and equalising politics. Such realism is *also* biopolitical. To assess the politics of literary realism means to assess both those dimensions.

I include a discussion of this biopolitical theory of the novel here because it can help clarify the specificity of Rancière's position. While Rancière does not address this biopolitical dimension of realism explicitly (it is too close, one suspects, to the problematic of representationalism that he leaves aside), traces of it can nevertheless be found in his work. Indeed, it is worth noting that realism is by no means an unambiguously positive term in his writings. For example, when Rancière summarises the trajectory of his entire work in the afterword to the English-language edition of *The Philosopher and His Poor* (2003 [1983][29]), he distances himself from realism, using the term 'realism' or the adjective 'realist' mostly in scare quotes, and to characterise what he calls in his political thought 'the police': 'the division of the sensible that claims to recognize only real parties to the exclusion of all empty spaces and supplements'.[30] Earlier on in that same afterword, he had already written of a '"realist" account [*compte*, 'count' or 'account' in English] of social parties',[31] even using the distinctively Foucaultian phrase 'governmental realism'[32] to refer to the optimising calculations of a utopian consensus democracy that practises such exclusion. His use of realism in this sense recalls his 'The End of Politics or The Realist Utopia', published in *On the Shores of Politics*, in which a similar understanding of realism can be found.[33]

To this 'governmental realism' of the 'police', this '"realist" account of social parties', Rancière opposes 'politics': 'the mode of acting that perturbs this arrangement by instituting within its perceptual frames the contradictory theatre of its "appearances"'.[34] 'Appearance', he writes earlier on in the afterword, 'is not the illusion masking the reality of reality, but the supplement that divides it':[35] 'It is properly a supplement to any "realist" account of social parties.'[36] For him, then, '[t]he essence of politics is dissensus', defined as 'the production within a determined, sensible world, of a given that is heterogeneous to it', in this way constituting an 'aesthetics of politics'.[37] 'Politics is aesthetic', he concludes, 'in that it makes visible what had been excluded from a perceptual field, and in that it makes audible what used to be inaudible.'[38]

Positing such an aesthetic politics as the essence of democracy, and contrasting it to the 'governmental realism' that the afterword sharply criticises, he writes:

> In the natural history of the forms of domination, only this supplement [of appearance] can bring forth democratic exceptionality. If equality is efficacious in the social order, it is by means of the constitution of this scene of appearance in which political subjects inscribe themselves

as a litigious, 'fictitious' supplement in relation to every account of social parties.[39]

Tying his comments here to his discussion of 'The Politics of Literature', one can conclude that it is such an inscription that the nineteenth-century French realist novel accomplishes. It provides the scene for the *theatrical* and *fictitious appearance* of *whatever* for *whomever*, thus supplementing the governmental realist account of literature's subject matter and audience at that time. Politics versus the police.

My own position, of course, is that some of what Rancière calls governmental realism is always also in effect in literature and the account of the world that it provides. But it is important to see how literature, in Rancière's view, also goes beyond this. I would characterise the shift that is accomplished in Rancière's thought about the politics of literature, and his discussion of the politics of literary realism in particular, as a shift from thinking realism within a representationalist framework (that would give rise to the biopolitical theory of the novel that I summarised above) to a thinking of realism within a performative framework. Indeed, Rancière is enabling one to think the politics of literary realism at a distance from realism's representationalist project, as a performative politics that would, through its staging rather than through its description, interrupt *any* 'realist' account of reality. Thus, it provides not so much a better, more perfect representationalist realism – one that would be achieved in view of the day when an entirely perfect representationalist realism may arrive (one could call it, for that reason, a messianic realism) – but a realism that reveals reality's internal, and political, split: the gap that separates any 'realist' reality from itself and can thus only be exposed performatively (in this sense, it is aesthetic rather than messianic).[40]

The reason why Rancière's theorisation of the politics of literature took many by surprise is thus that he locates the politics of literary realism not so much within its power of description (a representation that can always be recuperated by governmental realism) but within its politics of performance that manages to stage the gap separating reality from itself. Such performativity poses a formidable challenge to governmental realism; it cannot be exhausted by it. It is a 'mode of acting' that exists at the limit of representation, a politics that never coincides with the police. And the counterintuitive part of Rancière's thesis was, of course, that he found such a politics *in realism itself*, the exemplary genre of representationalism. Could there have been a better place to look?

Workers and workers' thought

To make all of this theory-talk a little more concrete, let me briefly consider one instance in Rancière's own writing where this performative realism is put into practice: Rancière's writings about the workers and the workers' thought. Let me first discuss these writings within the representationalist framework that Rancière casts aside, in order to then contrast this approach to the performative one. The texts I have in mind range from *Staging the People* and *The Intellectual and His People* (1975–85) to *Proletarian Nights* (1981) and *The Philosopher and His Poor*.[41] If one considers the realism of these works – their attempt to give an account of the workers and of workers' thought – through the lens of representationalism, they invite some obvious questions. What is the reality that any scholarly research on the workers seeks to write? Why, it is the reality of the workers! But how to write that reality if one is not a worker but a scholar? How can scholarly writing – or, for that matter, any writing – ever capture the reality of the workers, given that scholars aren't workers, that writing is considered to exist at a remove from working, and that workers are not usually considered to write? *La Parole ouvrière*, a collection of workers' writings ranging from 1830 to 1851 edited by Rancière and Alain Faure, seemed to address the issue by letting the workers speak for themselves: it simply published the workers' own writings.[42] Problem solved!

However, the representationalist project of 'letting the workers speak for themselves' is easily run aground. If, in this context, the workers' writings are somehow thought to represent the 'reality' of the workers, this would be a naïve presumption, similar to Foucault's presumption in his preface to the memoirs of the nineteenth-century French hermaphrodite Herculine Barbin, that Barbin's own account of her sexuality would somehow tell the truth about her sex – an outside that Foucault's *The History of Sexuality* had sought to deny.[43] Judith Butler has in this context asked what she refers to as 'the alternative Foucaultian question', namely: to what extent is Barbin's own account of her sexuality shaped by the narrative conventions of her time?[44] Indeed, it is not because the subject is allowed to speak that it automatically escapes the conventions that shape its speech. The same goes for the workers whose writing is published in *La Parole ouvrière*: it is one thing to let them speak, but quite another to assume that such speech would constitute the reality of the workers. Governmental realism arguably haunts one's self-representation just as much as it does one's representations of others and the world.

It is from this position that the strange style of Rancière's subsequent *Proletarian Nights* – and in general the style that characterises his entire oeuvre, one that Andrew Parker in his preface to *The Philosopher and His Poor* perceptively describes as measuring the distance between itself and the language in which it is written[45] – can be understood: as a writing that is scrupulously aware of its impossible realism, constantly questioning its representational claims, and maintaining a gap within the knowledge it produces, thus marking reality's refusal to enter into representation and arguably safeguarding it from biopolitics. However, the politics of Rancière's writing cannot be summed up by this representationalist point (and, likewise, Parker's perceptive description can in my view not be limited to the representationalist framework).

The issue that really matters from a Rancièrian perspective is that *La Parole ouvrière* shows that the workers *do* write, that writing does not exist at a remove from working. By doing so, *La Parole ouvrière* intervenes performatively, and not so much descriptively, in a distribution of the sensible in which writing and the workers are caught up, namely the distribution that assumes the two would be separate. As Rancière sees it, his book's contribution is not at all that it would somehow present the reality of the workers, at long last. No. It is that it breaks with the workers' age-old separation from the sphere of writing. That is where its political contribution lies.

While the issue of the representation of working-class thought is not entirely absent here – in the same way that it is not entirely absent in Rancière's theorisation of the politics of literature – it is important to see that Rancière's project lies elsewhere. If it can still be characterised as a realist one, it is a realism that performatively ruptures *any* reality of the workers. Instead of uncovering the real reality of the workers (versus another, false representation of them that was taken for reality), Rancière's work about workers performatively reveals a split within their reality that is resolved by various realist (descriptive) distributions of the sensible but exposed by their political, theatrical and fictitious – also realist, but performative – contestations. The aim is no longer to give an account of the people, but to 'stage' them, as the title of one of his books has it.

Houellebecq's realism

Rancière's position provides one with a productive framework to assess the contemporary realist novel's struggle with its own mission. This assessment is largely missing from Rancière's oeuvre, which remains limited to earlier periods of literary production (Virginia Woolf is about as contemporary as it gets). I want to consider in this context the French novelist Michel Houellebecq, who works in the realist tradition.

While pairing Houellebecq with Rancière may seem like an odd move given what seem to be their drastically different interests and philosophical outlooks – Houellebecq has been construed as a depressive nihilist whose work is characterised by sexism and racism; Rancière, by contrast, as an optimistic believer in democratic institutions whose guiding axiom is the presupposition of equality – Houellebecq has like Rancière engaged the problem of realism in his writing. In addition, 'work' has been a central concern in Houellebecq's oeuvre, perhaps even *the* central concern in all of his writings – to such an extent that Bernard Maris, the prominent economist who was killed in the terror attack on the magazine Charlie Hebdo in January 2015, wrote a short book about Houellebecq as an analyst of the contemporary economy.[46] If few would disagree that Houellebecq is a scandalous novelist, it is certainly worth noting that something like a scandal is also at the heart of Rancière's theorisation of politics, which always revolves around the scandalous, catachrestic fusion of two separate worlds into one ('Workers who write? Impossible!').[47]

I want to show, first of all, how Rancière's work can help us to understand Houellebecq's struggle with realism, and specifically its politics. Houellebecq will then also enable me to draw attention to an aspect of Rancière's theorisation of the politics of literary realism that has received little attention so far, and that in fact exposes a limit of his politics – a critical limitation that, when it comes down to it, may *only* be surpassable in literature.

In an article about Houellebecq's first novel, *Whatever* (the original French title was *Extension du domaine de la lutte*), literary critic Carole Sweeney has situated this novel and its first-person account of the life of a computer programmer within ongoing theoretical conversations about post-Fordism, the economic system that since the late twentieth century has replaced the Fordist economy.[48] Whereas the assembly line from Henry Ford's automobile factories and the increase it presents in the production of material commodities was central to Fordism and the capital it generated, post-Fordist capitalism (often associated with neo-liberalism) no longer revolves around the material commodity that is at the heart of Karl Marx's understanding of capital. Instead, post-Fordism thrives on 'immaterial labor' (Michael Hardt and Antonio Negri).[49] It is an economic system in which flexible workers – modelled, in the view of Luc Boltanski and Eve Chiapello, after the creative labourer: the artist, for example, or the writer[50] – work with their brains and minds, often for low salaries and minimal or no benefits, toward the production of fictitious capital (in Marx's definition, 'value in the form of credit, shares, debt, speculation, and various forms of paper money, above and beyond what can be realized in the form of commodities'[51]). Developments in technology and specifically the rise of high technology and digitisation are generally considered to have contributed greatly to this situation, whose most extreme contemporary articulation is arguably today's high-frequency algorithmic trading of financial instruments.

The 'cognitive' form of capitalism that this situation has created targets the brains and minds not only of its workers but also of its consumers, producing what Bernard Stiegler understands to be psychotic subjects without desire,[52] driven solely by the need to consume. Under post-Fordist cognitive capitalism, consumers and workers constitute a new proletariat that critical thinker Franco 'Bifo' Berardi calls 'cognitariat'.[53] It is the human being's brain and mind rather than its body that are proletarianised under current economic conditions. And these conditions are no longer limited to the poor: the rich are arguably also proletarianised in this situation, leading Stiegler to include Alan Greenspan and Ben Bernanke in his examples of today's proletarianised subjects.[54]

As one might guess, such an economic condition does not produce particularly interesting subjects for literary realism. Bret Easton Ellis was arguably still able to write an entertaining novel about one of the contemporary economy's proletarians, Patrick Bateman – a man who, while he is rich, has obviously been hollowed out by consumerism and is alive only in his murderous exploits, whether real or imagined.⁵⁵ But it can hardly be disputed that Bateman poses a challenge to realism: *American Psycho*'s surreal descriptions of torture and murder beg the question of why a contemporary realist novel about the post-Fordist economy would include such scenes – perhaps to make sure the novel stays entertaining, something that, had Ellis been limited to consumerism alone, would have been difficult to pull off? The protagonist, if one can still call it that, of Houellebecq's *Whatever* is less flamboyant, though also still decently paid. But his life under cognitive capitalism is dreary – so dreary that Houellebecq's novel explicitly wonders whether it still constitutes an appropriate subject for the realist novel.

Referring to Michel Biron's characterisation of Houellebecq's realism as 'second degree realism' or 'the idea of realism',⁵⁶ Sweeney notes that *Whatever* 'barely qualifies as a novel at all'.⁵⁷ Instead, the novel 'traces a moment of "vital exhaustion" that inevitably represents certain aesthetic challenges for the writer'.⁵⁸ Sweeney quotes from Houellebecq's fiction, which reflects on its own form: 'The novel form is not conceived for depicting indifference or nothingness; a flatter, more terse and dreary discourse would need to be invented.'⁵⁹ In Sweeney's perceptive reading, 'the novel presents the relationship between the "bad" subject of post-Fordism [. . .] who fails to reinvest his surplus in the affective or cultural domain and the corresponding aesthetic difficulty of constructing an appropriate novelistic discourse.'⁶⁰ Houellebecq's narrator in *Whatever* can be understood as one who 'ridicules narrative realism as the "pointless accumulation" of detail with "clearly differentiated characters hogging the limelight"'.⁶¹ At the same time, Sweeney notes that Houellebecq's fiction (as per the narrator of *Whatever*'s own admission) 'cannot altogether escape the lure of the idea of a kind of realism', thus yielding a realism for post-Fordist times.⁶²

Consider the distribution that must be in place for Houellebecq (and Sweeney) to arrive at these conclusions. First of all, there is the assumption that realism attempts to offer (impossibly so, of course) a living representation of the living. The realist novel is not a form that is fit to write a moment of what Houellebecq calls 'vital exhaustion'. Secondly, and in close relation to this, there is the assumption that the novel is not conceived for 'depicting indifference or nothingness': instead, its characters are engaged in the fullness of life. Finally, when it comes to those characters, they cannot be interchangeable. The realist novel needs to provide them with specific identities that must be laid out in distinct detail. These are, of course, all assumptions associated with the realist novel as a representationalist form. Within such a framework, the contemporary post-Fordist moment of cognitive capitalism poses a challenge to realism, for it offers a reality that is not worthy of representation. Given my characterisation of this representationalism as biopolitical earlier on, one must no doubt also note – and I will come back to this point below – the insistence on *liveliness* in these assumptions: the realist novel is a *living* representation of the *living*. It is not suited for the representation of the dead.

Perhaps unsurprisingly, the critical reception of Houellebecq's fiction has reinforced that representationalist framework and its biopolitical assumptions. When discussing Houellebecq's recent novel *The Map and the Territory*, for example, which once again problematises the aesthetic of realism in relation to the theme of work, prominent literary critic James Wood deplores that nothing in the novel 'is subjected to the longevity of narrative' and asks whether Houellebecq is 'really a novelist'.[63] Comparing Houellebecq to D. H. Lawrence, Wood identifies 'Lawrence's larger vision of life' as 'rich and substantial and ramifying'; Lawrence 'had a limitless faith in the novel's explanatory powers, in fiction's enormous capacity to be what he called "the bright book of life"'.[64] Houellebecq, of course, stands at the opposite end of that biopolitical credo. In Wood's reading, he is 'an unconvincing and incoherent novelist'.[65] Against the biopolitics of realism, Houellebecq is heralded as a writer (hardly a novelist) of death.

Rancière's discussion of the politics of literature, and specifically the politics of literary realism, enables one to shake up this conversation, and the general understanding of the politics of Houellebecq's realism (I am obviously not interested here in Houellebecq's personal politics, or the politics represented in his fiction). As I explained above, the key point about Rancière's theorisation of the politics of literary realism replaces the representationalist framework within which the debates about *Whatever* take place with a performative one. Such a performative realism would not so much seek to give an account of the reality of contemporary workers; its politics would not lie in its attempt to represent their reality, which may or may not challenge the aesthetic of the realist novel. Its performative politics would consist, rather (and here I go back to Rancière's discussion of the workers as I summarised it above), in the challenge that it poses to the distribution of the sensible that would separate these contemporary workers (subjects of cognitive capitalism) from writing. This point, which Rancière makes in the context of a discussion of nineteenth-century workers, becomes particularly important politically when it comes to the representation of workers in the post-Fordist economy, which is claimed (by some theorists, e.g. Boltanski and Chiapello) to have exhausted the workers' creative capabilities.[66]

In an economy that has arguably capitalised on the capabilities of creative workers, it seems politically important to show that these workers continue to write, and therefore have creative capabilities left that are not exhausted by capitalism. '"And yet some free time remains"', as the title of Sweeney's article has it. It seems important to distance this possibility from the actualisation of contemporary capital that, when it comes to one's creative capabilities, at times appears to be – and certainly at times is presented to be, not least by proponents of capital itself – total. In contrast to Rancière's publication of actual workers' writings, Houellebecq of course makes this move in the form of a fiction, and in that sense his book does not have the same 'evidentiary' status as Rancière's research. But it is worth noting that his fiction is a first-person narrative that includes, in addition to an account of its narrator's dreary life, excerpts of creative writing that the narrator is doing.

Perhaps unsurprisingly, given the continued dominance of the representationalist framework for the discussion of realism, and the continued (though less well recognised) attachment to the biopolitical credo within this framework, the performative politics of Houellebecq's realism has received no attention, even if it constitutes an interesting challenge to some contemporary discussions of post-Fordism. Houellebecq's novel does not offer its readers the reality of contemporary workers; instead, it reveals a split within that reality and the distribution of the sensible that governs it, challenging the workers' dissociation from writing, and specifically their creative exhaustion by capital.

This performative politics may strike one as slightly – or even entirely – off the mark when it comes to doing justice to Houellebecq's first novel. *Whatever* ends on a decidedly depressive note, in a peopleless forest near a town – Saint-Cirgues – that the narrator found on a Michelin road map he picked up earlier in the novel. While Houellebecq's jaded, proletarianised computer programmer notes that '[s]omething seems possible here', that '[o]ne has the impression of being present at a new departure', all of that just as suddenly 'evaporates', leading to the conclusion that that particular something 'will not take place' and that 'the goal of life is missed'.[67] And yet one is left, of course, as Sweeney already intimates in her remarks about Houellebecq's continued attachment, with a remarkable work of art: the narrator's account/ Houellebecq's novel.

It is worth noting that Houellebecq's later novel, *The Map and the Territory*, in which Michelin maps like the one used by the narrator in *Whatever* play a major role, ends with a similar scene, but on a different note. Like *Whatever*, *The Map and the Territory* takes work as its central concern and its main character is an artist, Jed Martin, who has engaged the theme of work in his painting and photography. In the novel's closing pages, Martin speaks in a rare interview given at the very end of his life about the artwork in which he had been quietly engaged. That is, the novel explains, he speaks about it while 'refus[ing] all comment'. 'I want to give an account of the world [. . .] I want simply to *give an account of the world* [Je veux rendre compte du monde [. . .] Je veux simplement *rendre compte du monde*],' Martin 'repeats for more than a page [of a forty-page interview] to the young journalist' who has come to see him.[68]

It would be a mistake to only read this as a statement in the realm of visual art, especially after the novel has worked hard to set up an identification between Martin, the artist, and Michel Houellebecq, the novelist, who also features prominently as a character in the book. The artist and the novelist share not just a mentality but also an aesthetic. When Martin states that he simply wanted 'to give an account of the world', and starts repeating this sentence for more than a page, the novel notes that the journalist 'turns out to be incapable of stopping this senile chatter', going on to say that 'this is perhaps for the best: the chatter of Jed Martin unfolds, senile and free, essentially concentrating on questions of diaphragm, amplitude of focusing, and compatibility between softwares.'[69] I read this moment in Houellebecq's oeuvre as a breakdown of realism and its representationalist project. It is a performative moment – Martin isn't so much describing the world as performing realism's programmatic statement of describing the world – that does not give way to a perfect, realist description of the world but to a 'senile and free chatter' about the technicalities of how such a realist description is accomplished (i.e. it gives way

The Politics of Realism in Rancière and Houellebecq 241

to technical conditions of production, rather than the world that is being represented). This appears to be a very different realism indeed.

So, how is one to imagine Martin's last works, in which he sought to give an account of the world? From the novel, one gathers that they are made on his property, a house surrounded by seven hundred hectares of land – mostly forested – that Martin was able to buy thanks to the immensely lucrative sale of his previous artworks. It seems Martin would drive his car out along the road traversing his property, stop it 'simply following the spur of the moment', and then leave a camera there – sometimes for a few hours, sometimes for an entire day or even several days – to film 'nature' (the novel notes that his frames would occasionally concentrate 'on a branch of a beech tree waving in the wind, sometimes on a tuft of grass, the top of a bush of nettles, or an area of loose and saturated earth between two puddles'[70] – but since such concentration happens only occasionally, one is left to assume that most of the time he is simply filming 'nature' in general). At a later stage, he would superimpose edited versions of these films – 'those moving plant tissues, with their carnivorous supplements, peaceful and pitiless at the same time', representations (as the novel puts it) of 'how plants see the world' – with his portrayals 'of industrial objects – first a cell phone, then a computer keyboard, a desk lamp, and many other objects', specifically 'those containing electric components'.[71] Such a process (realised digitally, I should add) produces

> those long, hypnotic shots where the industrial objects seem to drown, progressively submerged by the proliferation of layers of vegetation. Occasionally they give the impression of struggling, of trying to return to the surface; then they are swept away by a wave of grass and leaves and plunge back into plant magma, at the same time as their surfaces fall apart, revealing microprocessors, batteries, and memory cards.[72]

Around the same time, *The Map and the Territory* tells us, Martin started filming 'photographs of all the people he had known': 'he fixed them to a neutral gray waterproof canvas, and shot them just in front of his home, this time letting natural decay take its course.'[73] 'More curiously,' the novel continues, 'he acquired toy figurines, schematic representations of human beings, and subjected them to the same process.'[74] It is unclear whether these films are then also superimposed with the plant films – but the novel suggests this is the case when it speaks of 'those pathetic Playmobil-type little figurines, lost in the middle of an abstract and immense futurist city, a city which itself crumbles and falls apart, then seems gradually to be scattered across the immense vegetation extending to infinity'.[75]

How is one to interpret these works? One option would be, as the novel suggests, to focus on 'the human' and its disappearance: Martin's last works are, the novel suggests, 'a meditation on the end of the Industrial Age in Europe, and, more generally, on the perishable and transitory nature of any human industry'.[76] The films of the decaying portraits 'make themselves the symbols of the generalized annihilation of the human species'.[77] However, the closing lines of Houellebecq's novel focus not so much on what thus disappears – the human – but more on what such a disappearance reveals: 'Then everything becomes calm. There remains only grass swaying in the wind. The triumph of vegetation is total.'[78]

While the closing scene of *The Map and the Territory* clearly recalls the closing scene of *Whatever* – in both cases, Houellebecq ends the novel in a forest, with no people – the tone at the end of *The Map and the Territory* is 'triumphal' rather than depressive. If at the end of *Whatever* something does not happen, and a new departure is missed, at the end of *The Map and the Territory* there appears to be a new beginning. At this point, it would be a mistake to equate that new beginning with perfect realism: with a messianic realism that is able to give an account of the world. For the 'triumph of vegetation' that is accomplished at the end of Houellebecq's novel is obviously not to be read in a representationalist way – certainly not after the reader has just witnessed the breakdown of realism. Instead, the novel leaves the reader in Martin's work (and by extension in Houellebecq's work) with the *representation of* the total triumph of vegetation, a performative distance that brings one full circle to what can now be described as the fictitious but theatrical opening paragraphs of the book.

In a similar move, *The Map and the Territory* opens in the realist mode, describing a conversation between Jeff Koons and Damien Hirst. It soon turns out, however, that what is being described there is not so much an actual conversation, but Jed Martin's realist painting of this conversation: 'Koons's forehead was slightly shiny. Jed shaded it with his brush and stepped back three paces.'[79] With that revelation, the novel performatively liberates itself from the representationalist frame in which realism has for too long been caught, offering not so much a better, more perfect realism that would finally be able to write the reality of reality, but the appearance of a theatrical and fictitious supplement to reality that marks the gap or split within reality that no realist account can ever describe. In this sense, *The Map and the Territory* offers neither the map nor the territory, but the performative realism of an account exposing the internal difference of the world.

Democracy and equality of objects

I want to return, in closing, to an observation I made earlier on, namely that representationalist approaches to the realist novel assume that realism must seek to be a living representation of the living. Realism, as for example Wood presents it in his discussion of Houellebecq, is not particularly well suited to represent the dead. From the perspective of Rancière's discussion of realism, but remaining within the representationalist framework, one would have to object against Wood, and also against Houellebecq's assumptions about the novel form – he too thinks it is not fit for the deathly reality he wants to describe – that the realist novel did not necessarily start out as such a living representation of the living. Indeed, Rancière's own appreciation for it is decidedly object-oriented, if I can use this fashionable term: he appreciates its equal consideration of 'men and things' within its literary form.[80] In this, Rancière's appreciation for the realist novel's democratising and equalising politics seems to echo the mantra of object-oriented ontology that Ian Bogost offers in his book *Alien Phenomenology*: 'all things equally exist, yet they do not exist equally' (i.e. for the object-oriented ontologist, humans and objects share in existence equally, even if there are clearly differences between humans and objects).[81] Another object-oriented ontologist, Levi Bryant, has in his work offered the phrase 'democracy of objects',[82] which resonates with Rancière's work on literary realism. If Houellebecq's response to what he assumes the realist novel to be is *whatever* – the English translation of the more elaborate French title – Rancière turns that *whatever* into a key feature of realism's politics. Of course, within the representationalist framework, such a move would not escape, as I argued above, the realist novel's biopolitical credo: it would merely extend it to include not just non-humans, but also the non-living.

While an interest in non-humans may characterise Rancière's theorisation of the politics of literature, that interest is largely absent from his theorisation of politics. Indeed, Rancière tends to focus in his work on workers, and not on the objects they work with. If the non-human is present in his theory of politics (and certainly those who are construed as non-human are), it is so only in the sense that any assumption of non-humanness must be overcome in the name of equality. Politics is about becoming human. When he is discussing the politics of equality in *On the Shores of Politics*, for example, he writes of its 'humanising' power,[83] indicating the distinctly 'humanist' dimension of his work.

This leads into the question of whether, when it comes to the democratising and equalising politics that Rancière finds in the realist novel, the politics of literary realism – which includes the democracy and equality of objects – does not go further than Rancière's politics, which risks remaining caught in what Dominic Pettman in a discussion of the work of Giorgio Agamben has called an 'anthropological measure'.[84] Does not Rancière's politics, through what Rancière himself considers to be its humanist dimension, further a distribution of the sensible – specifically, the privileging of the human – that the politics of literary realism by Rancière's own account challenges?

All of that would mean that it is from the politics of literary realism that Rancière's own politics, and specifically a governmental realism that haunts it (namely, the privileging of the human), is challenged. That is a challenge that, in actual politics, might not mean much. But it does position literary realism as the ground from where Rancière's performative realism can be politically enacted, challenging even Rancière's own politics and the humanising impulse that informs it.

Notes

1. Jacques Rancière, *The Politics of Aesthetics*, trans. Gabriel Rockhill (New York: Continuum, 2004), 85.
2. Rancière, *Dissensus: On Politics and Aesthetics*, ed. and trans. Steven Corcoran (New York: Continuum, 2010), 152–68.
3. Rancière, *Mute Speech: Literature, Critical Theory, and Politics*, trans. James Swenson (New York: Columbia University Press, 2011).
4. Rancière, *Dissensus*, 154.
5. Ibid.

6. Ibid.
7. Ibid.
8. Ibid., 155.
9. Ibid., 156.
10. Ibid.
11. Gabriel Rockhill, 'Introduction: Through the Looking Glass – The Subversion of the Modernist Doxa', in Rancière, *Mute Speech*, 1–28.
12. Ibid., 13.
13. Ibid.
14. Ibid., 14.
15. Ibid.
16. Ibid. Looking ahead, I should note that the notion of 'performative speech' that is used here, in the sense of 'act and efficacious rhetoric', differs from the notion of 'performative realism' that I will propose later on.
17. Ibid.
18. I use the notion of the 'whatever' after Rancière, who proposed it himself in a lecture titled 'Auerbach and the Contradictions of Realism', which he delivered at the University of California, Los Angeles (UCLA), on 16 January 2015.
19. Rockhill, 'Introduction', 14.
20. Rancière, *Dissensus*, 157.
21. In this case as well, I take the notion of 'whomever' from Rancière's UCLA lecture.
22. Rancière, *Dissensus*, 158.
23. Ibid., 152.
24. Arne De Boever, *Narrative Care: Biopolitics and the Novel* (New York: Bloomsbury, 2013).
25. Ian Watt, *The Rise of the Novel: Studies in Defoe, Richardson and Fielding* (Harmondsworth: Penguin, 1970), 25.
26. Daniel Defoe, *Robinson Crusoe* (New York: Random House, 2001).
27. Yann Martel, *Life of Pi* (Orlando: Harcourt, 2001), viii.
28. Michel Foucault, 'The Right of Death and Power over Life', in *The History of Sexuality: An Introduction*, vol. 1, trans. Robert Hurley (New York: Vintage, 1990), 135–59.
29. While the English translation of the afterword is dated 2002, the French original that I consulted is dated 1998. I would like to thank the book's translator, Andrew Parker, for making the French original of the afterword available to me while I was preparing this chapter.

30. Rancière, 'Afterword to the English-language Edition', in *The Philosopher and His Poor*, ed. Andrew Parker, trans. John Drury, Corinne Oster and Andrew Parker (Durham, NC: Duke University Press, 2003), 226 (219–27).
31. Ibid., 225.
32. Ibid., 224.
33. Rancière, 'The End of Politics or The Realist Utopia', in *On the Shores of Politics*, trans. Liz Heron (London: Verso, 2007), 5–37.
34. Rancière, 'Afterword', 226.
35. Ibid., 224.
36. Ibid., 225.
37. Ibid., 226.
38. Ibid.
39. Ibid., 225.
40. I am mobilising a tension between the aesthetico-political and the theologico-political that is at the heart of Martín Plot's work on Rancière: Martín Plot, *The Aesthetico-Political: The Question of Democracy in Merleau-Ponty, Arendt, and Rancière* (New York: Bloomsbury, 2014).
41. Rancière, *Staging the People: The Proletarian and His Double*, trans. David Fernbach (London: Verso, 2011); *The Intellectual and His People: Staging the People Volume 2*, trans. David Fernbach (London: Verso, 2012); *Proletarian Nights: The Workers' Dream in Nineteenth-Century France*, trans. John Drury (London: Verso, 2012).
42. Jacques Rancière and Alain Faure, *La Parole ouvrière* (Paris: La Fabrique, 2007).
43. Foucault, 'Introduction', in *Herculine Barbin, Being the Recently Discovered Memoirs of a Nineteenth-Century French Hermaphrodite*, trans. Richard McDougall (New York: Pantheon Books, 1980), vii–xvii.
44. Judith Butler, *Gender Trouble: Feminism and the Subversion of Identity* (New York: Routledge, 1999), 125.
45. Andrew Parker, 'Editor's Preface', in Rancière, *The Philosopher and His Poor*, vii.
46. Bernard Maris, *Houellebecq économiste* (Paris: Flammarion, 2014).
47. I have discussed catachresis in this context in 'Feminism After Rancière: Women in J. M. Coetzee and Jeff Wall', *Transformations*, 19 (2011), available at <http://www.transformationsjournal.org/journal/issue_19/article_03.shtml> (last accessed 25 September 2015). In this article, which largely stays within a representational-

ist framework, I maintain a distinction between performative and aesthetic politics that I have since come to revise.
48. Carole Sweeney, '"And yet some free time remains ...": Post-Fordism and Writing in Michel Houellebecq's *Whatever*', *Journal of Modern Literature*, 33:4 (2010), 41–56.
49. See, for example, Michael Hardt and Antonio Negri, *Empire* (Cambridge, MA: Harvard University Press, 2000).
50. Luc Boltanski and Eve Chiapello, *The New Spirit of Capitalism* (London: Verso, 2007). I have also learned much in this context from Pascal Gielen, *The Murmuring of the Artistic Multitude: Global Art, Memory and Post-Fordism* (Amsterdam: Valiz, 2010).
51. Karl Marx, *Capital: Volume 3*, trans. David Fernbach (London: Penguin, 1991), 596–7.
52. Bernard Stiegler, with Frédéric Neyrat, 'Interview: From Libidinal Economy to the Ecology of the Spirit', trans. Arne De Boever, *Parrhesia*, 14 (2012), 9–15.
53. Franco 'Bifo' Berardi, *Precarious Rhapsody: Semiocapitalism and the Pathologies of the Post-Alpha Generation* (London: Minor Compositions, 2009).
54. Stiegler, *For a New Critique of Political Economy*, trans. Daniel Ross (Cambridge: Polity, 2010).
55. Bret Easton Ellis, *American Psycho* (New York: Vintage, 1991).
56. Biron quoted in Sweeney, '"And yet some free time remains ..."', 42.
57. Ibid., 43.
58. Ibid.; 'vital exhaustion' is a quote from *Whatever*.
59. Houellebecq quoted in Sweeney, ibid.
60. Ibid.
61. Ibid., 49; the quotes are again from *Whatever*.
62. Ibid.
63. James Wood, 'Off the Map', *The New Yorker*, 87:45 (23 January 2012), 78.
64. Ibid.
65. Ibid.
66. Rancière criticised Boltanski and Chiapello along these lines in a lecture titled 'Time, Narration, Politics' that he delivered at the West Hollywood Public Library, at the invitation of the MA Aesthetics and Politics program at the California Institute of the Arts, on 20 January 2015.
67. Michel Houellebecq, *Whatever*, trans. Paul Hammond (London: Serpent's Tail, 2011), 154–5.

68. Houellebecq, *The Map and the Territory*, trans. Gavin Bowd (New York: Knopf, 2012), 264. For the French original, see Houellebecq, *La Carte et le territoire* (Paris: Flammarion, 2010), 406.
69. Houellebecq, *The Map and the Territory*, 264.
70. Ibid., 265.
71. Ibid., 266.
72. Ibid., 267.
73. Ibid., 267–8.
74. Ibid., 268.
75. Ibid., 269.
76. Ibid.
77. Ibid.
78. Ibid.
79. Ibid., 3.
80. On this, see also Jane Bennett's criticism of Rancière in *Vibrant Matter: A Political Ecology of Things* (Durham, NC: Duke University Press, 2010), 104–8.
81. Ian Bogost, *Alien Phenomenology, or What It's Like to Be a Thing* (Minneapolis: University of Minnesota Press, 2012), 11.
82. Levi R. Bryant, *The Democracy of Objects* (Ann Arbor: University of Michigan Library, 2011).
83. Rancière, *On the Shores of Politics*, 33.
84. Dominic Pettman, *Look at the Bunny: Totem, Taboo, Technology* (Winchester: Zero Books, 2013), 76.

12

Literature, Politics and Action
Bert Olivier

> The philosophers have only *interpreted* the world, in various ways. The point, however, is to *change* it.
>
> Karl Marx, *Theses on Feuerbach*

The novel *The Woman Who Sparked the Greatest Sex Scandal of All Time* by Eli Yaakunah (2012), with its political theme of an individual's revolt against an ostensibly unassailable power, resonates conspicuously with the work of Jacques Rancière regarding the 'politics of literature'. For Rancière this implies that 'literature as literature' contributes to the configuration of the social world through 'a specific intertwining of ways of being, doing and saying'.[1] Rancière's novel understanding of literature bathes Yaakunah's novel in a less innocuous light than is usually the case with novels, which are routinely relegated to the aesthetic sphere in the modernist sense of the term, as belonging to a self-sufficient sphere of art, not having any representational bearing on the world of concrete things and events, least of all of a political nature. Neither is Rancière's conception 'aestheticist' in the postmodernist sense of the term, according to which all of reality – in the guise of language or discourse – must be understood as being subsumed under the aesthetic.[2] By insisting that literature shares in the transformation of the sensible world brought about by politics' structuring of experience, Rancière's conception is both revolutionary, in relation to aesthetic orthodoxy, and 'ancient', insofar as he returns to the meaning of 'aesthetic' that derives from the ancient Greek word for sense-perception, *aesthesis*.[3] Far from pertaining to a hermetic sphere of artistic experience, or a postmodernist sense of aesthetic reductionism, aesthetics, for Rancière, participates in the ultimately political demarcation of the world along the lines of what is spatio-temporally perceptible, conceptually intelligible and linguistically articulable.

Inversely, 'politics' is attributed a distinctly 'aesthetic' character by Rancière, but, without contradicting this sense of the term, a second, more explosive sense is encountered in his work, where he links it quasi-transcendentally[4] with 'equality', for example where he observes that politics is without a 'proper' foundation; instead, 'equality [...] is the nonpolitical condition of politics'. Moreover, contrary to what seems intuitively to be the case, it is not coterminous with party politics or the functioning of the state according to certain laws; 'it only appears as the figure of wrong'.[5] Politics, in other words, only emerges when people are excluded in some way or another from the 'polis' or community, and stake their claim to being part of it. The first characterisation of politics, in terms of a 'cluster of perceptions and practices that shape this common world', accommodates not only the second, more explosive meaning, above, but also the way that social reality is hierarchically and exclusively organised or arranged by what he terms the 'police' (discussed below).[6] In short, the first meaning of 'politics' highlights its aesthetic character of structuring the social world according to criteria of supposedly 'legitimate' or valorised perceptibility and intelligibility, while the second foregrounds its character as quasi-transcendentally intertwined with 'equality'. The latter marks those occasions when the political irruptively confronts any 'police'-organisation with politics in its naked form: the insistence that all human beings in the polis are equal to everyone else, regardless of their inclusion in or exclusion from the social order of the 'police'.

Yaakunah's *The Woman Who Sparked the Greatest Sex Scandal of All Time*

Yaakunah's novel unfolds the futuristic story of Ishtar Benten, who works at the Written Chronicles department of the Agency, earning a substantial salary for using her creative skills in the production of what may appear to be news stories, but are in fact fictions designed to fascinate if not mesmerise the unsuspecting, gullible, media-fascinated public with their sheer, but persuasive, mainly sexually oriented sensationalism, presented as 'news'. She arrives at the Agency one day to discover that she has been promoted to the Scriptwriting department, where she is to become one of the 'gods', who dictate the direction of historical events at all levels, from entertainment and the economy through to world politics. To cut a long story short, she discovers the existence of an organisation, cryptically called 'Friends of Elijah Lovejoy', and of the 'Rebel Reporters'.[7] By spreading news of what is actually occurring in society, these people, at great risk to their own lives, actively resist the political power of the Agency and its 'fictional', obfuscating determination of the course of events, from the mundane to the exalted. In *The Woman* there are no politicians; there are only actors, performing under the direction of an all-powerful oligarchy. The more Ishtar learns about the sway that the Agency holds over people's lives, the more her antipathy towards it grows. Her conscience having been awakened by her acquaintance with the Rebel Reporters, she resolves to revolt against the Agency through the fictionalising work that she has been doing, except that the latter is predicated on world domination through ideologically constrained fiction, while her revolt pitches her creative powers against the Agency, with predictable, possibly lethal repercussions for herself.

What the reader learns at the end of the novel is the self-reflexive truth that the subversive text by means of which Ishtar aims to undermine the hegemony of the Agency is identical to the novel he or she has been reading, which (at the conclusion of the narrative) she is on the verge of publishing under the pseudonym of 'Eli Yaakunah'.[8] This would make of it an autobiographical, in a sense documentary, novel. Moreover, she surreptitiously posts it in the public domain as a piggy-back file attached to the novel she was instructed to write about the Mexican president's fictitious sex scandal. This not only invites a harsh reprisal from the Agency when this eventually becomes apparent (after thousands of people have presumably already seen and downloaded it), nor is its self-reflexivity merely a reminder of its constructedness as literary artefact. It goes further, first, because the act of self-reflexivity positions Ishtar *both* within the fictional space of Yaakunah's (that is, what turns out to be her own autobiographical, documentary) novel *and* outside of it; and second, in that it reflects on the reader's implied complicity, through the act of reading and identifying with Ishtar, who narrates her story in the first person singular, the site of identification.[9] Because Ishtar's action introduces a moment of what Rancière calls dissensus into the diegetic space, this facilitates the possible subversion of the political status quo in fictional as well as extant social reality, given the conspicuous resemblance between the intra-fictional world (despite its being located in a projected future) and our own, as will be argued below. Furthermore, through its aesthetic capacity to 'partition the sensible' politically, the subversive narrative reaches out from the ostensible confines of fiction to infuse dissensus into the realm of common social and political experience in the early twenty-first century, by aesthetically shaping an alternative manner of perceiving an extant social domain no less politically subjugated than Ishtar's.

The distribution of the sensible, intra- and extra-fictionally

As is well known, the crucial phrase in Rancière's work is 'partition (or distribution) of the sensible', which means a specific manner in which the sensible world is structured, framed or configured regarding what is visible, audible, sayable and recognisable (axiologically as well as politically). This is reminiscent of Merleau-Ponty's phenomenological evocation of the sphere of perception as being structured 'horizontally' according to what is 'near' or 'further away' from the subject in terms of its perceptual intentionality, except that the 'distribution of the sensible' is not peculiar to the individual subject, but pertains to social space inhabited by political subjects.[10] If 'discourse' means the discursive-linguistic sphere shared by a number of people who have been subjectivised, or have become subjects, through the alignment of meaning and power along certain linguistic axes, for example patriarchal discourse as instance of the 'discourse of the master',[11] then the 'partition of the sensible' encompasses discourse as well as non-discursive qualities of social space such as visibility and audibility.[12]

Regarding Yaakunah's *The Woman*, one has to distinguish between two senses of the 'distribution of the sensible'. First there is the intra-fictional, narrative sense according to which the sensible is partitioned by the fictionalising ordering and transformation of social (political, economic) space by the 'Agency'. Or, to be more exact, by those individuals working for the Agency, who have been specially selected for their creative writing talents, harnessed towards the imaginative transformation and cratological reinforcement of the diegetic experiential world. These individuals construct the world at various levels of 'reporting' or 'scripting', hierarchically arranged from the lowest, of 'raw news' (already fictionalised to a certain degree), to the highest, of 'scriptwriting', where the 'scripts' produced by 'scriptwriters' anticipate, and dictate, what is to happen concretely in the world. Here one already notices the tendency, remarked on by Rancière, to relegate 'documentary' work, or art, to the lower social levels and reserve 'fictional' work for the higher echelons.[13] Their 'creative' aesthetic work therefore blatantly 'distributes the sensible' along cratological lines designed to maintain and entrench the power of the 'gods', or the handful of elite members of the Agency, aptly so-called because it comprises the hub of politically and economically momentous 'agency' or intervention globally. In the process intra-fictional society is structured as an instance of what Rancière calls 'the police', a concept modelled on the sense of the ancient Greek *polis*, denoting a closed arrangement of social space. In his employment of the term it represents a specific, exhaustive and hierarchical structuring of society, in such a way that 'everyone' ostensibly has a place in it.[14]

Secondly there is the extra-fictional 'distribution of the sensible' in which the novel participates as literature, which means that it ineluctably contributes to the 'intertwining of being, doing and saying' in the extant social sphere of the twenty-first century. This could either lead to a confirmation of the status quo and a shift towards the exacerbation of its characteristic attributes,[15] or it could set in motion, however infinitesimally, a modification – even, conceivably, a thoroughgoing transfiguration – of the social sphere that might subvert the current incarnation of the 'police'. The novel could therefore insert a moment of dissensus – a rupture in the valorised sphere of the sensible as it is currently stratified – into the police order.

What is the relationship between these two senses of the phrase here? Succinctly put, the first is an intra-novelistic thematisation of the second – a mirror of sorts, in which one may glimpse the way in which anticipatory projections, at the level of literary 'scripting', modify what is imaginable, visible, sayable and doable in the world of the novel. However, it differs from the second, extra-fictional instance of sense-distribution in terms of intention: the intra-fictional, aesthetic determination of what social reality *will be* is presented as intentional, deliberately orchestrated, and in a sense crude insofar as it represents a cynical manipulation of the lives of ordinary as well as prominent people via 'ontic' orchestration achieved through the media.

By contrast, the second, non-fictional case of partitioning the sensible – effected aesthetically by the novel in the extant world of commonly shared experience – is subtle, and not primarily a function of intention. To this one may add that the very structure of the novel's plot seems to be predicated on the efficacy of this second sense of the 'distribution of the sensible'. It concludes on a reflexive note that retrospectively alters the sense of the narrative by bathing it in the light of the possibility of a new experience of both the intra-fictional and the extant social world – one that would differ fundamentally from the contemporary embodiment of the 'police'. As Joseph Tanke remarks apropos of Rancière's understanding of the relationship between art/literature, on the one hand, and social reality, on the other, art changes the prevailing partitioning of the sensible 'through the creation of experiences that are opposed to it'.[16] *The Woman* does this by performing such a 're-distribution of the sensible' pertaining to the intra-fictional world, and by implication also of the social world in which the reader lives, because it creates an experience that is contrary to that of the sensible world of today as contingent instantiation of the 'police'.

With the three regimes of art distinguished by Rancière in mind – the ethical regime of images, the representative regime of the arts, and the aesthetic regime of art – one can discern evidence of at least two of them in *The Woman*.[17] The novel undoubtedly instantiates the aesthetic regime, insofar as there is no discrimination or prioritisation among things, objects or individuals represented. And yet, insofar as the writers and directors at the Agency are tasked to maintain, expand and reinforce the social and political status quo through the invention of fictions, or images – an activity of which they have the monopoly, and which does not tolerate any competition – one might say that their control of the aesthetic function of images resonates with the representative regime initiated by Aristotle. There is no Platonic proscription of images, but images are carefully deployed to serve and promote the interests of the ruling elites. This is achieved by enlisting art and writing selectively for the maintenance of a polis no less rigidly and hierarchically structured, through a particular partitioning of the sensible, than Aristotle's (or Plato's). One could therefore perceive in the Agency's fictionalising activities the hallmark of the representative regime, not merely in the fostering and preservation of a hierarchical 'police' order, but particularly in the manner in which certain modes of fiction (corresponding to different genres of art) are employed to represent the interests of people belonging to different classes. Paradoxically, however, judging by examples of Ishtar's sensational 'publications', written during her stint at Written Chronicles, some (if not most) of these belong to the aesthetic regime, given the range of topics that they cover and the sheer imaginative freedom of the writing. It seems to be a case of 'anything goes' to entertain the masses, as long as it has the anaesthetising effect that the Agency desires, in this way keeping the existing social strata intact, with the 'gods' aesthetically in control at the top.

Furthermore the novel, being the self-reflexive, fictional construction of a ruthlessly controlled, hierarchical 'police' order, evinces its status as belonging to the aesthetic regime insofar as irruptions of dissensus occur in the diegetic space ordered according to the parameters of police demarcation. Throughout the novel several literary inventions have the effect of dislocating the sensible boundaries erected by police strategies, conspicuous among them the inventive representation of characters that do not belong to the ruling class of 'gods'. These include the identity thief and prostitute Arianne (alias Reiyel) and the clown with whom Ishtar views Charlie Chaplin's *Modern Times*, *The Great Dictator* and *The Gold Rush*, with the obvious relevance of particularly the first two films for the novel's theme (such as the autocratic rule of the would-be dictator, but more importantly the effect that Chaplin's parody and ridicule have on it, exposing it as being untenable). The figure of the clown further points towards theatrical, fictionalising strategies of subversion – which are among the ways that equality manifests itself, according to Rancière – such as those that Ishtar witnesses the clowns and the 'buffoon' performing in the park. The effect of assigning important roles to several such characters in the plot is to introduce moments of dissensus and, through this, radical aesthetic as well as social and political equality into its fictional space.[18] This does not happen without implicating the social and political milieu of the reader as well, given the realisation that the text he or she has been reading is the aesthetic instrument (a virus of sorts) for inserting self-destruction into the otherwise hegemonic fabric of the fictional dominant order. What Ishtar does in the end is to unlock the space for the appearance of 'the part of those with no part' (who have by then amply proved their capacity for logos), and therefore to demonstrate the functioning of the unacknowledged presupposition of all political rule, namely equality. And although there is no seamless connection between her fictional revolutionary act and (potentially) those of readers in the existing social order – neither the novelist's possible revolutionary intention nor the literary character of the narrative can guarantee such an 'effect' – the context of reception can enable readers to recognise the resemblance between Ishtar's world and the extant world, which sets the stage for possible political action in the latter.[19]

The Woman therefore executes or performs a double repartitioning of the sensible: first, intra-textually, by exposing the ongoing construction of social reality by the Agency, in the process inviting revolt or rebellion, and second, extra-textually, by triggering recognition of the analogous construction of the social and political world in the realm of commonly shared experience globally today, and possibly (depending on a reader's receptivity) extending an exhortation to the reader to find ways of performing a comparative repartitioning of the sensible in the extant world. In this respect one might say that the novel prepares one for social revolution in the same manner that what Ian Parker calls the 'revolution in subjectivity', brought about by psychoanalysis in the clinic, prepares one for social revolution outside the clinic, by *bringing the subject face to face with her or his relationship with power*.[20] Parker stresses, however, that there is no guarantee that the subject will take the next step, as it were, even if he or she reconfigures his or her relationship with power in psychic terms. The same is true of readers' reception of *The Woman* and possible political action on their part.

In Rancièrian terms, the novel – functioning as an instance of the aesthetic regime – works as a kind of generative grammar for equality by being a mouthpiece for the logos of the part of those 'with no part', whom narrator Ishtar (or, at a different level, the pseudonymous Yaakunah) characterises as capable of speaking, instead of merely 'making a noise'. When she first catches the identity thief and 'pirate', Arianne, red-handed in her house, she listens to what the young woman has to say, and even participates in Arianne's hacking into the Agency's computer system to find information on her beloved Utu's whereabouts, thus initiating a portentous dual logic into her own identity – she is not exhaustively interpellated by Agency ideology, but can instead position herself outside it even as she serves its reinforcement. Furthermore, considering that Ishtar works for the Agency, symbolically representing the 'police' as embodiment of the exhaustive and exclusive structuring of the social and political order, Arianne introduces heterogeneity into Ishtar's life, with far-reaching consequences. What happens between them constitutes nothing less than 'politics' in the Rancièrian sense of the word, as does Ishtar's friendship with the clown who, by showing her the old Chaplin movies, stages a theatrical introduction of the political into the police order maintained by the Agency, in which Ishtar is complicit.[21] *The Woman* instantiates a text where equality is 'performed' intra-textually and potentially also 'outside' the literary text (with Derrida's dictum in mind, that 'there is no outside-text'), in the '(con-)text' of extant society.[22] This claim must be understood in the light of Rancière's observation that 'Politics occurs when there is a place and a way for two heterogenous processes to meet'.[23]

It is not only a matter of the introduction of equality, via the meeting of heterogeneous elements, into its textual fabric that makes *The Woman* an exemplary case of the aesthetic regime. There is a more radical sense of equality that it performs, insofar as it simultaneously affirms and erases the boundary between literature (art) and social reality: while it announces itself unapologetically as a 'novel', the experience that it affords the reader is one that surpasses the literary sphere along the trajectory launched by the aesthetic.

The convergence of theory and literature/art in the extant social world

For Rancière art and theory converge in a creative force field of sorts – to be able to make sense of the aesthetic function of literature vis-à-vis the projective or anticipatory transformation of the visible world, one has to scrutinise commensurate philosophical or (social-) scientific theories that resonate 'horizontally' with such literary partitions of the sensible,[24] and whose primary function is to make the role allocated to the arts in social reality intelligible. Such a 'force field' of sense, made accessible by the theoretical articulation of the conditions of intelligibility of the practice of art and literature, enables one to understand the aesthetic purchase that the artwork in question has on the social fabric. In Rancière's words, 'The simple practices of the arts cannot be separated from the discourses that define the conditions under which they can be perceived as artistic practices.'[25]

Given the reciprocal implications of the theoretical and the aesthetic, one has to turn to theories which comprise the 'historical-transcendental' touchstone for the comprehensibility of the aesthetic (and hence the political) function of Yaakunah's novel. It should already be apparent from what has been written above that Rancière's own philosophy of the arts – more particularly of the aesthetic regime – comprises an exemplary theoretical grid in terms of which the distinctly aesthetic-political functioning of *The Woman* as literature is comprehensible insofar as it participates actively in the reconfiguration of the perceptible world.

Relevant theories must further offer a conceptual grid for understanding the commensurability between the world of the novel and existing social reality, and for grasping the possibility of transmuting the social world 'aesthetically' along the defiles of the distribution of the sensible. Are there theories that have as their point of departure the manner in which late twentieth- and early twenty-first-century society is held in thrall by what is collectively referred to as 'the media', something that would chime with the role of the Agency in *The Woman*? If people in the world of the novel are largely duped by the 'news' created by the Agency – something the 'Rebel Reporters' resist by spreading 'real news' through 'heralds' and websites that survive briefly before being dismantled by the agents of the Agency – is it not the case that most people in the globalised world of the present are utterly dependent on what John Thompson (as early as 1990) calls 'mediated reality'? That is, in Thompson's theory, social actors' astonishing assumption that, to be the case, something has to be 'mediated' ('to be is to be televised') reverberates with the novel in question, which projects a world where political power relations are subordinated to or determined by aesthetic arrangement and rearrangement, in the guise of fictions deliberately constructed by the fiction-spinners of the Agency. Recall that these fiction-producers are those employed to imagine society and social or economic events according to the interests of the 'gods' of the Agency, and to hold these imagined occurrences up to a public who can, by and large, no longer distinguish between what is 'real' and what is merely imagined as being 'real'. The fictions, pitched at different levels of 'news', constitute the field of aesthetic possibilities for ordinary people's perceptions and behaviour, as well as the 'scripts' that the economic and political actors on the 'real-world stage' are expected to enact or perform, lest they be found wanting by the Agency, and be summarily removed.

One may wonder why the name of the author of *The Woman*, Eli Yaakunah, turns out to be a pseudonym, apparently, for Ishtar Benten, who initially appears to be a fictional narrator-character in a fictitious tale, but in retrospect assumes the imaginary role of a 'real' person who has written an ostensibly autobiographical novel.[26] Why then not present it as non-fiction, or a kind of journalistic, documentary text? Would that not have greater political impact? Rancière's conception of literature's political function makes it clear, however, that fiction poses its own dangers to the political status quo, particularly if it happens to be of an oligarchic nature. If the writer's name, 'Eli Yaakunah', were to be replaced by that of a historically existing person in the contemporary world, the novel would be less 'dangerous' in the sense of aesthetically (and therefore politically) active fiction, potentially subverting the current distribution of the sensible. Michel Foucault makes it explicit: 'How can one reduce the great peril, the great danger with which fiction threatens our world? The answer is: one can reduce it with the author. The author allows a limitation of the cancerous and dangerous proliferation of significations [...] The author is the principle of thrift in the proliferation of meaning.'[27] Evidently 'Eli Yaakunah' knows this only too well.

Furthermore, the title of the novel one reads (Yaakunah's, or Ishtar's, or, if these are both pseudonyms, an unknown author's) indexes the creative aesthetic-political function of the pervasive power (the Agency) in the narrative, and perhaps metonymically also of the corresponding hegemonic power in the extant world of the twenty-first century. After all, just as the Agency is responsible for setting the social scene, as well as setting in motion events that maintain and reinforce the political status quo, we live in a world where a pervasive economic and political power similarly dictates, to a large extent, the direction of events – although not *absolutely*, just as the Agency cannot make provision, infallibly, for the advent of an unpredictable event such as Ishtar's revolt. Some call this power 'Empire',[28] others name it 'disaster capitalism'[29] or the 'elites' of 'the space of flows',[30] although one could simply refer to it as 'liberal democracy', which condenses neoliberal capitalism and parliamentary democracy. No one should make the mistake of regarding the states that comprise the 'liberal democracies' as democratic, however; as Rancière indicates in *Hatred of Democracy*, they are, at best, oligarchies of some kind.[31] According to Hardt and Negri's reading of the global situation, all such states are complicit in engendering a novel, emerging, 'supra-national' and sovereign power, which they call 'Empire'.[32] Despite the democratising effect of the internet, their oligarchic power is kept intact by their military might and their hegemonic, 'oligopolistic' use of mainstream media like television and iconic newspapers (which are available online as well), such as the *New York Times*, the *Washington Post* and *The Times* of London.[33]

I would submit that everyone who is reasonably aware of the 'information society' in which we live – and this means the majority of literate people who make use of the internet, television, magazines and newspapers – would be able, intuitively, to recognise in Yaakunah's (Ishtar's) description of the fictional world controlled by the Agency a kind of exaggerated mirror image of our own. The context of reception of the novel predisposes readers to perceive similarities and differences between the fictional world and the extant social domain. This is important, as Rancière recognises. Commenting on the (im-)possibility of establishing rules of correspondence between 'committed' art and a commensurate politics, he notes: 'There are no criteria. There are formulas that are equally available whose meaning is often decided upon by a state of conflict that is exterior to them.'[34] From his subsequent elaboration it is clear that he regards the 'meaning' attributed to art or literature as something that depends 'on the times', that is, on the context of reception, which predisposes readers or critics to offer specific, related interpretations. It is no different with *The Woman*.[35]

The Woman and political action

Rancière's conception of the relationship between literature/art and politics in terms of the aesthetic dimension that they share, refreshing as it is in a world where the market seems to determine, predominantly, what is to count as 'aesthetic' as well as what is politically relevant, seems to me to falter at a crucial point, albeit through no fault of his. It comes as close as any theory, theoretical practice or philosophy can get to what is ultimately indispensable if one's objective is to dislodge a hegemonic, tyrannical power, as Yaakunah's novel demonstrates so graphically.[36] Rancière's work, like (and perhaps better than) that of Deleuze and Guattari and others before him, gives one a sound grasp of what literature can contribute aesthetically to the transformation of the political realm by boldly repartitioning the sensible realm in novel, electrifying ways, but he cannot impart, in a fail-safe manner, that final ingredient, namely (political) action. To be sure, saying or writing something is already a species of doing, as speech-act theory (among others) has it, but the virtue of Yaakunah's novel is finally to demonstrate the futility of stopping short of action, if one wishes to subvert a despotic force. When Ishtar posts the novel one has been reading on the internet, within everyone's reach, she performs the kind of action that carries with it the potential, but not the guarantee, for toppling the dominant power of the Agency. 'Her' novel is not merely a preparation for action, although it is that too regarding the potential action of others; it *enacts* or performs something that is a decisive political act, recognisable as such by the vital risk she takes in making it public.

Ishtar discovers her lover, Utu, to have changed his initial decision to expose the Agency (after his promotion to Advertising) to a resignation, on his part, that he is one of the 'gods'. In Machiavellian fashion he comes to accept that there will always be rulers and subjects, the elites and the masses, and that it is infinitely better to be a member of the former. He faces – and, given his position at the Agency, cheats – the mugger's choice, 'Your money or your life,' so that he retains both. Ishtar, however, does not make this decision, even if it means losing Utu. In true Lacanian fashion she faces the revolutionary's choice, 'Freedom or death,' and acts in the interests of freedom, even if it might entail her death – in which case she would still have affirmed her freedom.[37] After all, she publishes the novel she was ordered to write on a sex scandal that would bring a president down, which is (through the software programme she took from Arianne/Reiyel that hides files 'behind' others, in this case behind the one on the Mexican president) the electronic gateway to the very novel one has been reading, and she knows what to expect. Because the novel is written in the first person singular, one involuntarily identifies with the narrator, so that the culmination of the narrative in a potentially liberating but also potentially lethal act transfixes one with the experience, however vicarious, of having performed a revolutionary action. Along the trajectory of a radical modification of the prevailing, intra-textual distribution of the sensible, its extant counterpart is brought into question, and one is confronted with the challenge, if not the imperative, to act in a commensurate manner in the face of a global, comparably hegemonic situation. Ishtar's choice and her act of exposing the Agency brings across the irreducible difference between theory and action. It emphasises that action is inescapable if one wishes to rid the world of a colossal, tyrannical force.

To be sure, such a realisation on the part of the reader is not yet action, and yet, given the identification-mediated experience of finding oneself in the position of the narrator, Ishtar, however fleetingly, must ineluctably bring across the urgency of action in the face of a hegemon which unmistakably resembles the Agency in the novel. Why unmistakably? Because, in the light of what was said earlier regarding the extant social and political world – Empire, neo-liberalism, liberal democracy, disaster capitalism: these all denote the same 'police' state of affairs – even a moderately 'informed' reader of *The Woman* would have the knowledge enabling her or him to recognise the resemblance in question, as well as the imperative of action, instead of mere acquiescence. Only action could possibly insert a decisive fissure of what Rancière calls dissensus into the monodimensional fabric of the police order resembling that of the fictional Agency. To do so, as Ishtar does at the end of the narrative, is simultaneously to proclaim the equality of everyone with all others: she unmasks the Agency as the force maintaining the hierarchical order, or the specific distribution of the sensible, as something contingent, determined by the fictional-aesthetic interventions of the 'gods'. By exposing their cynical manipulation of the social order from 'inside' the edifice, as it were, Ishtar symbolically acknowledges her own and the other gods' equality with those who have 'no part' in the social order of exclusive plenitude enjoyed by the gods – from Arianne (or Reiyel) and the Rebel Reporters or Friends of Elijah Lovejoy, to the clown and the nameless thousands who eke out a livelihood in the trash mines of a world where there are no more minerals to be extracted from the earth.[38]

The question that obtrudes itself, however, is this: given the non-identity of theory and action, what is there which compels one to assume that the exemplary act of dissensus, revolt or resistance on the part of a fictional character may gain a purchase on the capacity for similar action shared by readers of the novel? Rancière's explicit answer to the question, whether political power is 'somehow inherent in works as they stand', leaves no doubt that artists cannot 'anticipate political effects of the work'.[39] This, to my mind, is one of the clearest indications on Rancière's part regarding the relation between literature and politics. For Rancière, as for Jacotot in the nineteenth century, the putative, qualitative gap between student and teacher, on which traditional pedagogics is founded, must be rejected, given the demonstrable ability of all human beings to approach novel experiences in such a way that they learn on the basis of what they (do not) know, that is, of what they stand to correct in the light of new insights.[40] In this sense, the schoolmaster is as 'ignorant' as his or her students, and they share a characteristic mode of knowledge acquisition. One need not be a philosopher, or a political scientist, for the penny to drop. Every literate person *can*, in principle, be subjectivised as a political subject when they reach this point in the novel. And although there is no guarantee that it will happen, everyone is capable of acting in a manner commensurate with Ishtar's, which could introduce dissensus into the homogeneous, monolithic police order of Empire. In this way the affirmation of the equality of everyone with everyone else could light up the mendacious features of a social world supposedly founded on 'equal human rights', but which excludes from its consensual order everyone who does not number among those who have been counted in terms of predetermined, exclusive criteria.[41]

The fact that Rancière has explicitly stated that there is no strict correlation between art or literature and politics is therefore consonant with my earlier argument. In response to a question from Gabriel Rockhill about his avoidance of the aesthetic notion of 'commitment', he says that 'there is no criterion for establishing a correspondence between aesthetic virtue and political virtue. There are only choices.'[42] Put differently: 'The core of the problem is that there is no criterion for establishing an appropriate correlation between the politics of aesthetics and the aesthetics of politics.'[43] To illustrate, Rancière elaborates on the multivocality of artworks like the novels of Dos Passos and the Dadaist paintings of Grosz or Dix, which could be construed interpretively in divergent ways, and concludes that 'Novelistic fragmentation or pictorial carnivalisation lend themselves just as well to describing the chaos of the capitalist world from the point of view of class struggle as to describing, from a nihilistic point of view, the chaos of a world where class struggle is itself but one element in the

Dionysian chaos.'[44] Moreover, he grants that the interpretation of such artworks depends 'on the times', just as I would argue that *The Woman*, understood in the present historical era, resonates conspicuously with the discontents of ordinary, working-class people in a world where a small percentage of people ('the 1%', reverberating with the 'gods' in the novel) own almost half of the world's resources, while the rest ('the 99%', chiming with Yaakunah's masses) have to make do with the rest.[45]

Moreover, insofar as the politics of a literary work may be identified, Rancière grants that it may amount to 'an act of political dissensus', which is exactly what the politics contingent upon Ishtar Benten's fictitious actions in the aesthetic realm constituted by *The Woman* instantiates, as I have argued.[46] The question remains whether the political aesthetics (such as the projection of a world where familiar perceptual parameters are drastically reconfigured) suggested under particular, historically contingent circumstances by an artwork such as *The Woman* can be linked, theoretically or otherwise, with political *action* on the part of readers, listeners or viewers of the artworks in question – action predicated on the possibility of reconfiguring the aesthetic contours of the extant social and political domain. Does Rancière make allowance for this? After all, the 'heterological' rupture of the social and political sphere constructed in the novel by Ishtar's actions may indeed amount to a 'way in which the meaningful fabric of the sensible is disturbed', with all the suggestiveness it entails regarding possible, perception-redistributing, revolutionary action on the part of reading subjects.[47] But is there any guarantee that this might happen? Or can a reading of the novel, like the psychoanalytic experience on the part of the analysand, at best bring about a 'revolution in subjectivity' that *might* turn out to be a preparation of the subject for a social or political revolution?[48]

Does Yaakunah's *The Woman* qualify, finally, as political literature in these terms? Does it successfully negotiate the precarious terrain between a decipherable meaning that potentially disrupts its own literary, sensible form, and a radically dislocating sense of the unsignifiable uncanny on the subject's part?[49] My answer would be in the affirmative because, first, seen in the context of current global power relations, the politics of the novel's aesthetic space is legible at two levels: the valorised police order maintained and reinforced by the Agency, and the politics of equality implied by the introduction of dissensus into this order by Ishtar's inexorable renunciation of its legitimacy. More importantly, the uncanny announces itself unexpectedly, but unmistakably, at that moment when readers register the implicit appeal directed at themselves by Ishtar's virtually unimaginable, death-defying action predicated upon the 'revolutionary's choice' on her part – 'freedom or death'. At that moment one is faced by an unspecifiable – hence uncanny – possibility inherent in quotidian reality: that of acting in a manner commensurate with Ishtar's resolute attempt to reconfigure the sensible coordinates of her world. In the reader's case it would mean facing the full might of the extant 'police' system of global liberal democracy, just as Ishtar has to face the annihilating force of the Agency. But that always remains a mere possibility. Not even the 'best' political literature or art can guarantee such action on the part of readers or viewers.[50]

Notes

1. Jacques Rancière, *Dissensus: On Politics and Aesthetics*, trans. Steven Corcoran (New York: Continuum, 2010), 107.
2. Allan Megill, *Prophets of Extremity: Nietzsche, Heidegger, Foucault, Derrida* (Berkeley: University of California Press, 1985), 2.
3. Joseph J. Tanke, *Jacques Rancière: An Introduction* (New York: Continuum, 2011), 49–50.
4. By 'quasi-transcendental' I mean that equality is for Rancière both the condition of possibility of politics as the announcement of a wrong suffered by some excluded or 'uncounted' people, as well as of its impossibility, that is, its distortion, by the 'police'; see Geoffrey Bennington, *Derridabase*, in Jacques Derrida and Geoffrey Bennington, *Jacques Derrida*, trans. Geoffrey Bennington (Chicago: University of Chicago Press, 1993), 276–7.
5. Rancière, *Disagreement: Politics and Philosophy*, trans. Julie Rose (Minneapolis: University of Minnesota Press, 1999), 61.
6. Rancière, *Dissensus*, 107.
7. Eli Yaakunah, *The Woman Who Sparked the Greatest Sex Scandal of All Time* (Charleston: CreateSpace Independent Publishing Platform, 2012), 96, 157, 161–72, 219–28.
8. Ibid., 225.
9. The mirror stage as formative of the function of the 'I' as revealed in psychoanalytic experience. In Jacques Lacan, *Écrits: A Selection*, trans. Alan Sheridan (New York: W. W. Norton, 1977), 1–7. See Bert Olivier, 'That Strange Thing Called "Identifying"', *South*

African Journal of Psychology, 39:4 (2009), 407–19; reprinted in *Intersecting Philosophical Planes: Philosophical Essays* (London and Frankfurt: Peter Lang Academic Publishers, 2012), 101–23.
10. Marcel Merleau-Ponty, *The Primacy of Perception and Other Essays on Phenomenological Psychology, the Philosophy of Art, History and Politics*, trans. James M. Edie (Evanston, IL: Northwestern University Press, 1964), 12–16.
11. Lacan, *The Other Side of Psychoanalysis: The Seminar of Jacques Lacan Book XVII*, trans. R. Grigg (New York: W. W. Norton, 2007).
12. Derek Hook, *(Post)Apartheid Conditions: Psychoanalysis and Social Formation* (New York: Palgrave Macmillan, 2013), 18–46.
13. Rancière, *The Politics of Aesthetics: The Distribution of the Sensible*, trans. Gabriel Rockhill (London: Bloomsbury, 2013), Kindle edition, loc. 1376.
14. Rancière, *Dissensus*, 499.
15. What comes to mind involuntarily when reading *The Woman* is Deleuze's 'Postscript on the Societies of Control' (1992), which describes a society already beyond the panoptical 'society of discipline' depicted by Foucault in *Discipline and Punish* (1995), insofar as control is no longer exercised through disciplinary mechanisms such as hierarchical observation or normalising judgement, but along rhizomatic networks of surveillance and economic (dis-)empowerment. In this respect the world projected in Yaakunah's novel instantiates an intensification of 'societies of control'.
16. Tanke, *Jacques Rancière*, 73.
17. Rancière, *The Politics of Aesthetics*, loc. 393–487.
18. Peter Hallward, 'Staging Equality: Rancière's Theatrocracy and the Limits of Anarchic Equality', in Gabriel Rockhill and Philip Watts (eds), *Jacques Rancière: History, Politics, Aesthetics* (Durham, NC, and London: Duke University Press, 2009), 140–57.
19. Rancière, *The Politics of Aesthetics*, loc. 1391.
20. Ian Parker, *Lacanian Psychoanalysis: Revolutions in Subjectivity* (London: Routledge, 2011), 196–9.
21. Hallward, *Staging Equality*, 144–51.
22. Derrida, *Of Grammatology*, trans. G. C. Spivak (Baltimore: Johns Hopkins University Press, 1976), 158.
23. Rancière, *Disagreement*, 30.
24. Rockhill, 'Introduction: Through the Looking Glass – The Subversion of the Modernist Doxa', in Rancière, *Mute Speech: Literature, Critical Theory, and Politics*, trans. James Swenson (New York: Columbia University Press, 2011), 5 (1–28).

25. Rancière, *Mute Speech*, 31.
26. Yaakunah, *The Woman*, 225.
27. This is not the place to go into the intricacies of the social or ontological status of the 'author' in relation to the 'narrator'. Suffice it to say that I am in agreement with Foucault's (1984) observations in this regard in 'What is an Author?', where he argues in favour of what he terms 'the author function', which corresponds to a plurality of distinguishable 'selves'. For example, the narrator indexed by the word 'I' (in the present case, Ishtar) is distinct from the person who supposedly wrote the text (Yaakunah), and both are different from the actual (here, unknown) subject who wrote the sentences comprising the narrative related by the narrator. All of them serve the author function, and are discernible in the text in question, even if it is as a mere 'trace' of absence. The 'author function' therefore allows one to navigate the terrain between the 'historical' author and the fictional author and narrator, as well as other 'functions' subsumed under this multivocal concept. See Michel Foucault, 'What is an Author?', in Paul Rabinow (ed.), *The Foucault Reader* (New York: Pantheon Books, 1984), 101–20.
28. Michael Hardt and Antonio Negri, *Multitude: War and Democracy in the Age of Empire* (London: Penguin Books, 2006).
29. Naomi Klein, *The Shock Doctrine: The Rise of Disaster Capitalism* (London: Allen Lane, 2007).
30. Manuel Castells, *The Rise of the Network Society*, 2nd edn (Oxford: Wiley-Blackwell, 2010), Kindle edition.
31. Rancière, *Hatred of Democracy*, trans. Steven Corcoran (London: Verso, 2014), 52.
32. Hardt and Negri, *Empire* (Cambridge, MA: Harvard University Press, 2001).
33. Ibid., 299–300.
34. Rancière, *The Politics of Aesthetics*, loc. 1059.
35. Ibid.
36. Ibid., loc. 1345–56.
37. Joan Copjec, *Imagine There's No Woman: Ethics and Sublimation* (Cambridge, MA: MIT Press, 2002), 17–19.
38. Yaakunah, *The Woman*, 140.
39. Rancière, *The Politics of Aesthetics*, loc. 1391.
40. Rancière, *The Ignorant Schoolmaster: Five Lessons in Intellectual Emancipation*, trans. Kristin Ross (Stanford: Stanford University Press, 1991), 1–18.
41. Hardt and Negri, *Multitude*, 270–3.

42. Rancière, *The Politics of Aesthetics*, loc. 1049.
43. Ibid., loc. 1069.
44. Ibid., loc. 1059.
45. Ibid.
46. Ibid., loc. 1069.
47. Ibid., loc. 1090.
48. Parker, *Lacanian Psychoanalysis*.
49. Rancière, *The Politics of Aesthetics*, loc. 1090.
50. That Rancière is in agreement with this is clear from his discussion of the prototypical political art of Brecht (see Rancière, *The Politics of Aesthetics*, loc. 1079).

Index

All main entries are in **bold**.

Adorno, Theodor W., 187, 211
aesthetic regime of the arts, 3, 4–6, 10–16, 46, 59, 72, 78, **79–85**, 90, 91, 144–5, 147–8, 150, 184–8, 192–6, 198–9, 202n, 207–10, 218–19, 254–8
Agamben, Giorgio, 92, 107, 244
Agee, James, 6, 10
Agrippa, Senator Menenius, 68, 69
Althusser, Louis, 2, 52, 80
Arcades Project, The, 190–7
Areopagitica, 88, 90
aristocracy, 154
Aristotle, 4, 30, 60, 61, 62, 64, 65, 82, 208, 254
Auerbach, Erich, 14, 26–8, 33, 36, 40, 172, 180n, 201n, 245n
avant-garde, 33, 36, 211

Badiou, Alain, 2, 5, 8, 9, 75n, 77, 80, 81, 83, 92, 99–100, 104, 106
Balibar, Etienne, 2
Balzac, Honoré de, 6, 9–10, 29, 30, 32, 58, 79, 134–5, 136, 169, 185, 193, 194
Barthes, Roland, 47
Bataille, Georges, 1
Baudelaire, Charles, 52, 189
Baumgarten, Alexander Gottlieb, 77–8, 82, 83
Beckett, Samuel, 210–11
Benjamin, Walter, 18–19, 46, 103, 111, **183–200**
Berardi, Franco 'Bifo', 236
Berman, Marshall, 103–4
Bigelow, Gordon, 130

biopolitics, 226, 229–30, 234, 238
Biron, Michel, 237
Blanchot, Maurice, 1, 8, 111
Bogost, Ian, 243
Borges, Jorge Luis, 10, 208
Bourdieu, Pierre, 61, 128
Bouvard et Pécuchet, 207–8, 214, 223
Brecht, Bertolt, 10, 107
Brooks, Peter, 171–3
Bunyon, John, 171
Burke, Edmund, 76, 84–5, 91, 95n, 104, 118
Butler, Judith, 233
Byron, Gordon Lord, 110

Cesarino, Cesare, 149
Chartism, 125–6, 129–34, 139
classicism, 3–4, 85
comedy, 4, 30, 70, 186
commodity, 159–60, 167, 177, 185, 191–6, 201n, 203n, 215, 236
communication, 2, 7, 50, 109, 184, 186–90, 193, 197–8, 204n
communism, 36, 38–9, 73
Corneille, Pierre, 86
Cuvier, Georges, 178

Daumer, Hans, 59
De Man, Paul, 83
Defoe, Daniel, 171, 222, 230
Deleuze, Gilles, 2, 7, 10, 26–7, 80, 115–17, 170, 261
democracy, 5, 6, 10, 80, 114, 133–5, 143–5, 151, 155, 160, 181n, 186, 215–16, 227, 231, 243–4, 259, 262, 265

democracy (*cont.*)
  of the letter, 6, 132–8, 140, 148, 209, 215
  of moments, 36
  of things, 7, 8, 58, 65, 215, 243–4
demos, 2, 4, 48, 60, 167–8
Deranty, Jean-Philippe, 14–15
Derrida, Jacques, 1, 8, 103, 257
Descartes, René, 83
detritus, 185–99, 223
disagreement, 76, 80, 147, 162n, 194
disciplinarity, 6, 42–3, 188, 230
dissensus, 8, 12–14, 66, 80, 90, 109–10, 119, 134, 159, 216–17, 231, 251–3, 255, 262–4
distribution of the sensible, 3, 4, 6, 7, 9, 13, 19, 20, 34–5, 50, 53, 76, 77–81, 82, 109, 157, 167, 168, 188, 198, 215, 217, 219, 220, 227, 234, 237, 239, 244, 252–7, 258–9, 262
Dubliners, 207, 217
Duncan, Isadora, 38

egalitarianism *see* equality
Eliot, George, 18, 129, 139, **164–79**
Eliot, T. S., 207
Ellis, Bret Easton, 236–7
emancipation, 15–16, 45, 47, 48, 52, 54, 55n, 63, 67–71, 72–3, 75n, 81, 146, 167–8, 185, 195–6, 204n
Epstein, Jean, 36
equality, 8, 11, 14–15, 37–8, 40, 44, 51, 54, 55n, 67–70, 75n, 80–1, 100, 113, 116–17, 134, 143, 148, 151, 154, 186–7, 196–7, 214–16, 227–8, 231, 235, 243–4, 250, 255–7, 262–5, 243–4
ethical regime of images, 3, 4, 5, 7, 58, 79, 91, 254
ethics, 12, 80–2, 84–5, 92

fiction, 25–41, 42–3
figures, 44–8
Flaubert, Gustave, 5, 7, 10, 15, 19, 47, 116–17, 134, 136, 165, 180n, 181n, 186–9, 194, 199, **207–16**, 223n, 227–9
Foucault, Michel, 2, 19, 43, 115, 173, 226, 229, 230–1, 233, 259, 267n
free indirect discourse, 135–8, 165, 180n

Gaskell, Elizabeth, 18, **125–41**
Godard, Jean-Luc, 46
Goethe, Johann Wolfgang von, 102–3
Greenberg, Clement, 33, 40, 84

Hammett, Dashiell, 138
Haraway, Donna, 47
Hawthorne, Nathaniel, 143, 154
Haywood, Ian, 129
Hegel, G. W. F., 5, 10, 12, 58, 66, 106, 114, 174, 202n
Heidegger, Martin, 1, 81–2
Heraclitus, 49
heresy, 88, 97n, 143–7
hermaphrodite, 233
Hirschman, Thomas O., 105–6
Hobbes, Thomas, 44, 101, 118, 147
Hobsbawm, Eric, 100–2, 107–8
Houellebecq, Michel, 226, **235–44**
Howells, William Dean, 164
Hugo, Victor, 115, 193, 195, 209, 228
humanity/-ism, 27, 30, 33, 34, 36, 39, 40, 42, 53, 101, 141, 155–8, 168–70, 173–5, 177, 192, 215–16, 226–30, 236, 241–4, 263

improper, 66, 69, 79, 150
infinity, 7, 76, 83, 91–2, 94n, 112, 152, 199, 208, 216, 242
intention, 12–14, 34, 45, 158, 171, 187, 191–5, 198–9, 212, 252–6

Jacotot, Joseph, 8, 51, 67–8, 72–3, 75n, 81, 112, 204n, 263
Jaffe, Audrey, 176
Jameson, Fredric, 9, 167–8, 171, 178–9, 180n, 181n, 223n
Joyce, James, 1, 19, 33, 36, 138, 207–23

Kafka, Franz, 1, 2, 116
Kant, Immanuel, 6, 45, 77–8, 81–2, 101, 102, 108, 109, 110, 192
Keats, John, 10, 107, 108–9, 112, 125
Kenner, Hugh, 212–13

Lacan, Jacques, 1, 65, 81, 261
literarity, 8, 10, 159, 161n, 166, 199, 216–18
literature, 5–6, 7, 112–13, 193–4, 199

politics of, 6, 10–16, 111, 147–8, 187, 198, 214–16, 222–3, 226–9, 232, 238, 244, 249
Luhmann, Niklas, 77
Lukács, Georg, 28–34, 39, 168, 170–2
Lyotard, Jean-François, 2, 80

Macherey, Pierre, 2
Madame Bovary, 135–6, 165, 167, 170, 186–7, 208, 211, 214, 227
Mallarmé, Stéphane, 1, 5–6, 10, 211
Malthus, Thomas, 18, 170, 173–5
Man with a Movie Camera, The, 36–40
Mandelstam, Osip, 6
Mann, Thomas, 33
Mannheim, Karl, 17, 104–7, 119
Map and the Territory, The, 226, 238, 240–3
Maris, Bernard, 235
Martel, Yann, 230
Marx, Karl, 59, 61, 63, 64, 73, 103, 104, 106, 128, 174, 236, 249
Marxism, 14, 16, 30, 31, 33, 36, 39, 61, 103, 104, 107, 114, 118, 195, 197
Mary Barton, 125–41
Melville, Herman, 2, 9, 18, 116, **143–60**
Michelet, Jules, 9, 58–9, 70–1, 144–5, 147–8, 188, 193, 195, 198, 203n
Middlemarch, 139, 176, 179
Mill on the Floss, The, **164–79**
Milton, John, 17, 76–93
mimesis, 3, 4, 10–11
Mimesis (book), 26–8
Moby-Dick, or The Whale, **143–60**
modernism, 6, 19, 28, 33, 39–41, 82, 84, 103, 168, 207–23, 227, 249
modernity, 5, 18–19, 28, 58, 77, **99–119**, 161n, 178–9, 207
molecularity, 7, 10–16, 115–17, 215–17
Mulligan Stew, 139
muteness, 2, 4–6, 11, 14–15, 58, 144, 148, 153, 158, 168, 191–3, 195–6, 211, 215, 220, 228–9

Nancy, Jean-Luc, 53, 80–2
narration, 26–7, 30, 37, 52, 95n, 132–8, 140–1, 150–8, 165–7, 169, 171–2

Nietzsche, Friedrich, 2, 103, 213
Novalis, 113

Of True Religion, 17, 76, 86–91
Ostranenie, 7

pamphlets, 86–91
Paradise Lost, 84–8, 91–2, 95n
Parker, Andrew, 234
Pasquier, Renaud, 53
petrification, 212–19, 227–8
philosophy, 53, 59, 60–6, 70, 72, 83, 132, 258
 French, 1–2
Plato, 2–3, 4, 50, 60–2, 65, 72, 79, 82, 91, 107, 115, 131, 145, 158, 254
police, 68, 69–70, 73, 80, 137, 218, 231–2, 250, 253–5, 257, 262–5
politics, 12–16, 66, 71, 73, 91, 99–100, 146–7, 219, 231, 243–4
 of literature *see* literature: politics of
poor, the, 18–19, 60–3, 66, **127–41**, 145–7, 218–23, 236
post-Fordism, 236–9
postmodernism, 6, 138, 227, 249
Pound, Ezra, 207–10
prose of the world, 5, 9, 174, 209
Proust, Marcel, 2, 9, 79, 116, 189–90, 192, 200

Quignard, Pascal, 48–9

Rancière, Jacques
 Aesthetic Unconscious, 86
 Aesthetics and its Discontents, 71, 79
 Aisthesis, 10, 15, 77, 114
 Disagreement, 60, 69, 195
 Emancipated Spectator, The, 59, 62, 72
 Flesh of Words, The, 9
 Hatred of Democracy, 107
 Ignorant Schoolmaster, The, 11, 51, 53, 67–8, 81, 112, 196
 Mallarmé, 9
 Mute Speech, 9, 11–12, 112–13, 227
 Names of History, The, 113, 118, 144–5, 183
 On the Shores of Politics, 48, 60, 61, 231, 244

Rancière, Jacques (*cont.*)
  Philosopher and His Poor, The, 59, 60–3, 73, 128, 132, 231, 233–4
  Politics of Literature, The, 10
  Proletarian Nights, 35, 107, 233
  Short Voyages to the Land of the People, 9, 108
realism, 5–6, 14, 18, 19, 29, 31–3, 47, 110, 127, 134, 136, 148, 165–9, 170–80, 208, 226–44
Red and the Black, The, 14
representationalism, 9, 17, 34, 47, 85, 148, 168, 170, 177, 216, 226–34, 238–40, 242–3
representative regime of images, 3–4, 5, 11, 34, 79, 84
revolution, 5, 15–16, 35–6, 40–1, 76–7, 99–110, 113–16, 118–19, 139, 144–5, 147, 178, 183–4, 186–8, 190, 193–5, 196, 199, 201n, 203n, 256, 261, 264
Rilke, Rainer Maria, 9–10
Robinson Crusoe, 230
Rockhill, Gabriel, 227–8, 263
romanticism, 4, 5, 6, 7, 12, 16, 72, 78, 82, 101–2, 112–14, 144–5, 147, 202n, 219
Ross, Kristin, 183
Rousseau, J.-J., 1, 34, 102, 103, 108
Ruskin, John, 164, 168–9, 173–4

Sanders, Mike, 129
Sartre, Jean-Paul, 1, 61, 107, 128, 187, 227
Sauer, Elizabeth, 87
Schiller, Friedrich, 16, 46, 72, 84, 109, 112
Schlegel, Friedrich, 101, 113, 116
Schmitt, Carl, 101–2, 111–12, 117
Sorrentino, Gilbert, 138
spectatorship, 12, 29, 45, 46, 48, 86
Spinoza, Baruch, 83, 116–17, 188
Stein, Gertrude, 210
Stendhal, 10, 14, 34, 207
Sternberg, Meir, 140
Stiegler, Bernard, 236
style, 2, 5, 8, 19, 53, 117, 134, 136, 159, 167, 170, 186–8, 195, 196, 198–9, 208–19, 221, 222–3, 227–8, 234
Sweeney, Carole, 235–7

Tel Quel, 1
Tennyson, Alfred Lord, 125, 130
Tentation de St Antoine, 207, 209, 213–14, 218
theatricality, 29, 32, 58–9, 62, 63–71, 72–3, 74n, 231–2, 234, 243, 255, 257
Tolstoy, Leo, 10, 29–30, 32
tragedy, 4, 17, 30, 31, 58–73, 103
translation, 48–53, 56n, 88, 125, 133, 138, 146

Ulysses, 207–23
Union of Soviet Socialist Republics (USSR), 5, 36–41

Vargo, Gregory, 129–30
Vertov, Dziga, 36–40, 79
Voltaire, 86

War and Peace, 32
Watt, Ian, 229–30
Whatever, 235–9
White, Hayden, 178
Whitman, Walt, 10
Winckelmann, Johan Joachim, 14, 108
Woloch, Alex, 168–9
Wood, James, 238
Woolf, Virginia, 2, 26–7, 35, 36, 210, 235
  To the Lighthouse, 26–7, 172
Wordsworth, William, 6, 9, 10, 79, 108–9, 118
Workers, 16, 39, 42, 61, 66, 69, 107, 111, 117, 127–35, 139, 143–6, 150, 154, 221, 226, 233–5, 236, 238–9, 244

Yaakunah, Eli, 20, 249–65

Zola, Émile, 10, 29–30, 32, 209

EU representative:
Easy Access System Europe
Mustamäe tee 50, 10621 Tallinn, Estonia
Gpsr.requests@easproject.com